THE USBORNE ILLUSTRATED ENCYCLOPEDIA

SCIENCE & TECHNOLOGY

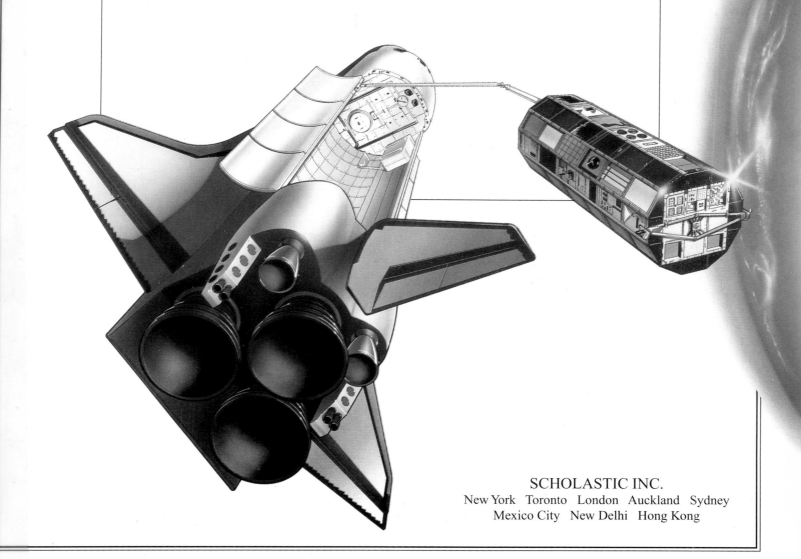

SCHOLASTIC INC.

New York Toronto London Auckland Sydney
Mexico City New Delhi Hong Kong

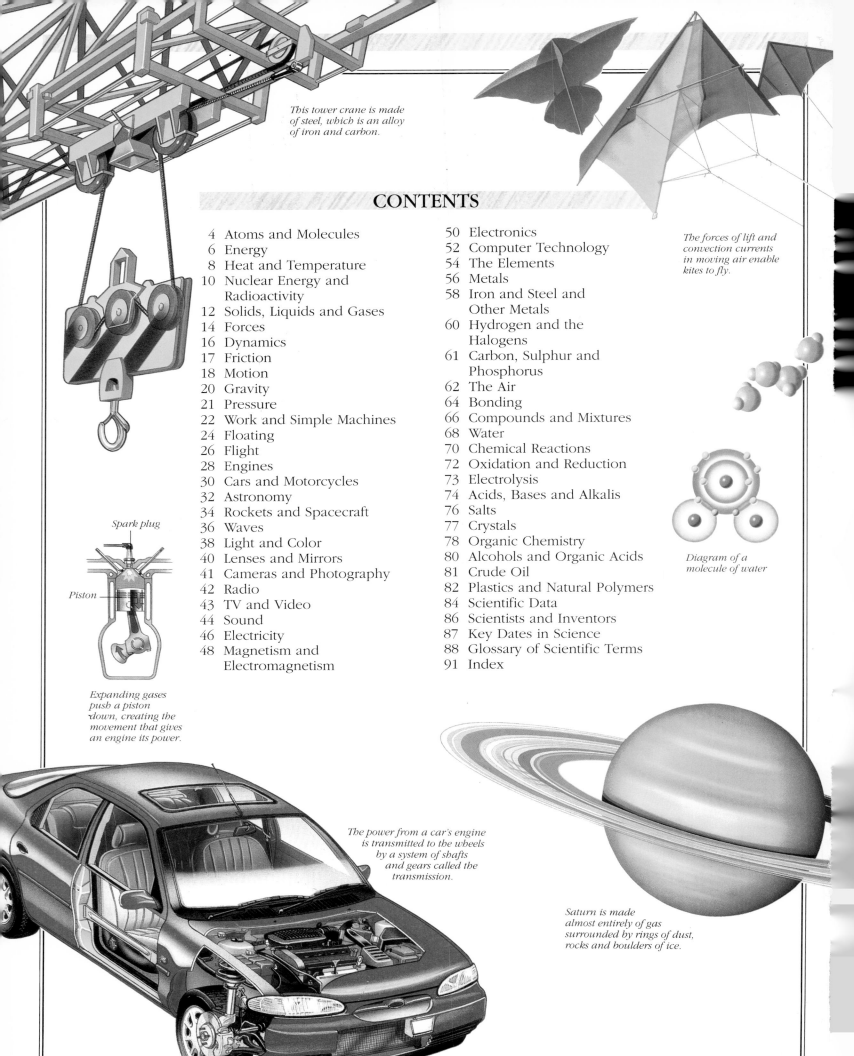

This tower crane is made of steel, which is an alloy of iron and carbon.

CONTENTS

The forces of lift and convection currents in moving air enable kites to fly.

Diagram of a molecule of water

Spark plug

Piston

Expanding gases push a piston down, creating the movement that gives an engine its power.

The power from a car's engine is transmitted to the wheels by a system of shafts and gears called the transmission.

Saturn is made almost entirely of gas surrounded by rings of dust, rocks and boulders of ice.

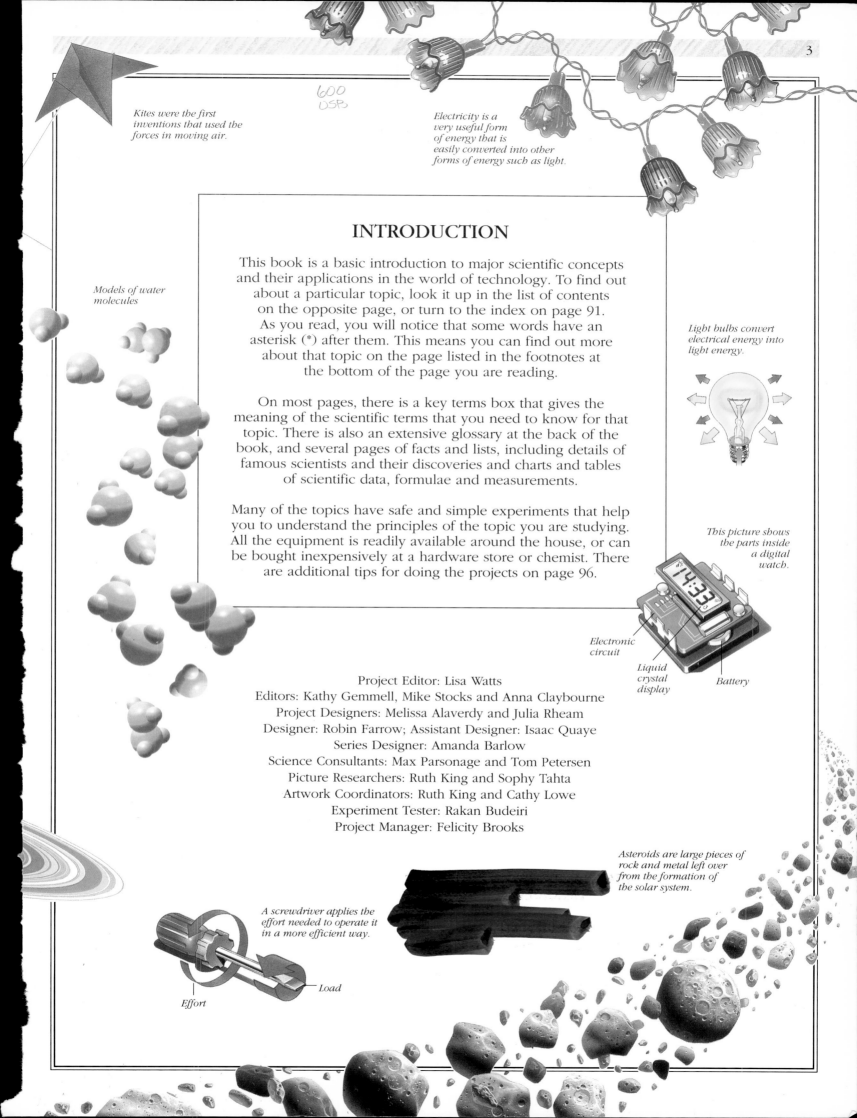

Kites were the first inventions that used the forces in moving air.

600 USB

Electricity is a very useful form of energy that is easily converted into other forms of energy such as light.

Models of water molecules

INTRODUCTION

This book is a basic introduction to major scientific concepts and their applications in the world of technology. To find out about a particular topic, look it up in the list of contents on the opposite page, or turn to the index on page 91. As you read, you will notice that some words have an asterisk (*) after them. This means you can find out more about that topic on the page listed in the footnotes at the bottom of the page you are reading.

On most pages, there is a key terms box that gives the meaning of the scientific terms that you need to know for that topic. There is also an extensive glossary at the back of the book, and several pages of facts and lists, including details of famous scientists and their discoveries and charts and tables of scientific data, formulae and measurements.

Many of the topics have safe and simple experiments that help you to understand the principles of the topic you are studying. All the equipment is readily available around the house, or can be bought inexpensively at a hardware store or chemist. There are additional tips for doing the projects on page 96.

Light bulbs convert electrical energy into light energy.

This picture shows the parts inside a digital watch.

Electronic circuit

Liquid crystal display

Battery

Project Editor: Lisa Watts
Editors: Kathy Gemmell, Mike Stocks and Anna Claybourne
Project Designers: Melissa Alaverdy and Julia Rheam
Designer: Robin Farrow; Assistant Designer: Isaac Quaye
Series Designer: Amanda Barlow
Science Consultants: Max Parsonage and Tom Petersen
Picture Researchers: Ruth King and Sophy Tahta
Artwork Coordinators: Ruth King and Cathy Lowe
Experiment Tester: Rakan Budeiri
Project Manager: Felicity Brooks

Asteroids are large pieces of rock and metal left over from the formation of the solar system.

A screwdriver applies the effort needed to operate it in a more efficient way.

Load

Effort

Atom

Table tennis ball

Earth

If atoms were the size of table tennis balls, by the same scale, table tennis balls would be as big as the Earth.

ATOMS AND MOLECULES

Atoms are the tiny particles of which all matter is made. It is impossible to imagine how small an atom is. A hundred million atoms side-by-side would measure only 1cm (less than half an inch), and a thin sheet of paper is probably a million atoms thick. There are just over a hundred different kinds of atoms and they join together to form all the different substances around us.

These balls represent atoms of oxygen (turquoise) and hydrogen (lilac) clinging together to form molecules of water.

HISTORY OF ATOMIC THEORY

The idea that everything in the universe is made up of atoms is not a new one. Philosophers in Ancient Greece, 2,500 years ago, believed that matter was made up of uncuttable particles that could not be cut any smaller. The word "atom" comes from the Greek word *atomos*, which means "uncuttable".

Although Ancient Greek philosophers debated the idea that matter was made of uncuttable particles, Aristotle (left) questioned this idea.

The term "atom" was first used by the British chemist, John Dalton, when he put forward his atomic theory in 1807. Dalton maintained that all chemical elements were composed of very small particles, called atoms, that did not break up during chemical reactions, and that every chemical reaction was the result of atoms joining or separating. Dalton's atomic theory provided the basis for the modern study of science.

John Dalton (1766-1844)

Dalton used symbols to represent one atom of each element or substance.

Zinc

Mercury   *Sulphur*

Early this century, scientists began to make models of the insides of atoms. Ernest Rutherford (1871-1937) showed electrons with a negative electric charge (see Atomic Structure, right) circling a positively charged nucleus. Neils Bohr (1885-1962) showed electrons following specific orbits. In 1932, James Chadwick (1891-1974) showed the nucleus made of particles called neutrons and protons. The large diagram on this page is based on models by Bohr and Chadwick.

Rutherford's model

ATOMIC STRUCTURE

Atoms are made of even smaller particles called subatomic particles. In the middle of every atom is its nucleus. The nucleus contains two types of subatomic particles, called protons and neutrons. A third type of subatomic particles, called electrons, move around the nucleus. There are many other kinds of subatomic matter, such as quarks, which are thought to be the matter of which protons and neutrons are made.

This diagram of an atom is based on models by Bohr and Chadwick (see left). It shows electrons moving at high speed around the nucleus in the middle.

The subatomic particles that make up an atom are held together by electrical charges. The protons have a positive electrical charge and the electrons have a negative charge. Neutrons have no electrical charge, so they are neutral.

The protons and neutrons form the nucleus of an atom.

Electrons have a negative electrical charge.

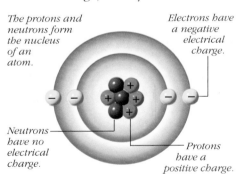

Neutrons have no electrical charge.

Protons have a positive charge.

Particles with opposite electrical charges are attracted to each other. The attraction between the negatively charged electrons and the positively charged protons in the atom's nucleus keeps the electrons around the nucleus. An atom usually contains an equal number of positively charged protons and negatively charged electrons. This makes the atom itself electrically neutral. The electrons exist in different energy levels, called shells, around the nucleus. Each shell can have a certain number of electrons and when it is full, a new shell is started.

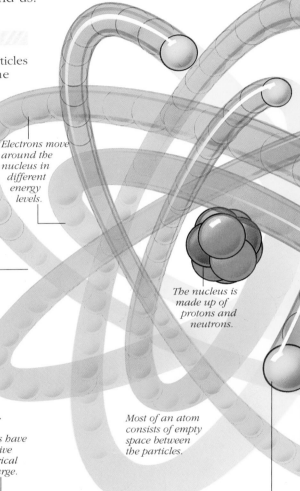

Electrons move around the nucleus in different energy levels.

The nucleus is made up of protons and neutrons.

Most of an atom consists of empty space between the particles.

The negatively charged electrons are held in their different energy levels by their attraction to the positively charged protons in the nucleus.

Although atoms are frequently represented by diagrams like the one above, scientists now believe that the electrons are in cloud-like volumes around the atom's nucleus, as shown in this electron cloud model.

In this picture of a molecule viewed through a scanning electron microscope, the colours show the different levels of density of electrons. The turquoise areas are the most dense.

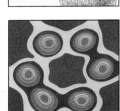

ATOMIC AND MASS NUMBERS

The number of protons in the nucleus of an atom is called the atomic number. An atom usually has an equal number of protons and electrons, so the atomic number also shows how many electrons it has. Different atoms have different numbers of protons.

The nucleus of a phosphorus atom contains 15 protons, and 16 neutrons, so its atomic number is 15.

The nucleus of a gold atom contains 79 protons, and 118 neutrons so its atomic number is 79.

The more protons and neutrons an atom has, the greater its mass (the measurement of the amount of matter in the atom). The total number of protons and neutrons in an atom is called its mass number. The mass number of phosphorus (shown above) is 31. Electrons are left out of the calculation as they add so little to the mass of an atom. A machine called a mass spectrometer can be used to help identify atoms by sorting them by mass.

This picture shows a carbon atom. It has six protons and six neutrons, so its mass number is 12. It has two electrons in its first energy level and four in the second.

ISOTOPES

Most atoms exist in a number of different forms, called isotopes. Each form has the same number of protons and electrons, but a different number of neutrons. So all the isotopes of an atom have the same atomic number, but they have different mass numbers. The mass number of the isotope of an atom is written beside its name.

Proton — *Neutron*

C-12

These examples show the three isotopes of carbon. Carbon-12 has six neutrons and six protons. Carbon-13 has seven neutrons and six protons and carbon-14 has eight neutrons and six protons.

C-13

C-14

Isotopes have different physical properties but their chemical properties are the same. Most of the atoms in an element* (a substance made up of only one type of atom) usually belong to one isotope, with smaller amounts of the other isotopes.

MOLECULES

Atoms are rarely found on their own. They usually cling together to form molecules or other, larger structures. A molecule is a group of atoms that are bonded* together to form the smallest piece of a substance that can exist on its own. They are much too small to be seen with the naked eye.

Right: this diagram shows two atoms of hydrogen bonded to an atom of oxygen to form a molecule of water. The atoms are held together by the electrical charges in their particles.*

Model of a molecule of water, H_2O

When studying molecules, scientists often use models to represent them. There are two main types of models: ball-and-spoke models and space-filling models.

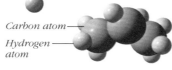

Ball and spoke model of a molecule of chlorine (Cl_2)

Space-filling model of a molecule of sulphuric acid (H_2SO_4)

Ball-and-spoke model of a molecule of methane (CH_4)

Carbon atom

Hydrogen atom

Space-filling model of a molecule of propane (C_3H_8)

In ball-and-spoke models, the bonds that hold the atoms together are shown as sticks, while in space-filling models the atoms are shown clinging together. A model does not look like an actual molecule, but it is a simple and useful way of showing the different atoms that form the molecule.

CHEMICAL FORMULAE

A chemical formula shows the atoms of which a substance is made and in what proportions. Each atom is represented by a symbol, which is usually the first letter of its name in English, or another language such as Latin or Arabic.

For example, a molecule of carbon dioxide is made up of two atoms of oxygen and one atom of carbon and the formula for carbon dioxide is CO_2. The figure "2" shows the number of oxygen atoms in the molecule.

Right: a molecule of carbon dioxide, CO_2

Oxygen atoms

Carbon atom

Left: a molecule of ammonia, NH_3, which is made up of an atom of nitrogen and three atoms of hydrogen.

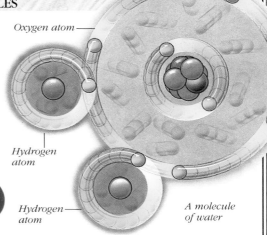

Oxygen atom

Hydrogen atom

Hydrogen atom

A molecule of water

SEE FOR YOURSELF

This experiment helps to show how the molecules in a substance are held together by the forces of attraction between them. Fill a glass to the brim with water.

Gently slide several coins into the glass until the water bulges above the rim of the glass.

The pull between the water molecules is strong enough to hold some water above the level of the glass. This pulling force at the surface of water is called surface tension.*

KEY TERMS

Atom The smallest particle of an element that still has the chemical properties of that element.

Atomic number The number of protons in the nucleus of an atom.

Electron A negatively charged particle that exists around the nucleus of an atom.

Element A substance made up of one kind of atom and which cannot be broken down by a chemical reaction to form simpler substances.

Isotope An atom that has a different number of neutrons and so has a different mass number from the other atoms in an element.

Mass number The total number of protons and neutrons in the nucleus of a particular atom.

Neutron A subatomic particle with no electrical charge in the nucleus of an atom.

Proton A subatomic particle that has a positive electrical charge in the nucleus of an atom.

ENERGY

Without energy, nothing could live or grow, and there would be no movement, light, heat or noise. Energy can take many different forms: heat, light, sound, microwaves and electricity are all different forms of energy. For anything to happen, energy is needed, and whenever anything happens, energy is converted from one form to another. Nearly all the energy on Earth comes from the Sun.*

Foods such as chips, potatoes, cereals and bread, contain large amounts of stored energy.

The energy from the Sun is the equivalent of that supplied by 100 million large power stations.

FORMS OF ENERGY

Energy can exist in many forms and the different forms make different things happen. As well as heat,* light* and sound,* there are other forms such as chemical energy, kinetic energy and potential energy.

A light bulb gives out light and heat energy.

Heat energy

Light energy

Electrical energy

Sound energy travels as waves. We hear sounds when the waves make our eardrums vibrate.

Chemical energy is energy that is released during chemical reactions. Food, and fuels such as coal, oil and gasoline, and also batteries,* are storages of chemical energy.

Food is a storage of chemical energy that is released by chemical reactions in your cells.

SEE FOR YOURSELF

In this matchbox "paddleboat", energy stored by a twisted rubber band is changed into kinetic energy that moves the "boat" forward.

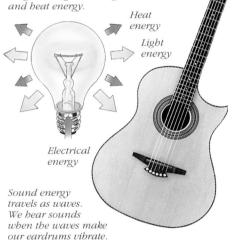

Used match

Rubber band

Place a piece of cardboard in the rubber band and twist it to wind up the band.

Float the boat in some water.

Moving objects have kinetic energy, the energy of movement. The faster something moves, the more kinetic energy it has. As it slows down, it loses kinetic energy.

When a moving object hits a stationary one, some of its kinetic energy is transferred to the stationary object, making it move.

Animals convert some of the energy from their food into kinetic energy.

The moving marble transfers kinetic energy to the stationary marble.

Potential energy is the energy an object has because of its position in a force field, such as a field of gravity* or magnetism.* Substances that can be stretched or squashed, such as elastic and springs, have potential strain or elastic energy.

A pendulum has its maximum potential gravitational energy when it is in its highest position.

As a hairspring gradually unwinds, it releases energy that turns the parts in a mechanical watch.

Plants take energy from sunlight and use it to make their food, which is a store of chemical energy.

ENERGY CONVERSION

The law of conservation of energy states that energy can never be created or destroyed. Whenever anything happens and energy is used, it is converted into a different form.

Chemical energy in batteries is changed to electrical energy in a flash-light.

Electrical energy is changed to light and heat energy in the bulb.

An "energy chain" is a useful way of showing how energy is converted from one form to another. The pictures below show the energy changes that take place in a power station, where the energy in coal is converted into electrical energy.

Coal is the fossilized remains of plants that grew long ago. It is a chemical storage of energy that came from the Sun.

When the coal is burned, the chemical energy is converted to heat energy, which is used to heat water to make steam.

The steam turns turbines, producing kinetic energy - the energy of movement.

The kinetic energy is converted to electrical energy in a generator (see Generating Electricity).*

Appliances such as lamps, TVs, heaters and audio equipment convert electrical energy into light, heat and sound.

The final forms in most energy chains are heat and light. Even this energy is not lost, but it spreads out into the environment and is very difficult to harness for any useful purpose.

*Heat, 8; Light, 38; Sound, 44; Batteries, 47

*Sun, 32; Gravity, 20; Magnetism, 48; Generating Electricity, 47

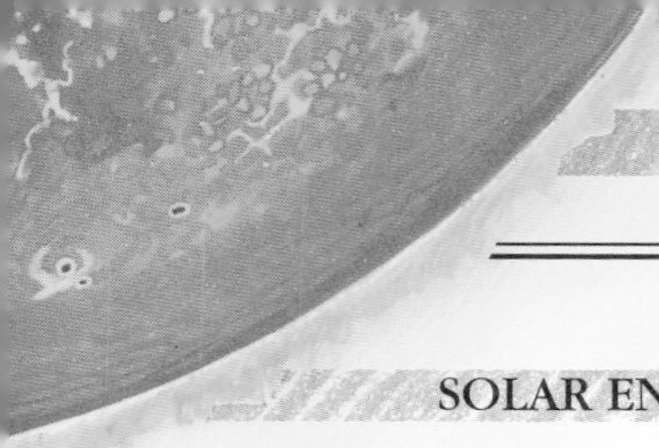

SOLAR ENERGY

The energy from the Sun reaches the Earth in the form of electromagnetic energy,* the only energy that can travel across space. It can be used to generate electricity using a solar cell,* or to heat water using solar collectors.

Sun's rays

Solar collector panels absorb heat from the Sun.

Left: cutaway view of a solar collector panel. Heat from the Sun is absorbed by the black absorber panel which heats the water in the pipes.

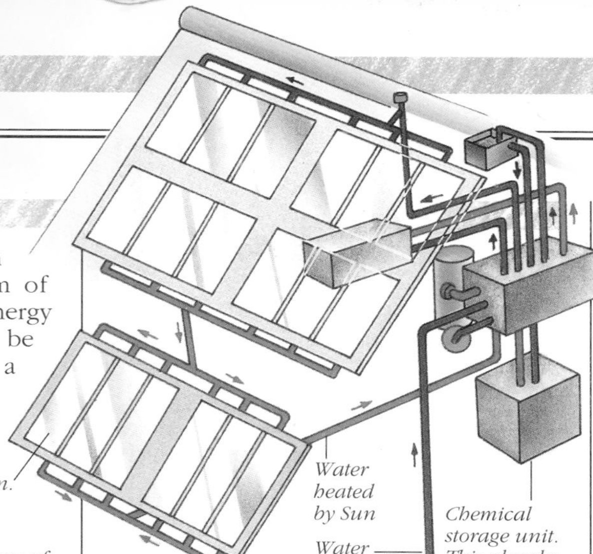

Absorber panel   *Pipe*

Water heated by Sun

Water supply

Cutaway view of a roof with a solar heating system. The hot water is for domestic use, and for the central heating system.

Chemical storage unit. This absorbs surplus heat which is stored and released when it is needed.

ENERGY RESOURCES

We need energy to heat and light houses, to cook food and provide the power for factories and cars. This energy can be obtained by burning fuels, or by other methods such as hydroelectric power.

About half the world's population uses wood, dung or charcoal to provide the energy that they need for cooking and heating.

Wood, coal, oil, and natural gas are called nonrenewable fuels because they can only be used once. Other sources of energy, such as the Sun, wind and water, are called renewable energy resources because they generate power without themselves being used.

Renewable energy 5%   *Nuclear energy* 3%*

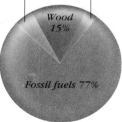

Wood 15%

Fossil fuels 77%

This pie chart shows the percentages of the different power resources that are used to generate energy for homes and industry.

Coal, oil and natural gas are called fossil fuels because they formed from the fossilized remains of plants or animals. About 20 percent of the world's energy comes from coal. When fossil fuels burn, they release carbon dioxide and other gases into the air and they are partly to blame for problems such as acid rain* and the greenhouse effect.*

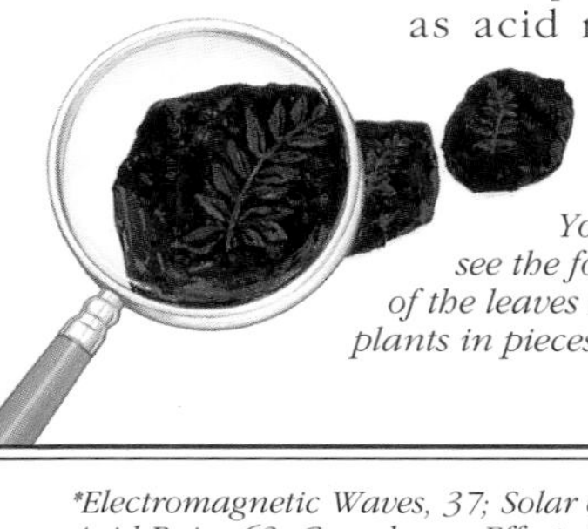

You can sometimes see the fossilized remains of the leaves of prehistoric plants in pieces of coal.

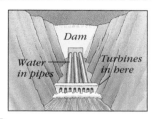

Dam

Water in pipes   *Turbines in here*

Hydroelectric power stations use the kinetic energy in the moving water from a dam to turn turbines that generate electricity.

Only about five percent of the world's energy is generated by renewable energy resources such as hydroelectric power, solar energy (see above) and wind power. Biogas from rotting waste matter is another renewable energy resource.

When organic matter rots, it produces gases including methane, the main substance in natural gas. Biogas can be burned to heat buildings and water.

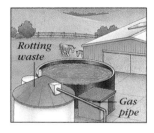

Rotting waste

Gas pipe

The wind has been used for thousands of years to power sailing ships and windmills. It can also be used to generate electricity or pump water.

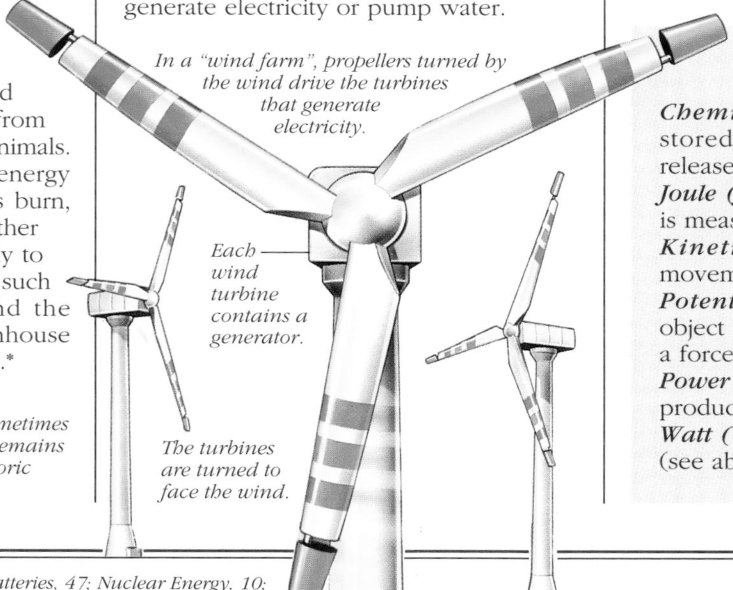

In a "wind farm", propellers turned by the wind drive the turbines that generate electricity.

Each wind turbine contains a generator.

The turbines are turned to face the wind.

MEASURING ENERGY AND POWER

Energy is normally measured in very small units called joules (J). A thousand joules is a kilojoule (kJ).

An ordinary sized apple (100g) contains 150kJ of chemical energy and the same mass of milk chocolate contains 2,335kJ.

Power is the energy used in a certain time and it is measured in units called watts (W). One watt is equal to one joule per second. The more energy a machine or appliance produces in a certain period of time the more powerful it is.

60 watt light bulb

100 watt light bulb

A 60 watt light bulb uses 60 joules of energy each second and a 100 watt bulb uses 100 joules a second.

ENERGY EFFICIENCY

Machines and appliances take one form of energy, for example, electricity, and change it into another form of energy. Machines are described as efficient if they change most of the energy that is used to power them, into the useful form of energy that is needed.

Most cars are very inefficient. An average sized car engine converts only about 15 percent of the chemical energy in gas into kinetic energy. The rest is converted into heat.

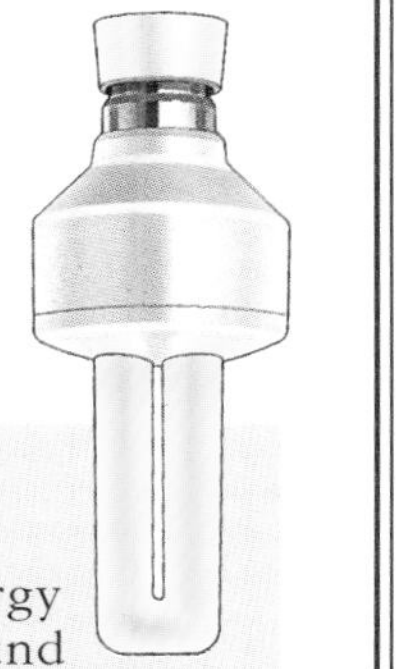

Energy-saving fluorescent tube lights are more efficient than normal light bulbs because they turn more of the electrical energy into light and waste less as heat.

KEY TERMS

Chemical energy Energy stored in a substance and released during a chemical reaction.
Joule (J) The unit in which energy is measured.
Kinetic energy The energy of movement.
Potential energy The energy an object has because of its position in a force field.
Power The rate at which energy is produced or used.
Watt (W) The unit in which power (see above) is measured.

*Electromagnetic Waves, 37; Solar cell, see Batteries, 47; Nuclear Energy, 10; Acid Rain, 63; Greenhouse Effect, 63

HEAT AND TEMPERATURE

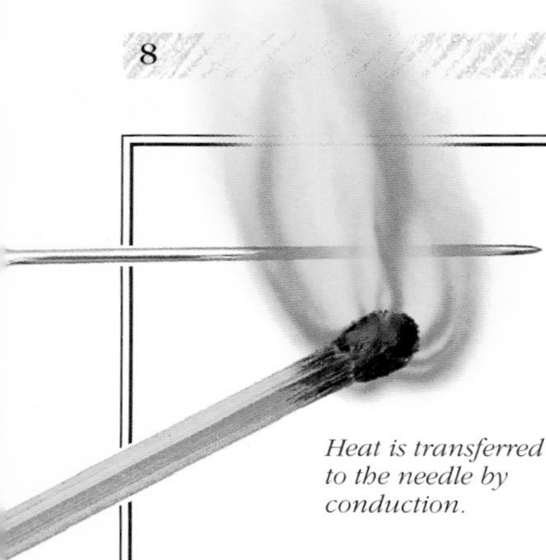

Heat is a form of energy* that flows from one place to another because of a difference in temperature. Temperature is a measure of how hot something is. Heat can be transferred by conduction, convection or radiation. Radiation from the Sun provides the warmth that makes life on our planet possible.

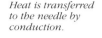

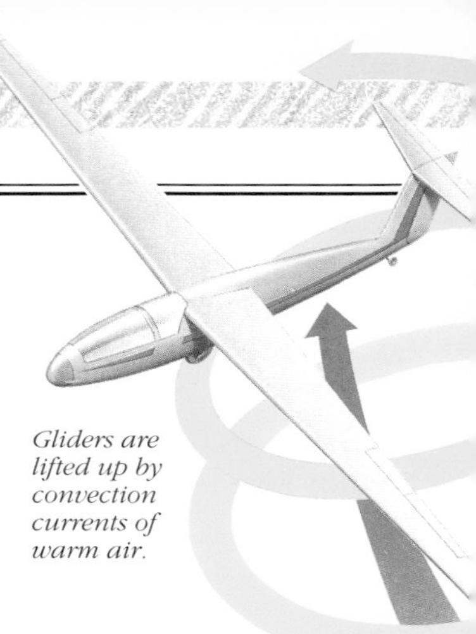

Heat is transferred to the needle by conduction.

Gliders are lifted up by convection currents of warm air.

HEAT ENERGY

Heat is a form of energy* and when a substance absorbs heat, its internal energy increases. Internal energy is the sum of the kinetic energy and the potential energy of the particles of which the substance is made. Kinetic energy is the energy that makes the particles in a solid vibrate and they have potential energy because of the forces between them (see Energy*).

If a solid is heated, the kinetic energy of its particles increases and as it expands, the potential energy of its particles also increases.

Heat energy flows from hot objects to cooler ones and continues to flow until they are at the same temperature. When a substance loses heat, its internal energy decreases.

When ice melts, it absorbs heat energy from the liquid around it, and lowers the temperature of the liquid.

Heat, and other forms of energy, are measured in joules (J) after the English scientist James Joule (1818-89). Joule was the first scientist to recognize that heat is a form of energy. Using a machine like the one shown on the left, he measured how much potential gravitational energy in falling weights was needed to raise the temperature of the water by stirring it.

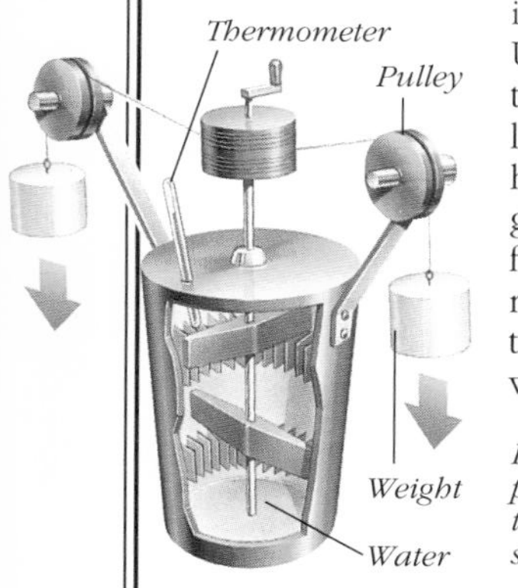

Thermometer

Pulley

Weight

Water

Falling weights made the paddles in the container turn, causing the water to swirl about and heat up.

It takes 4,200J to raise the temperature of 1kg (2.2lb) of water by 1°C (1.8°F).

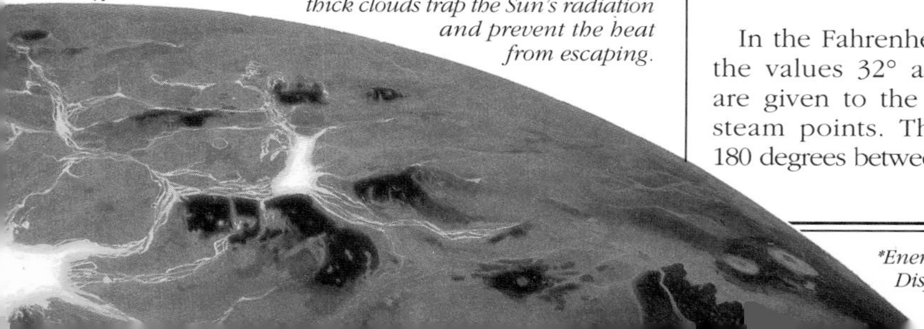

On Venus, the temperature is around 480°C (896°F) because thick clouds trap the Sun's radiation and prevent the heat from escaping.

TEMPERATURE

Temperature is a measure of how hot something is. If the same amount of energy is supplied to equal masses of two substances at the same temperature, they will reach different temperatures. Substances are said to have different specific heat (or thermal) capacities.

*Above: oil
Right: water*

The same amount of heat makes oil hotter than water.

The different heat capacities of the land and the sea cause sea breezes. In the day, the land heats up faster than the sea.

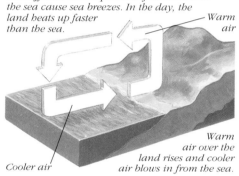

Warm air

Cooler air

Warm air over the land rises and cooler air blows in from the sea.

Temperature can be measured in degrees Celsius (°C) or Fahrenheit (°F), or on the absolute temperature scale. The Celsius scale has two fixed points: ice point (0°C) and steam point (100°C). Each Celsius degree is one hundredth of the difference between these two points.

Left: an early Celsius thermometer. The Celsius scale was invented by Anders Celsius (1701-44), a Swedish astronomer. Right: the Celsius and Fahrenheit scales

Steam point	
212°F	100°C
32°F	0°C
Ice point or freezing point	

In the Fahrenheit scale, the values 32° and 212° are given to the ice and steam points. There are 180 degrees between them.

The absolute temperature scale starts at a point called absolute zero, which is -273°C. This is the temperature at which no more energy can be removed from a substance and it is the lowest temperature possible. Kelvins (K), the unit used by this scale, are the same size as Celsius degrees.

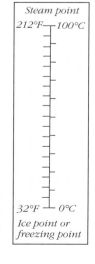

The Kelvin scale is used for scientific work.

THERMOMETERS

A thermometer is an instrument for measuring temperature. It may contain a liquid that expands when heated, or a wire whose resistance* to electric current changes if the temperature changes.

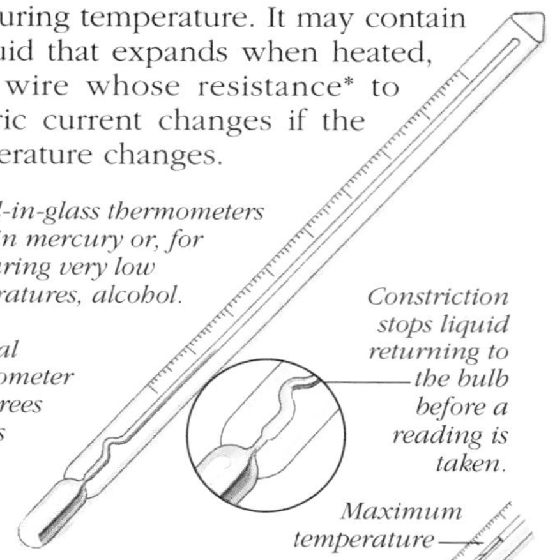

Liquid-in-glass thermometers contain mercury or, for measuring very low temperatures, alcohol.

Clinical thermometer in degrees Celsius

Constriction stops liquid returning to the bulb before a reading is taken.

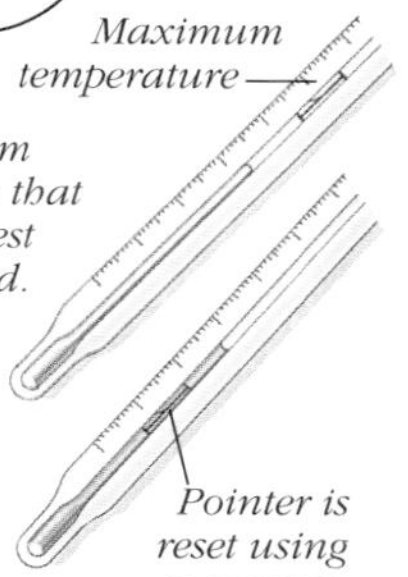

Maximum temperature

Right: maximum and minimum thermometers contain pointers that record the highest or lowest temperature reached.

Above: a digital thermometer contains an electronic component that is sensitive to heat. It shows the temperature on a digital display.

Pointer is reset using a magnet.

| 35 | 36 | 37 | 38 | 39 | 40 |

Above: liquid crystal thermometers contain liquid crystals that change colour when they are heated.*

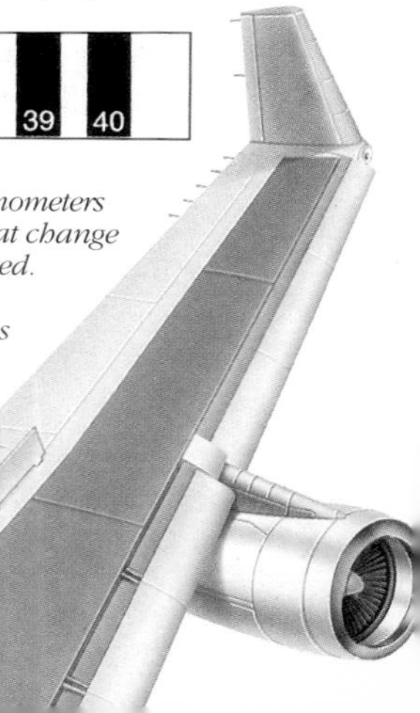

Aircraft have tiny devices called thermistors under their wings that measure the temperature of the air.

Energy, 6; Resistance, 50; Liquid Crystal Displays, 77

CONVECTION

Convection is the main way that heat energy is transferred in liquids and gases. When a liquid or gas is heated, the part nearest to the heat source expands and becomes less dense, so it rises. The cooler, denser liquid sinks towards the heat source. The upward currents of hot liquid or gas are called convection currents.

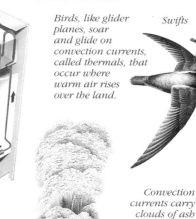

Fridges are kept cold by convection currents. Cool air near the top of the fridge sinks, while warmer air rises to be cooled.

Convection current of warmer air

Convection current

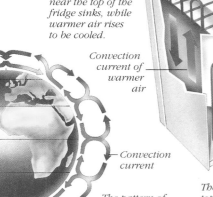

The pattern of winds around the world are caused by convection currents that occur because more of the Sun's energy falls near the equator. As the air is heated, it expands and rises and colder, denser air rushes in, creating a wind.

The air near the top of the fridge is cooled by gas, such as freon, in these pipes.

Birds, like glider planes, soar and glide on convection currents, called thermals, that occur where warm air rises over the land.

Swifts

Convection currents carry clouds of ash from volcanoes into the upper atmosphere. Dust from the eruption of Mount St. Helens in 1980 affected the world's climate for several years.

Mount St. Helens volcano

CONDUCTION

Conduction is the way that heat energy is transferred in a solid. The energy of the particles nearest to the heat source increases and they vibrate and pass on some of their energy, spreading heat through the substance.

Metals heat up quickly as they are very good conductors of heat.

Handles are made of wood or plastic which do not conduct heat easily.

Metals* are good conductors of heat because they have free-moving electrons that carry heat energy through the metal. Substances that conduct heat slowly, such as wood and water, are called insulators. Air is a good insulator and materials that trap air, such as wool and polystyrene, are good insulators.

Heat energy from a desert fox's ears is transferred to the air by conduction and spreads away by convection.

Fat and feathers insulate birds such as penguins, helping to keep them warm.

RADIATION

Radiation is heat energy that travels in waves, called infrared waves, which are a type of electromagnetic wave.* Radiation does not depend on the movement of particles, and this is the only form of energy that can travel across a vacuum (a space that is completely empty of air or other matter).

Heat from the Sun travels by radiation at 300 million metres (328 million yards) per second. It takes about eight minutes to reach the Earth.

Very hot objects such as light bulbs and electric fires, also radiate heat. Dark coloured objects absorb heat radiation while light colours reflect radiation and stay cool.

Left: light bulbs radiate heat.

Light surfaces reflect radiation.

In Antarctica, the snow reflects over 90 percent of the radiation from the Sun back into the atmosphere. The surface receives very little heating, so the air remains cold.

VACUUM FLASKS

A vacuum flask is a container for keeping liquids at a constant temperature. It has two glass containers, one inside the other, with a vacuum (a space with no air in it) between them. The vacuum prevents the transfer of heat by conduction or convection (see left), and the very shiny surfaces reduce the heat transfer that radiation produces.

Stopper

Outer glass wall

Inner glass wall

Protective case

Vacuum

HEAT AND EXPANSION

Most substances expand when they are heated because, as their particles vibrate more vigorously, they push each other farther apart. Gases and most liquids expand more than solids because their molecules have more energy to break free of the forces that hold them together (see Kinetic Theory*).

The steel strings on a guitar expand in the heat from stage lights and have to be frequently tightened to keep them in tune.

Machine head for tightening the strings

Different solids expand at different rates. This can be seen in a bimetallic strip, which is used in thermostats - devices that switch on and off in response to a change in temperature.

A bimetallic strip is a strip of copper and iron fixed firmly together. When heated, the copper expands more than iron, causing the strip to bend outwards, breaking the electrical circuit.

Strip of copper and iron

Electrical circuit to heater

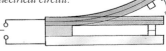

SEE FOR YOURSELF

This experiment shows the warm air rising by convection from your body. Trace and cut out the propeller shape on page 96 and then balance the tracing paper on a pencil.

Convection current of warm air

Hold pencil near tip

A convection current of warm air causes the propeller to spin around. If your hands are not warm enough, rub them together for a minute or two.

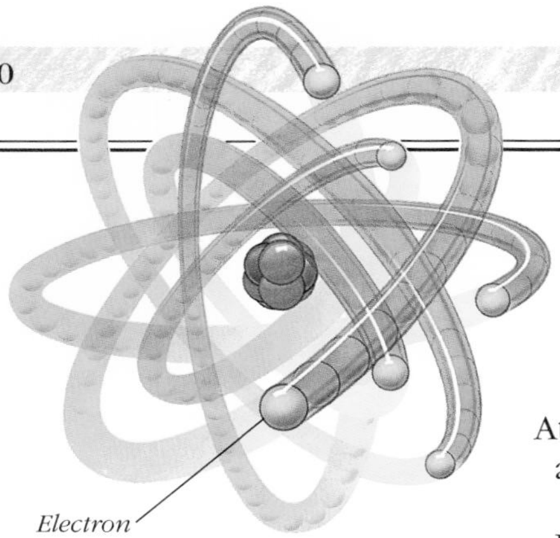

NUCLEAR ENERGY
AND RADIOACTIVITY

Atoms,* the particles of which all matter is made, hold a vast amount of energy in their nuclei. This energy is released as radiation by radioactive substances. Radiation is dangerous for living things, but nuclear reactions can supply the power to generate electricity, and radiation has important uses in medicine.

Electron

An atom consists of a nucleus surrounded by clouds of particles called electrons.

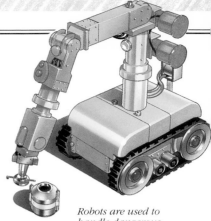

Robots are used to handle dangerous radioactive substances.

RADIOACTIVITY

Radioactivity is the release of radiation from the nuclei of unstable atoms.* Most atoms that have a large number of protons in their nuclei are unstable, but many smaller atoms have radioisotopes (radioactive isotopes - see Key Terms).

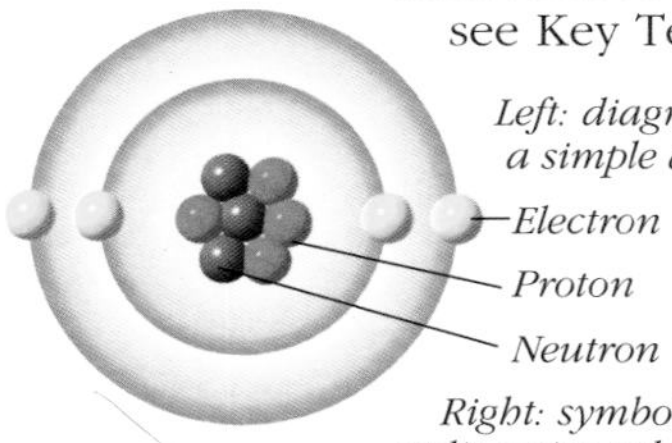

Left: diagram of a simple atom

—*Electron*
—*Proton*
—*Neutron*

Right: symbol for radioactive substances

Radioactivity occurs because the atoms are attempting to become stable. There are three main types of radiation: alpha particles, beta particles and gamma rays. They are named after the first three letters of the Greek alphabet.

An atom throws off alpha and beta particles from its nucleus first, and then, if it is still unstable, gamma radiation. The three nuclei shown in the picture below are all unstable and each one is emitting a different type of radiation.

α
Alpha

β
Beta

γ
Gamma

Left: the Greek letters used for the three different types of radiation.

Beta particles are very high energy electrons emitted when a neutron in the nucleus decays.

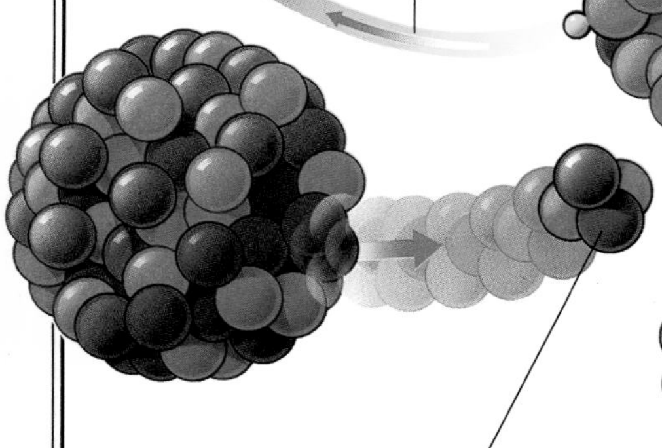

Alpha particles move slowly and are stopped by substances thicker than paper. They are identical to the nuclei of helium atoms and scientists think helium is created by natural radioactivity in the Earth. Beta particles are more powerful and penetrating than alpha particles and they move almost at the speed of light.

Helium is used to fill balloons.

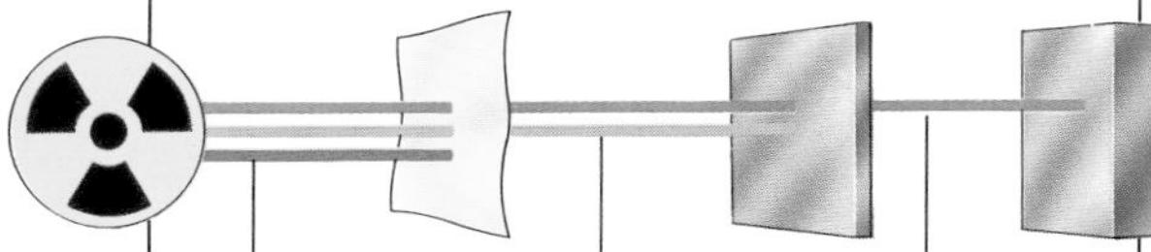

Alpha particles travel less than 10cm (4in) and are absorbed by thick paper.

Beta particles have a range of 1m (3.3ft) in the air and are absorbed by 1mm (0.04in) of copper.

The intensity of gamma rays is halved by 13mm (0.5in) of lead or by about 120m (131yd) of air.

Radioactive substances are transported in thick lead containers to prevent any radiation from escaping. Exposure to radiation can cause burns, cataracts and cancer.

Radiation is measured using a Geiger counter that gives off a series of clicking noises when radiation is present.

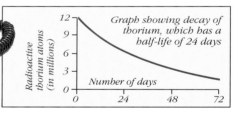

After ejecting particles, a nucleus has a new atomic number (see Key Terms) and becomes the nucleus of a different element. This is called radioactive decay. If the new element is also unstable, the decay process will continue until there are atoms with stable nuclei.

For example, when plutonium-242, whose mass number is 242, gives off an alpha particle, which has a relative atomic mass of four (two protons and two neutrons), it becomes uranium-238, whose mass number is 238.

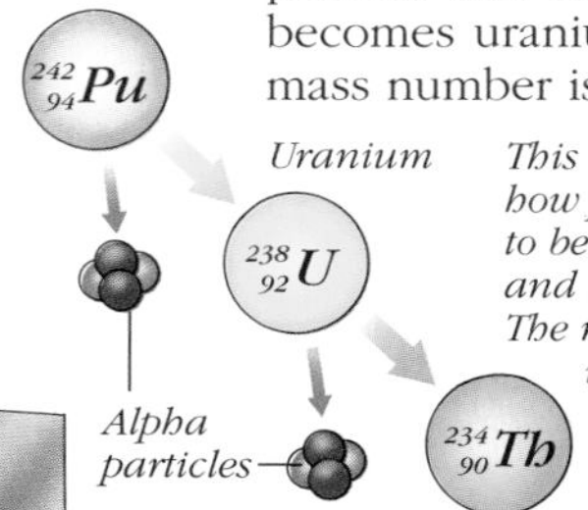

Plutonium

$^{242}_{94}Pu$

Uranium

$^{238}_{92}U$

Alpha particles

$^{234}_{90}Tb$

Thorium

This diagram shows how plutonium decays to become uranium and then thorium. The mass numbers are written above the atomic numbers.

The length of time it takes for the nuclei of an element to decay is called its half-life. This is the time taken for half of the nuclei in a sample to decay. Every element has a different half-life. Radium-221 has a half-life of 30 seconds while uranium-238 has a half-life of 4.5 thousand million years.

Graph showing decay of thorium, which has a half-life of 24 days

Radioactive thorium atoms (in millions)

12
9
6
3
0

Number of days

0   24   48   72

KEY TERMS

Atomic number The number of protons in the nucleus of an atom.

Electron A negatively charged particle that exists around the nucleus of an atom.

Half-life The time taken for half the atoms in a sample to decay.

Isotope An atom that has a different number of neutrons and so has a different mass number from the other atoms in an element.

Mass number The total number of protons and neutrons in a nucleus.

Neutron A subatomic particle with no electrical charge in the nucleus of an atom.

Proton A subatomic particle that has a positive electrical charge in the nucleus of an atom.

Alpha particles are clusters containing two protons and two neutrons. They are identical to the nucleus of a helium atom.

Gamma rays are very high energy electromagnetic rays that move at the speed of light.*

NUCLEAR REACTIONS

There are two types of nuclear reactions: nuclear fusion and nuclear fission. Fusion means "joining" and during nuclear fusion, two small nuclei combine to form a larger one. Nuclear fusion only takes place at extremely high temperatures and releases huge amounts of radiation energy.

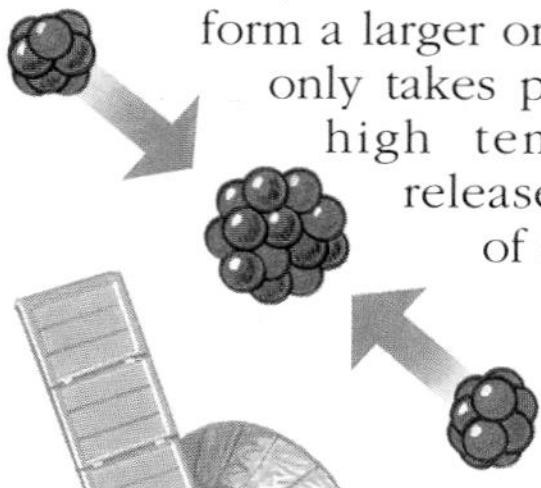

During nuclear fusion two small nuclei join to form one large one.

In 1992, the COBE satellite detected ripples of radiation that support the theory that the Universe was formed in a huge explosion known as the "big bang".

Fission means "splitting apart" and nuclear fission occurs when the nucleus of an atom is bombarded with neutrons.

This occurs in radioactive substances, or in a machine called a particle accelerator. The nucleus splits open, releasing neutrons and large amounts of radiation energy.

During nuclear fission a nucleus splits open forming two or more new nuclei.

World War II atomic bomb

Radioactive plutonium

NUCLEAR WEAPONS

Nuclear weapons use nuclear reactions to generate huge amounts of uncontrolled energy that creates a massive explosion. In World War II, the USA dropped atomic bombs on the cities of Hiroshima and Nagasaki in Japan, killing hundreds of thousands of people. Atomic bombs use nuclear fission reactions (see left). Hydrogen bombs use nuclear fusion.

Mushroom-shaped cloud from an atomic bomb

NUCLEAR POWER

The energy released during nuclear reactions can be used to generate electricity, and to power submarines and aircraft carriers.

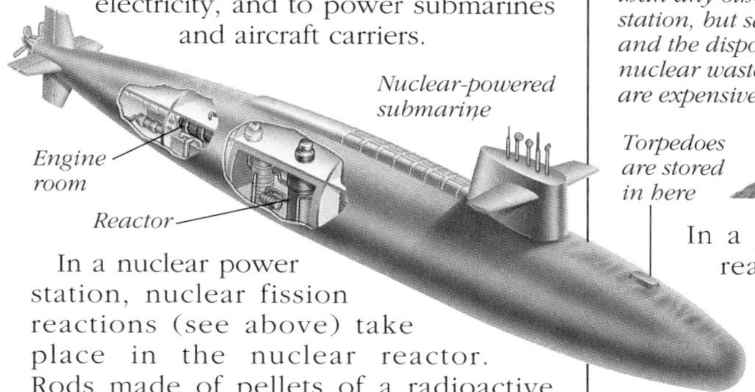

Nuclear-powered submarine

Engine room

Reactor

In a nuclear power station, nuclear fission reactions (see above) take place in the nuclear reactor. Rods made of pellets of a radioactive substance such as uranium are bombarded with neutrons. Their nuclei split up, releasing radiation and more neutrons which set up a chain reaction.

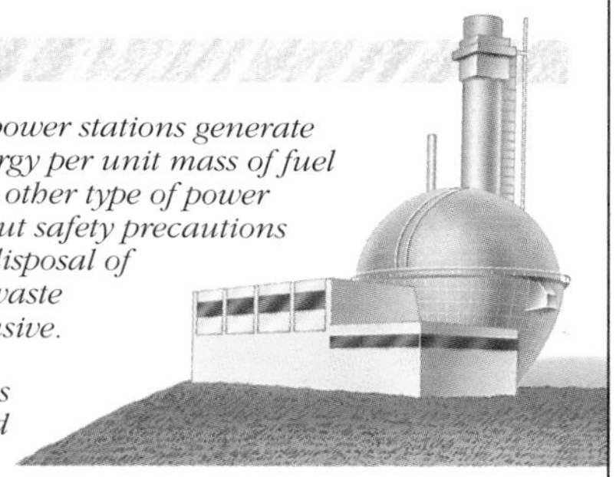

This diagram shows the main parts of a pressurized water reactor where nuclear energy is used to generate electricity. Nuclear fission reactions take place in the core of the nuclear reactor (1). The energy released heats pressurized water in the primary water circuit (2).

Nuclear power stations generate more energy per unit mass of fuel than any other type of power station, but safety precautions and the disposal of nuclear waste are expensive.

Torpedoes are stored in here

In a pressurized water reactor like the one shown in the diagram below, the energy released in the core of the reactor is used to heat water to make steam. The steam turns the turbines that generate the electricity.*

Pellets of nuclear fuel

CARBON DATING

Carbon dating is a method of calculating the time that has passed since living matter died. All living things contain a small amount of carbon-14, a radioactive isotope of carbon. Carbon-14 has a half-life (see Key Terms) of 5,700 years. When living things die, the carbon-14 decays and is not replaced, so the age of the remains can be calculated.

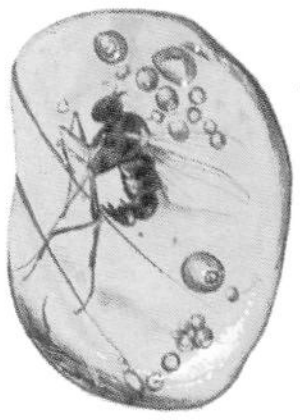

Five thousand year old insect in amber

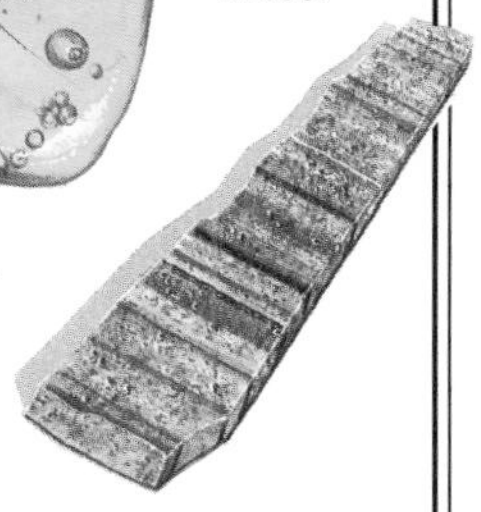

Lava from different volcanic eruptions can be dated using carbon dating on insects and pollen trapped in the lava.

OTHER USES OF RADIOACTIVITY

In industry, radiation is used to check the thickness of sheets of paper and plastic. Tiny irregularities can be detected by measuring the amount of beta radiation that passes through the sheets. Food, such as fruit and meat, can be "irradiated" with gamma rays to keep it fresh.

In hospitals, doctors use radioactive tracing to follow a substance through a patient's body. For example, to see how a patient's body deals with sugar, they can attach some carbon-14 to molecules of sugar and track the radiation given off by the carbon-14.

Untreated strawberry

"Irradiated" strawberry after two weeks

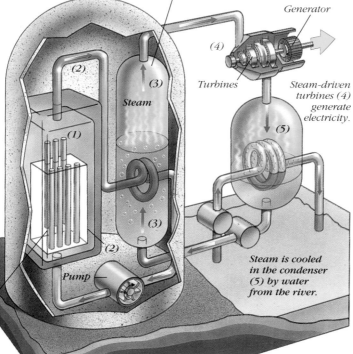

Heat from the primary water circuit heats the water in the secondary circuit to make steam (3).

Generator

(4)

Turbines

Steam-driven turbines (4) generate electricity.

Steam

(2)

(3)

(1)

(5)

(3)

(2)

Pump

Steam is cooled in the condenser (5) by water from the river.

Workers wear masks and clothes to protect them from radioactive dust, and a device that records any exposure to radiation. Uranium rod

Radiotherapy uses carefully controlled doses of radiation to kill cancer cells, which are living cells that are growing in a disorderly way.

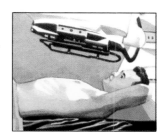

SOLIDS, LIQUIDS AND GASES

Most substances can exist in three different forms: as solids, liquids or gases. These are called the states of matter. The change from one state to another is caused by heating or cooling, or by a change in pressure. For example, when water, a liquid, is heated it becomes a gas called water vapour (steam). The theory that explains the properties of solids, liquids and gases is called the kinetic theory and it is based on the idea that all substances are made up of moving particles.

An ice cream melts and becomes a liquid in the heat of the Sun.

In rainforests, raindrops quickly evaporate to form water vapour in the air.

THE KINETIC THEORY

Many of the ideas in science have not yet been proved, but are held to be true because they explain what scientists observe happening. The kinetic theory explains the properties of solids, liquids and gases in terms of the energy of the particles of which they are made.

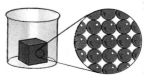
The particles in a solid have least energy and cannot break free of the attraction between their particles. They vibrate around fixed positions.

Heating a solid gives the particles more energy so they can break free of their neighbours. This makes the solid melt and become a liquid.

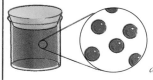

The particles in a gas have even more energy. They easily move far apart and spread out through all the available space.

Heating a substance gives the particles more energy, enabling them to move around faster and change from one state to another (see Changes of State).

BROWNIAN MOTION

The movement of particles in liquids and gases is known as Brownian motion, after a British biologist named Robert Brown. In 1827, Brown observed how tiny grains of pollen moved around randomly in a liquid, but he could not explain what caused this movement.

The ziz-zag movement of pollen grains in water can be easily seen under a microscope.

In the 20th century, the German-born scientist, Albert Einstein, explained that the movement of particles in a liquid or gas is caused by the particles being hit by the invisible molecules of the fluid in which they are floating.

CHANGES OF STATE

When a solid is heated, its temperature rises and its particles gain energy until it reaches its melting point. The particles now have enough energy to break free of their neighbours and the solid melts. Further heat causes the liquid to rise in temperature until it reaches its boiling point and the particles break free of each other completely and the liquid becomes a gas.

The heat from a flame melts candle wax, but the wax sets as it drips away from the flame.

Mercury melts at -40°C (-40°F).

Geysers are jets of boiling hot water and steam heated by volcanic rocks in the Earth's crust.

When a substance cools, the process is reversed. When a gas cools to its boiling point, it condenses and becomes a liquid. When a liquid cools to its melting point, it sets or freezes and becomes a solid. Some substances, for example, carbon dioxide* change from solid to gas without passing through a liquid form. This is called sublimation.

Cavities filled with groundwater

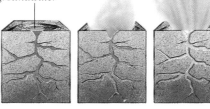
Geysers occur when groundwater heated by hot volcanic rocks begins to boil. As the water turns to gas, the pressure builds up in the channels between the rocks and the geyser erupts, shooting a jet of steam and water into the air.

Different substances change state at different temperatures and a substance is classified as a solid, liquid or gas depending on its state at room temperature (20°C or 68°F).

Nitrogen dioxide boils at 21°C (70°F) and becomes a gas at room temperature.

Chlorine boils at -35°C (-31°F) and is a gas at room temperature.

Sulphur melts at 119°C (246°F).

Copper melts at 1083°C (1981°F).

Diamond melts at 3750°C (6782°F).

The temperature at which a substance melts or boils changes if it contains traces of any other substances, or if the pressure is different. The air presses down on the Earth with a force called atmospheric pressure.* Standard pressure at sea level is often referred to as one atmosphere.

Thermometer

At the top of Mount Everest (8,848m or 29,028ft), where the pressure is less than one atmosphere, pure water boils at 71°C (160°F), while at sea level, it boils at 100°C (212°F).

At higher altitudes, the atmospheric pressure is less so it is easier for the particles in a liquid to escape into the air, and their boiling points are lower.

Scientists think there is no water on Mars because the atmospheric pressure is very low, so any water immediately boils and evaporates.

Dry, lifeless surface of Mars

---

*Carbon Dioxide, 63; Iodine, see The Halogens, 60; Pressure, 21

SURFACE TENSION

The molecules on the surface of a liquid are strongly attracted to each other. This creates a force called surface tension that makes the liquid seem to have a "skin".

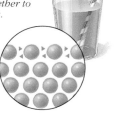

Surface tension pulls molecules of liquid together to form drips.

The molecules on the surface of a liquid are spaced farther apart than inside the liquid and this strengthens the forces of attraction between them.

The force between the molecules is strong enough to support very light objects, such as particles of dust or even insects, on the surface of the water.

Pond skaters can walk on the surface of the water as they are not heavy enough to break the skin-like surface of the liquid.

EVAPORATION

Some of the molecules on the surface of a liquid have more energy than others, and they escape, or evaporate, into the air. Liquids are evaporating all the time, even when they are not being heated. When a liquid is evaporating, its temperature falls because the average energy of the molecules that are left in the liquid has fallen.

When people sweat, the droplets of water absorb heat from the skin and evaporate. This cools the skin.

KEY TERMS

Atom The smallest particle of an element that still has the chemical properties of that element.
Kinetic energy Energy that takes the form of movement.
Molecule Two or more atoms chemically bonded together to form the smallest particle of a substance.
Particle An atom, molecule or ion.
Pressure The force exerted over a given area by a solid, liquid or gas.

GASES

A gas is a substance that has no definite volume or shape. According to the kinetic theory (see left), the molecules in a gas have enough energy to break free of the forces between them, and they spread out to fill the available space. This is called diffusion.

Balloons stretch as the gas spreads out to fill them.

— Air

After fifteen minutes, the air and bromine in the jars on the left become mixed by diffusion as their molecules spread through the two jars.

Bromine gas   Gases mixed by diffusion

Smells, such as the scent of flowers, are gases that travel through the air by diffusion.

The pressure of a gas depends on the rate at which its molecules hit the sides of its container. If the volume of a gas at a constant temperature is decreased, for example, by reducing the size of its container, its pressure increases because the gas molecules hit the container's walls more often. The pressure will also increase if more gas is pumped into the container.

The pressure of the air pushing against the walls inside this inflatable life-raft gives it its shape.

When heated, the molecules in a gas move around faster and become even further apart as the gas expands and becomes lighter. If the gas is not allowed to expand when heated, its pressure increases.

Metal sphere filled with boiling water   Steam

This ancient Greek toy uses the pressure of steam to turn the sphere at the top.

Steam

Hot air balloons float as the air in their balloons is lighter than the air around them.

VOLUME, MASS AND DENSITY

Volume is the amount of space a solid or liquid occupies. It is measured in cubic metres (m^3) or cubic feet (ft^3). The volume of a rectangular solid is found using this formula: length x breadth x height. The volume of a liquid can be found by pouring it into a measuring cylinder.

Eureka can

The volume of an irregularly shaped solid is measured by finding how much liquid it displaces.

The mass of a solid, liquid or gas is the amount of matter it contains. Mass can be measured in kilograms or pounds. Mass is different from weight, which is a measure of the strength of the pull of gravity* on an object.

Unknown mass   Known mass

Mass is measured by weighing a substance and comparing its mass with a known mass.

Density is a measure of how tightly packed the particles are in a substance. For example, molecules of metal are packed more tightly together than molecules of cork or paper, so metals have a higher density than cork. Density is found by dividing the mass of an object by its volume, and it is measured in kilograms per cubic metre (kg/m^3) or pounds per cubic foot (lb/ft^3).

The density of a liquid is measured using a hydrometer. The hydrometer floats near the surface in a dense liquid, as only a small volume of liquid needs to be displaced to equal the weight of the hydrometer (see Why Things Float).*

SEE FOR YOURSELF

This experiment shows the effects of the surface tension of a liquid. Fill a clean saucer with water and sprinkle some flour or talcum powder on it.

Let a couple of drops of liquid detergent fall into the centre of the saucer and see what happens.

The detergent* destroys the attraction between the molecules and breaks the surface tension. The tension between the molecules near the sides of the saucer pulls the powder towards the sides.

*Gravity, 20; Why Things Float, 24; Soaps and Detergents, 80

FORCES

A force is any push or a pull on an object. When you pick up an object you are exerting a force on it. If you leave it sitting where it is, there are still forces acting on it, but they cancel each other out. Forces can make things move faster or slower, stop, change direction, or change size or shape.

The force of the Earth's gravity* makes seeds fall to the ground.

The forces acting on a yo-yo make it spin as well as go up and down.

TYPES OF FORCES

Forces affect objects in many different ways. There are forces you can see, such as a foot kicking a ball, and invisible forces, such as magnetism.* A single force acting on an object will make it start to move, or move faster. Two equal forces acting in opposite directions try to change the object's size or shape.

Forces that need two or more objects to be touching each other are called contact forces. You are using contact forces when you move an object with your hands.

Some forces do not need objects to be touching. The forces that act at a distance include the force of electricity,* the force of magnetism* and the force of the Earth's gravity.*

The force of gravity* makes objects accelerate downward.

The force of the wind makes sycamore seeds spin as they fall.

When you kick a football, the single force of your kick makes the football start to move.

As you catch a ball, the pushing force of your hands makes the ball slow down and stop.

If you step on a ball, the equal forces of your foot pushing down and the ground pushing up squash it.

The force of lift* keeps a helicopter in the air.

The force of friction* makes pencil lead rub off onto paper.

The spherical shape of bubbles is caused by a force called surface tension.*

Static electricity* attracts these leaves to a piece of rubbed amber.

Compasses work by the force of the Earth's magnetism.*

A magnet attracts tacks without touching them.

To prevent buildings falling down, they must be designed so that the many forces acting on them are in equilibrium (see right).

St. Basil's Cathedral in Moscow

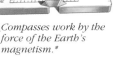

In a tug of war, the team that pulls with the most force wins.

MEASURING FORCES

The strength of a force is measured in newtons (N), after the English scientist, Sir Isaac Newton (1642-1727). One newton of force causes a mass of 1kg (2.2lb) to accelerate one meter per second per second. This is only about the force needed to lift a glass.

It takes a 500N force to lift this 50kg (110lb) mass.

A spring balance measures how many newtons a force is exerting. The spring, which is fastened at one end, is stretched by the force. Hooke's Law states that the extension of a material is proportional to the force stretching it. So the more the spring stretches, the more newtons the force is applying.

The scale gives the strength of the force in newtons.

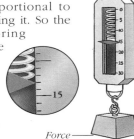

Force

VECTOR AND SCALAR QUANTITIES

Forces have magnitude (strength) and direction. In physics, things that have both these quantities are called vector quantities. Acceleration and velocity are vector quantities. A quantity that has magnitude but no direction is called a scalar quantity. Temperature and speed are both examples of scalar quantities. They can be low or high, but they do not have a direction.

Temperature has only magnitude, so it is a scalar quantity.

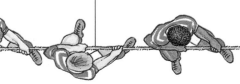

*Electricity, 46-47; Friction, 17; Gravity, 20; Lift, see How Planes Fly, 26; Magnetism, 48; Surface Tension, 13

COMBINING FORCES

There is usually more than one force acting on an object. They all combine to create a single force called the resultant. If the strength and direction of all the forces is known, it is possible to calculate the resultant force and predict the way in which the object will move.

The resultant force on this boat moves it forward and to the right.

Individual forces acting on the boat are the force of gravity* pulling it down, upthrust* pushing it up, the current pushing it sideways, the rudder swinging it around, the wind pushing it forward and resistance from the water pushing it backward.

EQUILIBRIUM

There are forces acting on an object even when it is not moving. The forces are all balanced, so they cancel each other out and the object is said to be in equilibrium. For example, the force of gravity* pulls down on a book on a shelf, while the shelf pushes up on the book with an equal force. The resultant force is zero, so there is no change in its motion.

Each side of an arch exerts the same amount of force.

This dancer is standing perfectly still.

He is exerting equal force on each leg, so he is in equilibrium.

If both of these tug of war teams pull the same amount, the rope will be in equilibrium and will remain stationary.

TURNING FORCES

To turn something around a fixed point, for example a door around its hinges, a force with a turning effect is needed. The fixed point is known as a fulcrum or pivot. It is much easier to turn something around a fulcrum if the force is applied at a distance. This is why doors and gates have their handles at the opposite edge from the hinges.

Fulcrum

It is easier to undo this bolt by holding the wrench at the end, as the force is then farthest from the fulcrum.

The force of a turning effect is called a moment. The moment around a fulcrum is found by multiplying the strength of the force by its distance, at right angles to the force, from the fulcrum. Moment is measured in newton meters (Nm) and can be either clockwise or counterclockwise in direction.

The force of the water pushing against the rudder of this boat causes the turning effect.

Rudder

A lifted wheelbarrow has a clockwise and a counterclockwise moment around the fulcrum.

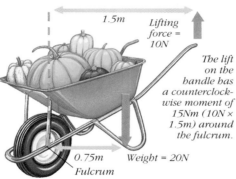

1.5m

Lifting force = 10N

The lift on the handle has a counterclockwise moment of 15Nm (10N × 1.5m) around the fulcrum.

0.75m

Weight = 20N

Fulcrum

The weight has a clockwise moment of 15Nm (20N × 0.75m) around the fulcrum.

Turning forces can be in equilibrium just like any other forces. When the clockwise and counterclockwise moments are equal, they cancel each other out and there is no change in turning motion.

KEY TERMS

Contact forces Forces that need objects to be touching.
Fulcrum The fixed point around which a turning effect takes place.
Moment The turning effect of a force, which is measured in newton metres (Nm).
Newton (N) The unit in which force is measured.
Resultant force The total effect of all the forces acting on an object.

ELASTICITY

When forces act on an object that cannot move, they may change its size or shape. Some substances, like rubber, return to their original form when the force is removed. These are called elastic substances.

A trampoline is elastic. When the forces stretching it are removed, it goes back to its original shape.

The amount that an elastic substance will stretch obeys Hooke's Law, which states that the stronger the force, the greater the stretch. But if something is stretched beyond its elastic limit, Hooke's Law no longer works. The elastic limit is the point at which a substance alters when it is stretched.

A rubber band is elastic, but will snap if you stretch it too far.

Some materials do not return to their original form after being stretched and they change shape permanently. This is called plastic behavior.

Clay is permanently altered when it is squeezed, even when the squeezing force is removed. It behaves in a plastic way.

SEE FOR YOURSELF

To see forces of equilibrium in action, you can build a tower of playing cards.

Each card exerts the same amount of force on its neighbors.

If you remove one card, the forces acting on the structure are no longer in equilibrium and the tower collapses.

Flat platform

*Gravity, 20; Upthrust, see Why Things Float, 24

DYNAMICS

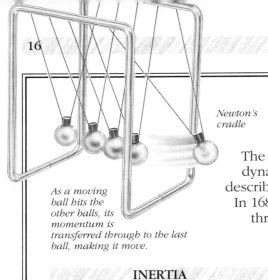

Newton's cradle

As a moving ball hits the other balls, its momentum is transferred through to the last ball, making it move.

Fulmar

Albatross

The study of how forces affect movement is called dynamics. Principles called inertia and momentum describe how easily objects both start and stop moving. In 1687, the English scientist, Isaac Newton, formulated three laws of motion that explain the principles governing the movement of all objects.

Because of its size, a large bird has greater momentum than a smaller one and can glide much farther.

INERTIA

Objects resist any change in their movement. This tendency, called inertia, applies to both stationary and moving objects. The inertia of a stationary object makes it hard to get moving. If already moving, inertia makes the object want to continue moving in a straight line. It takes a force* to overcome inertia.

The force of friction overcomes the inertia of this moving toy truck, slowing it down.

The larger an object's mass, the more inertia it has. A big animal has to exert more force to change its movement than a small one. Twice the mass means twice the inertia.

This adult elephant has five times as much mass as the baby. Its inertia is five times as great.

In a car crash, it is inertia that makes the people inside continue moving. Safety features such as seatbelts and airbags help overcome this inertia.

Without the restraining force of the seatbelt or protective airbag, the inertia of this crash test dummy would send it through the windscreen.

NEWTON'S LAWS OF MOTION

Isaac Newton made important discoveries on many subjects, including motion,* gravity* and light.* His three laws of motion have had a major influence on all scientific thinking.

Isaac Newton (1642-1727)

Newton's first law states that if an object is not being acted on by a force, it will either stay still or continue moving at a constant speed in a straight line. This is the principle of inertia (see left).

When this truck stops, it will take a force to overcome its inertia and start it moving.

Newton's second law states that any force acting on an object will change its motion. How much it changes depends on the object's mass and the size of the force.

The same force of wind will move a pine cone less than a leaf because the cone's mass is greater.

Newton's third law states that when a force acts on an object, the object exerts an equal force in the opposite direction. The first force is called the action and the second is the reaction.

A ball exerts a force on a bat, felt as the slowing down of the bat, that is equal and opposite to the force the bat exerts on the ball.

MOMENTUM

Momentum is a measure of an object's tendency to carry on moving. It is found by multiplying the object's mass by its velocity. The greater the mass and the velocity, the more the momentum. Like velocity, momentum is a vector quantity,* which means it has both size and direction.

This trolley's mass is 10kg (22lbs) and its velocity is 1m/s north. Its momentum is 10kg m/s north.

An object with a small mass can have the same momentum as an object with a large mass, providing it is moving faster.

This trolley has a mass of 2kg (4.4lbs) and a velocity of 5m/s. Its momentum is also 10kg m/s north.

According to Newton's third law (see left), when two objects collide, each one applies a force to the other. The momentum gained by one object equals that lost by the other because the total momentum stays the same just before and after the collision. This is called conservation of momentum.

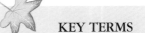

The pink ball transfers momentum through the blue ball to the red ball. As their masses are the same, the red ball accelerates to the speed the pink ball was travelling before the collision.

KEY TERMS

Force One of several forms of push or pull on an object.
Mass The amount of matter an object contains.
Velocity The speed an object travels in a particular direction.

FRICTION

When a moving object is touching another object, like a coin sliding across a table, the moving object slows down. The force that causes this is called friction. The rougher surfaces are and the harder they press together, the more friction there will be. Friction occurs in liquids and gases as well as between solids.

Friction between a bow and violin strings makes them vibrate to create sound.

New shoe

Old shoe

Constant friction with the floor means a ballet dancer's shoes only last a few weeks.

USING FRICTION

Friction is useful in some situations and damaging in others. If there were no friction at all between surfaces, it would be impossible to grip anything.

Running shoes have rough rubber soles to increase friction with the ground.

Many kinds of machines make use of friction. With too little friction between the tires and the surface of the road, drivers would not be able to stop their vehicles from sliding around.

The pattern on the surface of a tire is called the tread. It improves the tire's grip on the road.

Water and mud lessen friction because they act as lubricants (see Reducing Friction). The grooves on the tire channel water or mud through them.

Some devices need friction to be able to work at all. Friction between a match and a matchbox generates enough heat for chemicals in the match head to burn. Most brakes work by using friction to slow down the wheel.

A match lights due to friction with the box.

Brake pads press against this wheel, causing enough friction to slow it down.

Rubber brake pads

Ridges on the soles of ski boots increase friction when walking on snow.

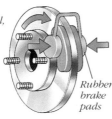

Skis are very smooth and have little friction with the snow, which makes them slide very easily.

REDUCING FRICTION

High levels of friction between machine parts is damaging. It causes wear and tear, and some of the energy needed to run the machine is wasted in heat instead of movement.

You feel heat from friction by rubbing your hands. If you rub for too long, wear and tear occurs in the form of blisters.

No surface is perfectly smooth, not even glass or shiny metal. Under a microscope, smooth surfaces look bumpy or jagged. Oil is smoother than any solid surface, so it allows objects to slide across each other more easily. A liquid used like this is called a lubricant.

A layer of oil between moving metal surfaces reduces friction.

Magnification shows how rough a metal surface is.

Bearings are devices in machines that bear some of the weight of the moving parts, so reducing the friction between them. They turn the sliding action of two moving surfaces into a rolling action.

Ball bearings lie around the axle of a wheel. They rotate as the wheel turns.

SEE FOR YOURSELF

You can see how bearings reduce friction using some marbles and a big book. First push the book along the floor without the marbles. Notice how much friction there is.

Marbles

Put marbles under the book. Push again. The marbles roll between the book and the ground, reducing friction.

FRICTION IN AIR AND WATER

Air resistance is the friction that occurs between air and any object moving through it. In space, there is no air, so there is no friction.

Space shuttle launching satellite*

Below left: air friction slows down the shuttle as it enters Earth's atmosphere and makes it glow red hot.

To reduce air resistance, vehicles are designed so they are streamlined. Streamlining lets the air flow over cars in smooth lines, which helps them to go faster and also to use less fuel.

Car testers use jets of smoke and strands of wool to test the way air flows over new cars.

Water is denser than air, so more friction acts on objects moving through water. The more streamlined a ship is, the faster it can travel. Fish and sea mammals such as whales, have naturally streamlined bodies that allow them to move through water easily.

A diamond-shaped hull cuts through water easily.

Water flows easily over a whale's streamlined body.

*The Space Shuttle, 35

MOTION

In physics, motion is the study of how something moves, whether it is a planet moving around the Sun or an arrow flying through the air. An object's motion is usually described in terms of its velocity and acceleration, and its motion only changes if a force, or several forces, acts on it.

This dart is flying through the air at a speed of 10 metres per second (m/s).

A bouncing ball accelerates on the way down...

...and decelerates on the way up.

SPEED

Speed is a measure of how fast an object is moving. The average speed of a moving object can be calculated by dividing the distance it has travelled by the time it has taken to do so.

This migrating tern has flown 90km (56 miles) in two hours. Its average speed is 45kph (28mph).

Speed is a scalar quantity (see Forces*). This means that it measures the amount of speed a moving object has, but not the direction in which it is moving. In physics, metres per second (m/s) is the unit of measurement most often used to express speed. The speed of light* is 300 million m/s. Light is thought to travel faster than anything else in the Universe.

This cyclist has gone 500m (547yds) in 36 seconds. The calculation below gives her average speed.

$$\text{Average speed} = \frac{\text{Distance (metres)}}{\text{Time (seconds)}}$$

$$\text{Average speed} = \frac{500}{36} = 13.89m/s$$

The speed of a moving object can change from moment to moment. For example, a sprinter runs slowest when setting off at the start of a race. His speed at that point will be slower than his average speed. A measure of someone or something's speed at any particular moment is called its instantaneous speed.

In 1994, the world record for the 100m race was 9.86 seconds. This is an average speed of 10.14m/s. After running 1m of a 100m race, a sprinter's instantaneous speed might be 3m/s. After a few more metres, it could be as high as 11m/s.

VELOCITY

Velocity is similar to speed, but it measures the direction in which an object is travelling as well as its speed. This makes velocity a vector quantity (see Forces*). The velocity of a moving object can change even if its speed remains exactly the same because a change in direction changes the velocity.

The path of the car

Turning circle

Although this car is travelling at a steady speed of 10kph (6.2mph), its velocity is changing all the time because it is always changing direction.

Velocity is measured in metres per second (m/s) in a particular direction. If a woman walks four metres north in one second, her velocity is 4 m/s north. Relative velocity is the velocity a moving object appears to have when viewed from another moving object.

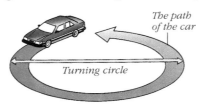

These stunt jets are both flying at a velocity of 83m/s in the same direction.

The velocity of one jet relative to the other (from the point of view of either) is zero.

The velocities of the leading and losing sprinters are 3.1m/s south and 3.0m/s south. The velocity of the leader relative to the loser (from the loser's point of view) is 0.1m/s south.

ACCELERATION

Acceleration is a change in the velocity (see left) of an object, that is, a change in its speed or direction. In physics, acceleration is measured in metres per second per second, or m/s². This is not as confusing as it looks. If something accelerates at 1m/s² (1 metre per second per second), it gets faster by one metre a second every second.

When they first leave the plane, skydivers accelerate at a rate of 9.8m/s².

When skydivers open their parachutes, they will suddenly decelerate (see below).

A decrease in velocity is called negative acceleration, or deceleration. Any change in speed or direction means that an object accelerates, or decelerates, as both affect velocity.

Car manufacturers usually consider acceleration in kilometres (or miles) per hour per second. This is simply using different units to measure the same thing.

This Porsche 959 accelerates from 0-100kph (62mph) in 3.9 seconds. This works out at an average acceleration of 7.1m/s².

If a car is travelling at a steady 50kph (31mph) in one direction, its acceleration is zero. This is because neither its speed nor its direction are changing.

A cheetah can accelerate from 0-70kph (43mph) in a shorter time than most cars can.

TERMINAL VELOCITY

When something falls through air, it accelerates, at a decreasing rate, until it reaches its maximum constant velocity. This is called its terminal velocity. Skydivers start to accelerate the moment they jump from a plane. They continue accelerating, but at a slower and slower rate, until they reach a speed of about 200kph (124mph). This is their terminal velocity and their acceleration is now zero.

Any object falling through a gas or liquid will eventually reach its terminal velocity. The object stops accelerating when the forces acting on it become balanced.

These skydivers accelerate, at a slower and slower rate, until they reach their terminal velocity.

The pull of gravity* is the force that makes an object accelerate downwards. But as it starts to move, it experiences resistance, or friction,* from the gas or liquid it is falling through. The faster the object falls, the stronger the resistance becomes, until it eventually equals the force of gravity. The object stops accelerating at this point and has reached its terminal velocity.

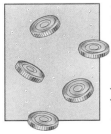

Coins reach the bottom of an empty well quicker than a full one, as the terminal velocity of an object is slower in water than in air. This is because there is more friction in water, so the forces become balanced earlier, and the coins stop accelerating sooner.*

KEY TERMS

Acceleration The change in velocity over a certain amount of time.
Centripetal force A force that keeps an object moving in a circle.
Speed The distance an object travels in a certain amount of time.
Velocity The speed an object moves in a particular direction.

MOTION IN A CIRCLE

All moving objects try to travel in a straight line (see Dynamics*). The force which makes some turn in a circle instead is called a centripetal force. Centripetal force is any force that constantly pulls towards the centre of a circle.

Centripetal force

Earth

Moon

The force of the Earth's gravity is a centripetal force on the Moon, keeping it moving in a circle.*

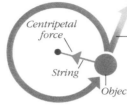

Centripetal force

String

Object

Without the string pulling it in, the object would move off in this direction.

If you tie a small object to a piece of string and whirl it around your head, the pull of the string on the object is a centripetal force. As long as you whirl fast enough, the object will not fall in on you. If you let go of the string, you remove the centripetal force and the object will fly off at a tangent, as when an athlete throws a hammer.

The Sun's force of gravity on the Earth and the other planets is the centripetal force that causes them to circle the Sun, keeping them in the solar system.*

To throw this hammer, the athlete first has to get it moving.

He pulls on the wire to make the hammer move in a circle.

The athlete's pull is a centripetal force acting on the hammer.

The faster the hammer moves, the more centripetal force is needed.

The hammer flies off when the centripetal force is removed.

GYROSCOPES

Gyroscopes are wheels that spin very fast within a free-moving frame. The circling motion of a gyroscope is complicated, but its main feature is that the frame can tilt very steeply without falling over, so resisting the force of gravity.*

Frame

This gyroscope resists gravity when spinning. When it slows down, it will wobble and fall over.

Gyroscopes are very useful in transport. Ships use gyrostabilizers, which are fins that stick out into the sea, connected to a gyroscope. The gyroscope resists any motion of the fins. This steadies the ship against the rolling of the waves.

SEE FOR YOURSELF

You can see the effect of centripetal force yourself, by using a shallow plastic bowl and a marble.

Put the marble in the bowl and move the bowl so that the marble moves in a circle.

When it is moving fast enough, the marble will fly out. The centripetal force is not strong enough to keep it moving in such a tight circle.

GRAVITY

The force of gravity attracts objects to each other. This applies to all objects, but we do not notice the attraction unless one of the objects is very large, like a planet. It is the pull of the Earth's gravity that makes objects fall to the ground when dropped. Even the seas are affected by gravity, as the pull of the Moon causes tides.

The force of the Sun's gravity keeps a belt of rocks, called asteroids, orbiting around it.

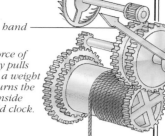

Clock hand

The force of gravity pulls down a weight that turns the cogs inside this old clock.

GRAVITY, MASS AND WEIGHT

The strength of the pull of gravity between two objects depends on how far apart they are and their masses. Mass is the amount of matter that an object contains and this never varies. Any two objects, such as two apples, are attracted to each other, but as their masses are both small, the force of gravity between them is insignificant.

The attraction between these small objects is so tiny that it cannot be felt.

On the other hand, the force of gravity between the Earth and any object is extremely noticeable because the mass of the Earth is so large.

The pull of the Earth's gravity makes any object, such as this horse chestnut, fall to the ground.

Weight is a measure of the pull of gravity on an object's mass. The weight of an object in your hands is in fact the force of the Earth's gravity pulling it down. The farther away an object is from the center of the Earth, the less the pull of gravity on it. Because of this, you weigh slightly less at the top of a mountain than at the bottom. You would weigh much less on the Moon, because the Moon's gravity is only a sixth as strong as the Earth's.

On the Moon, astronauts weigh only one sixth of what they do on Earth, but their mass never changes.

Below: tides move up and down our shores due to the pull of the Moon's gravity, which holds great bulges of water still as the Earth's surface spins far below.

CENTER OF GRAVITY

Gravity acts on every part of an object, but there is one point where the object's whole weight seems to act. This is its center of gravity. An object can often be balanced at its center of gravity.

Regular shaped and symmetrical objects, like this handweight, have their center of gravity exactly in the middle.

Center of gravity

A stable object returns to its original position when tilted. Center of gravity is the key to stability. If an object tilts so its center of gravity is outside its base, it will fall over.

Tightrope walkers use long poles to adjust their center of gravity so that it is always over their feet on the rope.

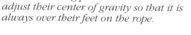

GRAVITY AND TIDES

Tides are caused by the pull of the Moon's gravity as it orbits the Earth. The pull is greatest on the side of the Earth nearest the Moon, causing the water to rise up in a great bulge. This bulge of water is a high tide.

High tide — *Earth* — *Low tide*
Low tide — *Moon*
High tide

On the opposite side of the Earth, the Moon's pull is so weak that the water moves outward, away from the Moon. This creates another bulge and another high tide. Low tides occur in the areas between high tides. There are two high tides and two low tides every twenty-four hours, the time it takes for the Earth to rotate around its axis.

When the tide goes out, the receding waves leave ripples and channels in the sand.

Objects with their center of gravity low down, near their base, are stable. Those with a high center of gravity are not stable and topple over easily.

The center of gravity of this weight is directly below the point from which it is suspended.

This lifeboat has a low center of gravity, which makes it very stable. If it does capsize, it will easily right itself.

A wide base helps an object's stability. A motorbike is much less stable than a racing car because its base is so much narrower.

A stationary motorbike will fall over when tilted because its center of gravity lies outside its base.

Racing cars are built to be very stable. The center of gravity is low and the wheels are wide apart.

SEE FOR YOURSELF

You can find the center of gravity of any shape using a plumbline (a string with a weight on it), a pin, a pencil and some cardboard.

1. Pin a cardboard shape to a bulletin board so that it hangs freely.

2. Hang the weighted string from the pin.

3. Pencil in the line the string follows.

The center of gravity is at the exact spot where all the lines cross.

4. Repeat twice, pinning the shape at different places.

PRESSURE

A needle will go through a piece of cloth, but with the same amount of force, a pencil will not. The differently shaped points of the needle and pencil exert different amounts of pressure. Pressure is everywhere. It operates many machines and affects our weather. Solids, liquids and gases all apply pressure to the surfaces they touch.

Divers' suits protect them from the high pressure in deep water.

The weather is affected by atmospheric pressure. Atmospheric pressure is measured on a barometer.

WHAT IS PRESSURE?

When a force* acts on an object, at right angles to it, it is exerting pressure. The amount of pressure depends on the strength of the force and the area over which it is applied. For example, you will sink into soft snow wearing normal shoes but not if you wear large snowshoes. Your weight is the same in both cases, but snowshoes spread the weight over a wider area. This reduces the pressure.

Caribous' wide feet act like snowshoes, spreading the weight to reduce pressure on the snow.

A sharp knife cuts better than a blunt one because its force is applied to a smaller area.

Pressure is measured in pascals (Pa), after the French scientist Blaise Pascal (1623-62), who made many discoveries about air pressure.

PRESSURE IN FLUIDS

Fluids (liquids or gases) change shape according to their container, so they press against more surfaces than a solid object does. Pressure in any fluid acts in all directions.

The water in a fish tank exerts pressure against the sides as well as the bottom. The tank itself only exerts pressure downward.

Air inside a beach ball pushes out in all directions, keeping it blown up.

SEE FOR YOURSELF

This experiment shows how air pushes out in all directions. You need a book and a paper bag.

Put the book on the bag and blow into the bag.

Air pressure increases inside the bag and lifts the book.

HYDRAULIC MACHINES

Hydraulic machines are machines powered by liquid pressure. A liquid cannot be squashed, so if you press one part of the liquid, pressure increases throughout and the liquid has to move somewhere.

A hydraulic hose helps power this robot arm.

Car brakes are hydraulic. Brake fluid is pushed through the brake system, forcing the wheels to decelerate.

As the driver presses the pedal, a piston (1) pushes brake fluid through a cylinder (2). The brake fluid goes down a pipe into two more cylinders (red arrows) where it pushes more pistons out. These press brake pads (3) against a disk (4) in the wheel. The friction this causes slows down the wheels.

PNEUMATIC MACHINES

Pneumatic machines are driven by the pressure of gases,* usually air. Unlike liquid, air can be compressed into a small space, greatly increasing its pressure. A pneumatic drill is powered by a piston which squashes air inside the drill to a very high pressure.

The compressed air inside a pneumatic drill pushes out with enough force to power a chisel to crack rock.

A foam and water fire extinguisher is a pneumatic machine which uses compressed carbon dioxide gas.

By squeezing the handle (1), you release carbon dioxide gas from a canister (2). The high pressure gas pushes down on a mixture of water and detergent (3), forcing it up a tube (4) and through a hose (5), where it shoots out as a jet of foam and water.

ATMOSPHERIC PRESSURE

Atmospheric pressure is the weight of air pressing down on the Earth's surface. Over 1 square meter (10 square feet), the weight of air pressing down is heavier than a large elephant. Air pressure is greatest near the ground, and reduces with height. At 10,000m (30,000ft) above the ground, where jumbo jets fly, air pressure is very low as there is less air pressing down.

Aircraft have pressurized cabins so people can breathe high up.

Even with pressurized cabins, your ears "pop" in a plane as atmospheric pressure becomes lower than the pressure of the air inside your ears.

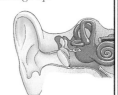

Atmospheric pressure is measured in millibars (mb). Weather changes as the pressure changes, with low pressure signaling bad weather and high pressure bringing a settled, fine spell.

The usual atmospheric pressure at sea level is 1,013mb. This can fall to 910mb in a hurricane.

WORK AND SIMPLE MACHINES

In physics, simple machines are devices like levers and screws. They make physical work easier to do by taking the effort needed to operate them and using it in a more efficient way. Simple machines are often used together to make more complex machines, such as drills and clocks.

The wheel, one of the most important devices ever invented, forms the basis of many machines.

This hand drill is powered by a wheel which turns when the handle is turned.

Wheel
Drill bit

WORK AND POWER

Work is the scientific term for when a force* makes an object move. The object moves in the direction that the force is acting. Work is only being done when the object is moving.

Work is done when the pulling force of the cattle and the pushing force of the man move the plough.

Work transfers energy* from one object to another and, like energy, is measured in joules (J). One joule equals the work done (and energy used) when a force of 1 newton (N) moves an object 1 metre (3.25ft).

If this man pushes the box with a force of 100 newtons for 3 metres, he performs 300 joules of work.

Power is the rate at which work is done, or energy is transferred. It is measured in watts (W), after James Watt (see Engines*) and is worked out by dividing the work done by the time it takes to do it.

It takes twice as much power to move the box in one minute than to move it in two minutes.

KEY TERMS

Effort The force needed to operate a simple machine.
Fulcrum (or **pivot**) The point about which a lever turns.
Joule (J) The unit of measurement for energy and work.
Load The force that a simple machine overcomes.
Newton (N) The unit in which force is measured.
Power The rate that work is done or energy used, measured in watts (W).
Work The distance an object moves times the force moving it.

EFFORT AND LOAD

To move any object, you need to overcome a force called the load, which is often the weight of the object. A simple machine helps you do this by taking the force of your effort and applying it more efficiently.

The effort is the force that turns the handle.

The load is equal to the force applied by the screwdriver, which is greater than the effort.

By dividing the load by the amount of effort used, it is possible to find the force ratio of a simple machine.

Squeezing the nutcracker handles takes an effort of 1N. The load force needed to crack the nuts is 4N, so the force ratio of the nutcracker is 4:1.

Effort

If the force ratio is 4:1, the load which the machine overcomes is four times greater than the effort used. Machines like this are force magnifiers.

WHEELS

When a wheel turns around an axle, a bigger force is exerted at the axle than at the wheel's edge. Some machines, such as steering wheels, use wheels to increase force in this way. The bigger the wheel is, the more easily the axle turns.

Horn

Axle

Turning the wheel on this phonograph exerts a big enough force at the axle to power the whole machine.

Phonograph

When the axle is turned, the wheel converts the axle's circular motion into a straight line motion that can move loads across the ground. The wheel turns a greater distance than the axle because it is much bigger.

Wheels on a roller boot turn around axles to move the boot in a straight line.

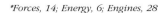

LEVERS

A lever is a rod that turns at a fixed point, called a fulcrum or pivot, making it easier to dislodge heavy weights. There are three classes of lever, each with a different arrangement of the fulcrum with the effort and load (see left).

A class one lever has the fulcrum between the effort and the load.

Effort

Load   Fulcrum   Load   Fulcrum

A class two lever, has the load between the effort and the fulcrum.

Effort

Fulcrum

A class three lever (right) has the effort between the load and the fulcrum.

Load

The further the effort is from the fulcrum, the easier a lever is to use (see Turning Forces*). This means that longer levers are generally the most useful.

GEARS

Gears are used to change speed in many different kinds of complex machines, from cars to clocks. They do this by changing the size of a turning force.*

This gear changes the size and direction of the turning force.

Gears consist of two or more toothed wheels that fit into each other, so that turning one wheel turns the other. A large gear makes a smaller gear turn faster and vice versa.

A mechanical pendulum clock works through a complicated system of geared wheels.

Pendulum

SCREWS

A screw has an axle and a thread which work together like an inclined plane (see below right) wrapped around a cylinder. The axle is the cylinder and the thread is the inclined plane.

— Axle

— Thread

You turn a corkscrew many times to get it into a cork, but this is easier than pushing it straight in.

The force of turning a screw around its thread is converted to a straight line force along the line of its axle. The straight line force drives the screw into an object.

A spiral staircase works like a screw. You walk further, but it is easier than climbing straight up.

PULLEYS

Pulleys help lift heavy loads and are often used in lifts and cranes. The load is attached to a rope which passes around one or more grooved wheels. When the other end of the rope is pulled, the load is lifted.

Right: pulleys let you pull down instead of up, so you can use your weight to help.

The more wheels a pulley has, the easier it is to lift a load, as its weight is spread out over more rope.

This crane pulley can lift a load four times as heavy as a one-wheel fixed pulley, as the load is spread out over four ropes.

SEE FOR YOURSELF

To see how a class one lever works, put a pencil under the middle of a flat strip of wood or metal, such as a strong ruler. Put a book on one end.

Press down on the other end of the ruler to raise the book.

Load

Fulcrum

Effort

Try changing the position of the pencil under the ruler. You will find that the longer the lever, the easier it is to lift the weight.

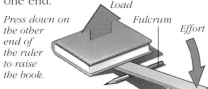

USING SIMPLE MACHINES

Simple machines are used in a variety of different ways to make up more complex machines. Our bodies, and those of many animals perform tasks with the help of in-built simple machines.

Archimedes' screw was an early device for pumping water from rivers or lakes.

Handle

Axles

Water was drawn up on the inclined planes of a turning screw.

A propeller is a simple form of screw, that pulls ships and aircraft through the water or the air.

Handle

Big gear wheel

Small gear wheel

Gears on a whisk increase the size of the turning force needed to turn the handle, so that the blades turn very fast.

Blades

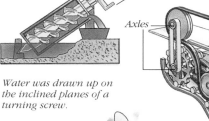

Fulcrum

A lobster's claws, or pincers, are third class levers.

Downward force

A human tooth is a wedge. It pushes food apart as it cuts down.

Wheels power the steps and handrails on an escalator. The wheel rims move far further than the axles do.

An axe turns the downward force of the swing into a sideways cutting force. The blade is a wedge like a tooth (see above).

A fan is a third class lever. When you wave it, your wrist acts as the fulcrum.

INCLINED PLANES

An inclined plane is just a slope, like a ramp or a staircase. It is easier to move an object up an inclined plane than vertically upwards, because you travel further, so less force is needed for the same amount of work.

80m (264ft) slope

10m (33ft) vertical

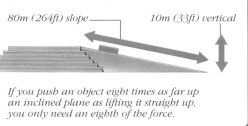

If you push an object eight times as far up an inclined plane as lifting it straight up, you only need an eighth of the force.

The Ancient Egyptians, who built the pyramids, may have used inclined planes, in the form of spiral slopes, to push enormous blocks of stone up to the tops. Some of the tallest pyramids were about 146m (480ft) high.

Drill bit

Drive shaft

Gears

An electric drill combines gears and a screw at the tip, called a bit. The gears change the speed that the bit rotates, so that you can drill a hole quickly or slowly.

The pyramids were probably built using inclined planes (see left).

Fulcrum

Scissors are levers. The blades are sharp wedges that force surfaces apart.

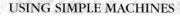

Catamarans have two hulls so they float very high in the water.

FLOATING

Why do some substances float in water, but not others? And why are there so few substances that are able to float in air? By understanding the principles of floating (and sinking), engineers can build ships out of metals that are heavier than the water they float in, and design airships and hot-air balloons that can float in the air.

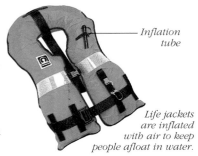

Inflation tube

Life jackets are inflated with air to keep people afloat in water.

WHY THINGS FLOAT

When an object is put into water, it pushes aside, or displaces, some of the water. It takes up the space that the water was in, and the level of the water rises. According to legend, the ancient Greek scientist Archimedes (287-212BC) realized how objects displace water when he got into the bath.

This is a medieval picture of Archimedes making his discovery.

Water pushes back against an object placed in it with a force called upthrust, or buoyancy. When the upthrust is the same as the weight of the object, the object floats. At this point, the weight of the object and the weight of the water it displaces are equal.

This plastic duck is so light that it needs only a small upthrust force to float.

The strength of the downward force (the weight) depends on the overall density of an object. Density is a measure of the amount of matter in an object (the mass) compared to its size.

A steel ball is heavier than an apple of the same size because it is denser. Its matter is packed more tightly together. The apple floats (just), but the steel ball sinks.

For an object to float in water, its density needs to be less than the density of water. If not, the water cannot provide enough upthrust to support it. The relative density of an object is its density when compared to the density of water. The relative density of water is 1, so an object will sink if its relative density is more than 1, but float if it is less than 1.

Water	Cork	Air
1	0.2	0.0012
Aluminum	Steel	Copper
2.7	8	9

This shows the relative densities of various different substances.

Nearly all metals are denser than water.

HOW SHIPS FLOAT

Modern ships are made of steel, which is eight times denser than water. The reason ships do not sink is because their overall density is lower than water.

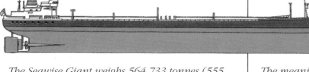

The Seawise Giant weighs 564,733 tonnes (555, 697 tons) and is one of the world's biggest ships. Its size helps to create a huge upthrust force.

Ships are not made from solid steel, but contain lots of empty space. Also, their large size spreads their weight over a wide area, and creates a lot of upthrust in the water.

ARCHIMEDES' PRINCIPLE

Archimedes' principle states that the upthrust (see Why Things Float) acting on an object is equal to the weight of the fluid that the object displaces. An object sinks into a fluid, such as water, until the force of the upthrust from the fluid is equal to the object's weight. Then the object floats.

Archimedes

PLIMSOLL LINES

Plimsoll lines on the side of a ship show how heavily it can be loaded in different conditions. For example, because cold water is denser than warm water, a ship floats higher in cold water. This means that it can carry more weight. Fresh water is less dense than saltwater, so in fresh water a ship will float lower and can carry less weight. Plimsoll lines were invented by Samuel Plimsoll (1824-1898).

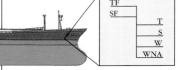

TF	
SF	
	T
	S
	W
	WNA

When the water level reaches the appropriate line, the ship is fully loaded.

The meaning of the letters is shown below:

TF *Tropical fresh water* S *Summer saltwater*
SF *Summer fresh water* W *Winter saltwater*
T *Tropical saltwater* WNA *Winter N. Atlantic*

SEE FOR YOURSELF

To see upthrust in action, drop a ball of modeling clay into a glass of water. The clay will sink and the water level will rise. Mark the new water level with a felt-tip pen.

Now shape the same piece of clay into a boat and float it gently in the water. This time the water level rises even higher. The boat pushes aside more water than the ball shape, so the force of the upthrust is stronger.

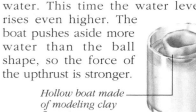

Hollow boat made of modeling clay floats in water

FLOATING IN AIR

Objects float in air for the same reason that they float in water. The air pushes back against them with a force called upthrust (see Why Things Float). Few things can float in air because it is so light, but hot-air balloons can float because hot air is less dense than cold air. Gases, such as helium, which are lighter than air, are also used to make things float.

Helium gas cells

Metal frames

This airship and the balloons on the left are filled with helium gas, which is lighter than air.

SHIPS AND BOATS

Ships and boats once relied on the wind or human strength for their power. The development of engines* enabled ships to use propellers to drive them through the water and there are now newer inventions such as hydrofoils.

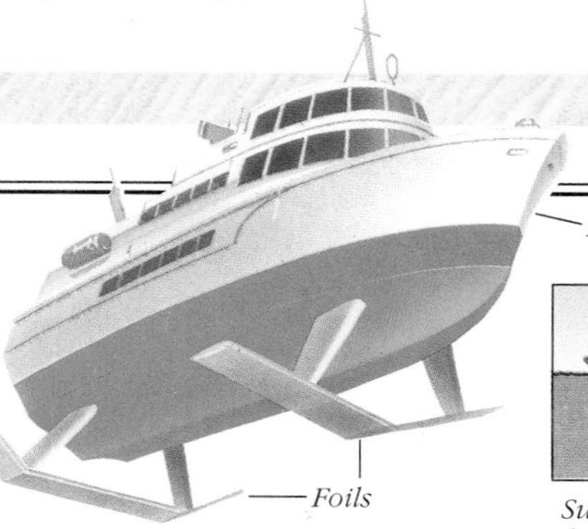

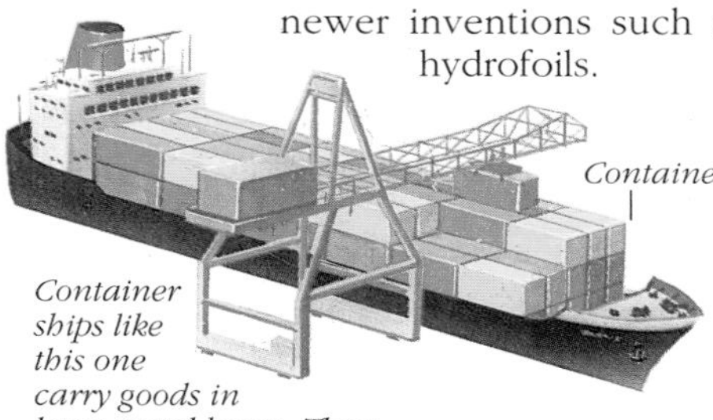

Container ships like this one carry goods in large metal boxes. These can be loaded or unloaded quickly by cranes. One ship can carry about 2,000 containers.

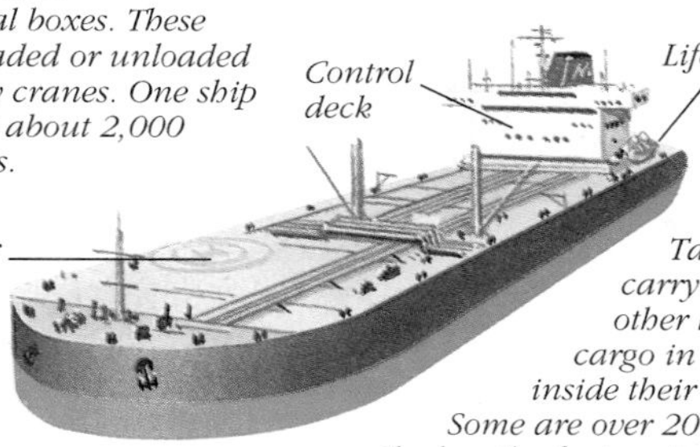

Containers

Control deck

Helicopter landing pad

Lifeboat

Tankers carry oil or other liquid cargo in tanks inside their hulls. Some are over 20 times the length of a tennis court.

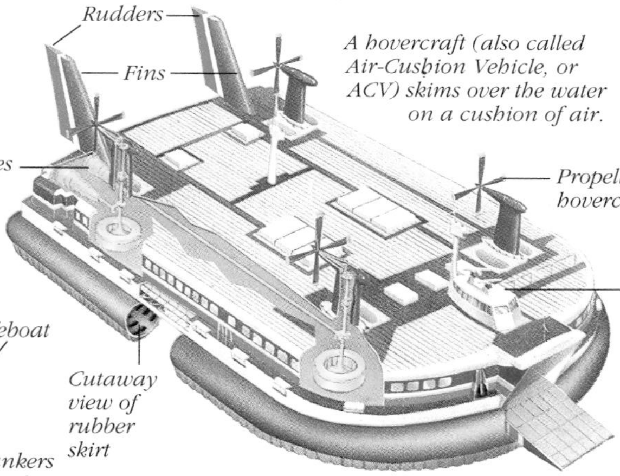

Hydrofoils have stilts attached to underwater "wings" called foils. When a hydrofoil speeds up, its hull lifts out of the water, reducing water resistance.

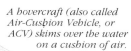

Hull

Foils

A hovercraft (also called Air-Cushion Vehicle, or ACV) skims over the water on a cushion of air.

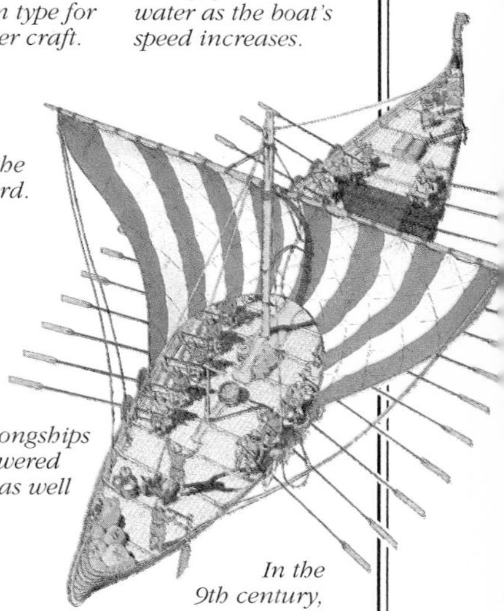

Rudders

Fins

Engines

Propellers drive the hovercraft forward.

Control cabin

Cutaway view of rubber skirt

Surface-piercing foils are the most common type for passenger craft.

Ladder foils emerge from the water as the boat's speed increases.

Viking longships were powered by oars as well as sails.

In the 9th century, the Vikings used ships like this to raid many coastal towns in Western Europe.

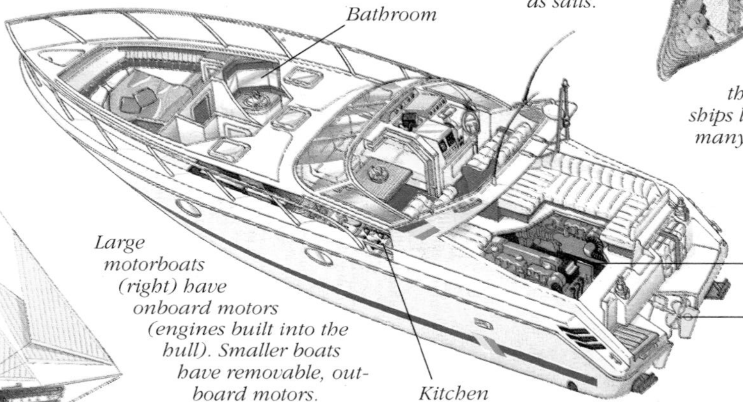

Bathroom

Large motorboats (right) have onboard motors (engines built into the hull). Smaller boats have removable, outboard motors.

Engine

Propeller

Kitchen

The Great Britain (1843) was the first iron ship with a screw propeller* driven by a steam engine*. It also had sails.

Clippers in the 1820s (left) could travel up to 37kph (23mph) because they had so many sails.

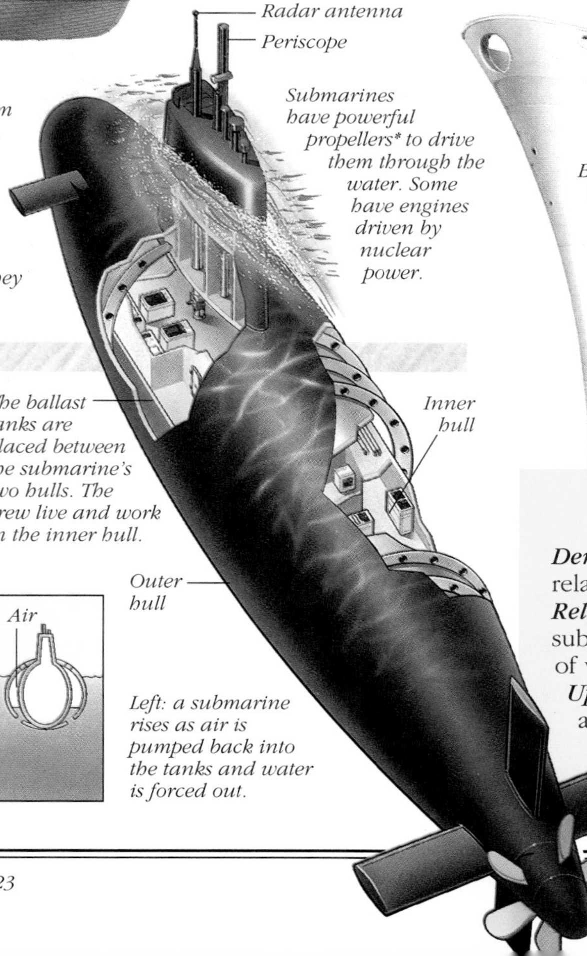

Radar antenna

Periscope

Submarines have powerful propellers* to drive them through the water. Some have engines driven by nuclear power.

Before air travel, liners were the best way to travel long distances. They are now used mainly for vacations.

SUBMARINES

Submarines can dive and surface by altering their relative density (see Why Things Float). They carry large containers called ballast tanks. When air is expelled from these tanks and replaced with water, the submarine's density increases and it dives. When it needs to surface, air is pumped back into the tanks and water is forced back out. This makes the submarine less dense, and it rises to the surface.

The ballast tanks are placed between the submarine's two hulls. The crew live and work in the inner hull.

Inner hull

Outer hull

Ballast tank

Right: a submarine dives as its ballast tanks are filled with water.

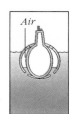

Air

Left: a submarine rises as air is pumped back into the tanks and water is forced out.

KEY TERMS

Density The mass of an object in relation to the space it takes up.
Relative density The density of a substance in relation to the density of water.
Upthrust The force pushing up on an object when it is placed in a fluid such as water or air.

*Engines, 28; Propellers, see Work and Simple Machines, 23

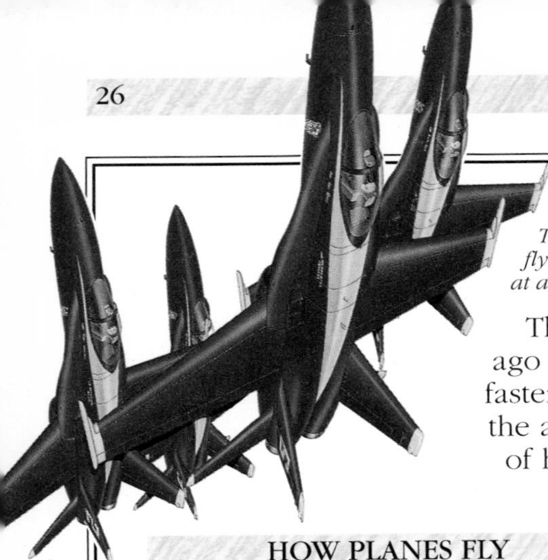

The Blue Angels fly in formation at airshows.

FLIGHT

The first powered flight took place less than a century ago and lasted only twelve seconds. Now planes can travel faster than the speed of sound, and helicopters can hover in the air without moving. The wings of planes and the blades of helicopters have a special shape which helps them fly.

Kites were the first inventions that used the forces in moving air.

HOW PLANES FLY

Planes can fly because of the shape of their wings. The wings are curved on top and flatter underneath. A bird's wings have the same shape. It is called an aerofoil.

Cross-section of an aerofoil shape

Curved on top

Flatter underneath

The air above an aerofoil wing has farther to travel than the air under it. When the flow of a gas such as air gets faster, its pressure* is reduced because it becomes less dense. This is called Bernoulli's principle. Because of this, the slower air flowing under the wing has a higher pressure and pushes up on the wing. This force is called lift.

Cross-section of an aircraft wing

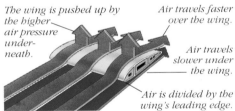

The wing is pushed up by the higher air pressure underneath.

Air travels faster over the wing.

Air travels slower under the wing.

Air is divided by the wing's leading edge.

Gliders are very light and the lift from their wings is strong enough to overcome the downward pull of gravity.* Heavier aircraft, such as jumbo jets, need a force called thrust to stay in the air. Thrust is the force that moves a plane forwards. Birds generate thrust by flapping their wings, but planes need engines.*

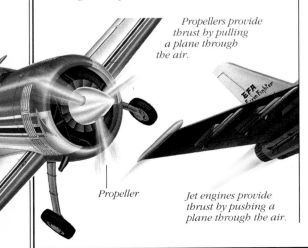

Propellers provide thrust by pulling a plane through the air.

Propeller

Jet engines provide thrust by pushing a plane through the air.

The more thrust an engine provides, the faster the plane goes. This greater speed also improves the lift on the aircraft. The faster the wings are moving through the air, the greater the difference in air pressure above and below them, because of Bernoulli's Principle.

The arrows on this picture show the four forces of flight.

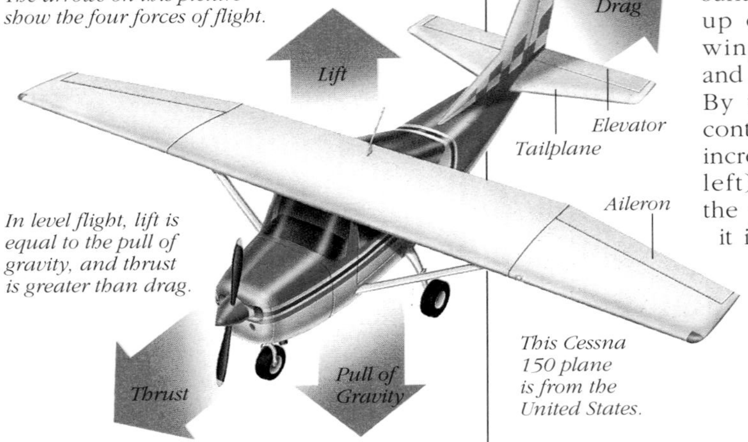

Lift

In level flight, lift is equal to the pull of gravity, and thrust is greater than drag.

Thrust

Pull of Gravity

This Cessna 150 plane is from the United States.

Drag, or air resistance, is another force acting on a plane. Air resistance is the force of friction* that occurs when something moves in air. Air resistance increases as speed increases, so very fast aircraft are streamlined to reduce drag. A streamlined plane is designed so that air moves around it more smoothly. Concorde (see right) is a good example of a streamlined plane.

SEE FOR YOURSELF

You can create a working aerofoil wing with a strip of paper 25cm x 5cm (10in x 2in) and a pencil.

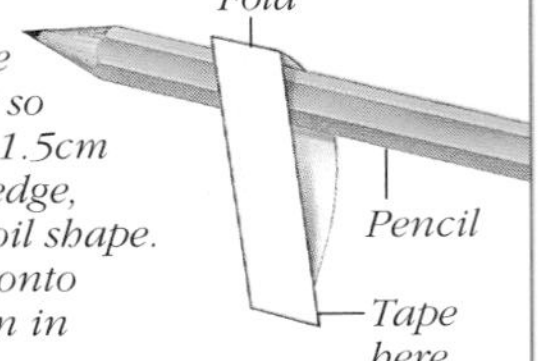

Fold the paper in half, then tape the two ends together so one end is about 1.5cm (0.5in) from the edge, making an aerofoil shape. Slide the aerofoil onto a pencil, as shown in the picture.

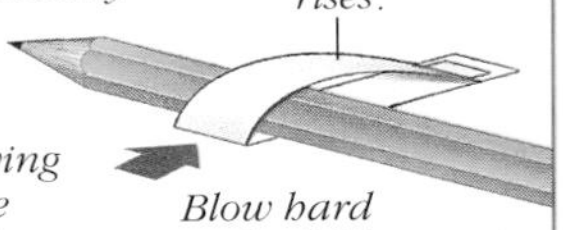

Fold

Pencil

Tape here.

Blow hard and steadily at the fold. The difference in air flow above and below the wing makes it rise (see How Planes Fly).

Wing rises.

Blow hard at the fold.

HOW PLANES ARE CONTROLLED

A plane needs to be able to move up and down, and to turn and bank (tip) to each side. To do this, the wings and tail are fitted with hinged flaps. These are known as control surfaces. They are made up of ailerons on the wings, and elevators and a rudder on the tail. By using a particular control surface, a pilot increases the drag (see left) on that part of the plane. This pushes it into a new position, as shown in the diagrams below.

Rudder

Drag

Tailplane

Elevator

Aileron

These diagrams show how control surfaces work.

Turning to the left or right is called yawing, and is controlled by the rudder on the tail fin.

Rudder

When turning, a plane also banks. This is called rolling and it is controlled by the ailerons on the wings.

Aileron

Moving up and down is called pitching and is controlled by the elevators on the tailplane.

Elevator

KEY TERMS

Aerofoil The special wing shape which creates the force of lift.
Drag The force of air resistance which slows a plane down.
Lift The upwards force created by the shape of a plane's wings.
Thrust The force which moves a plane forwards.

PLANES AND HELICOPTERS

The design of aircraft varies depending on their function. Some planes can land on water, and some helicopters can lift huge weights. The pictures below show different types of aircraft.

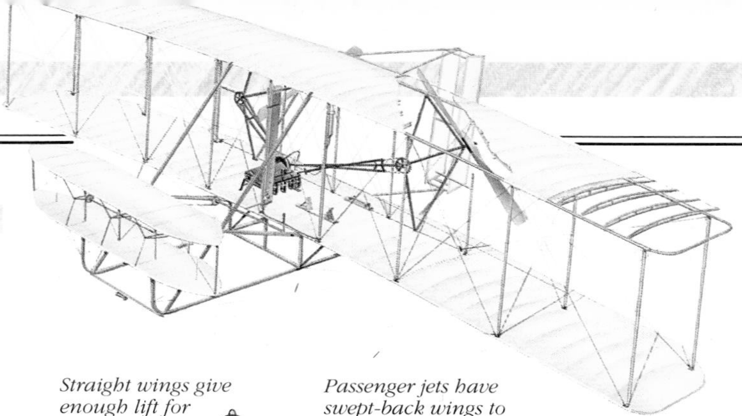

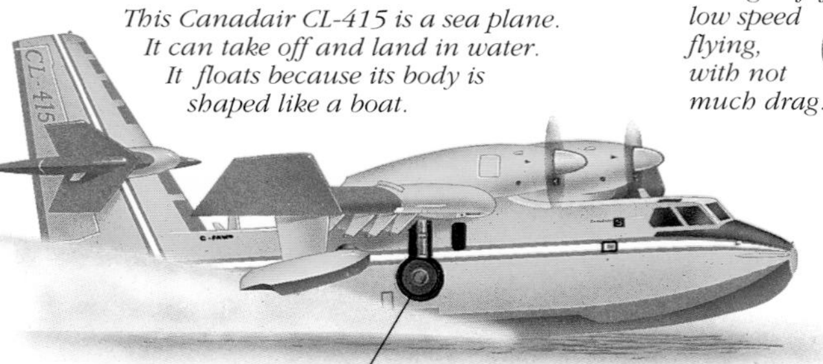

This Canadair CL-415 is a sea plane. It can take off and land in water. It floats because its body is shaped like a boat.

This plane also has wheels so it can move on land. Planes like this are called amphibians.

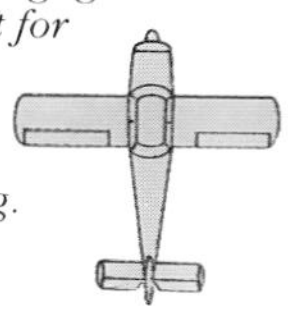

Straight wings give enough lift for low speed flying, with not much drag.

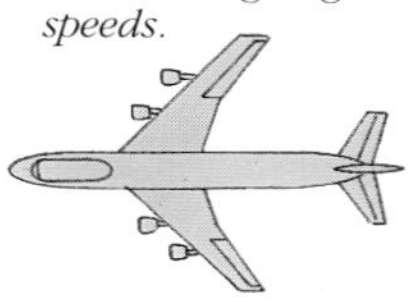

Passenger jets have swept-back wings to reduce drag at greater speeds.

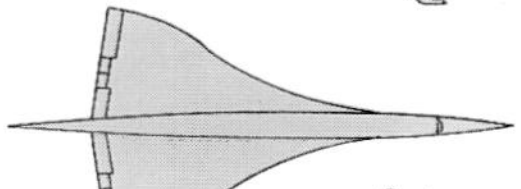

Supersonic aircraft, which fly faster than the speed of sound, have delta-shaped wings.

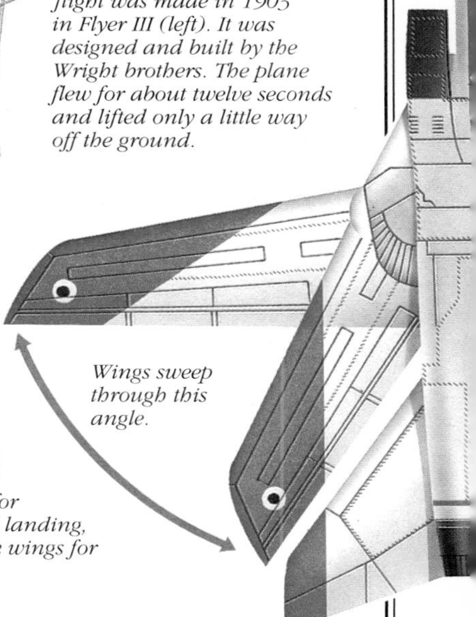

The first successful powered flight was made in 1903 in Flyer III (left). It was designed and built by the Wright brothers. The plane flew for about twelve seconds and lifted only a little way off the ground.

This Panavia Tornado is a swing-wing jet fighter. Its movable, or variable geometry wings allow it to have straight wings for slow flying and landing, and swept-back wings for high speed.

Wings sweep through this angle.

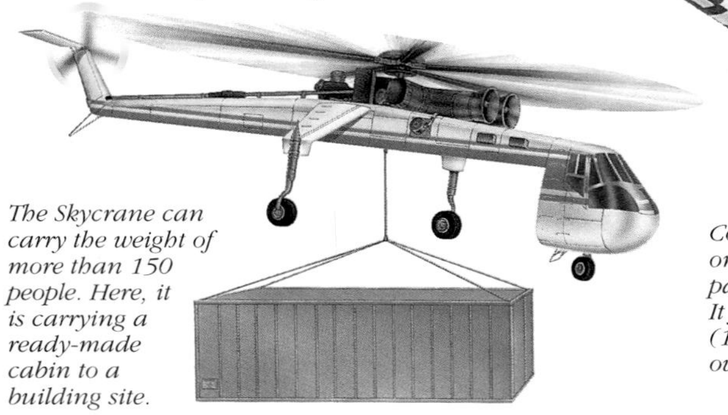

The Sikorsky Skycrane carries heavy loads to places which cannot be reached in any other way.

The Skycrane can carry the weight of more than 150 people. Here, it is carrying a ready-made cabin to a building site.

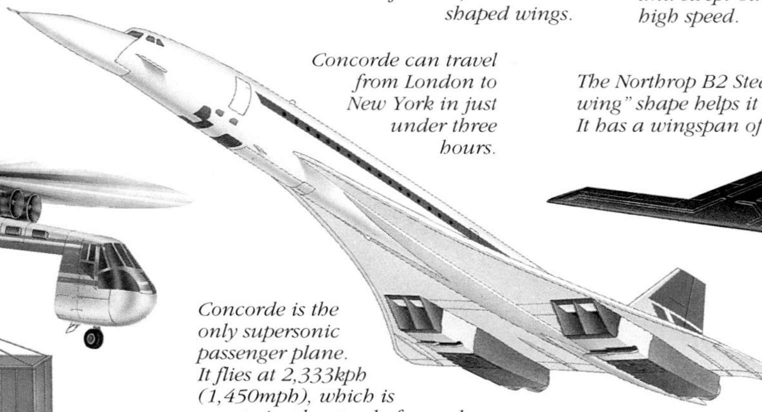

Concorde can travel from London to New York in just under three hours.

Concorde is the only supersonic passenger plane. It flies at 2,333kph (1,450mph), which is over twice the speed of sound.

The Northrop B2 Stealth bomber's strange "flying wing" shape helps it to avoid radar detection. It has a wingspan of over 52m (170ft).

The Stealth bomber is made of special radar-absorbent materials.

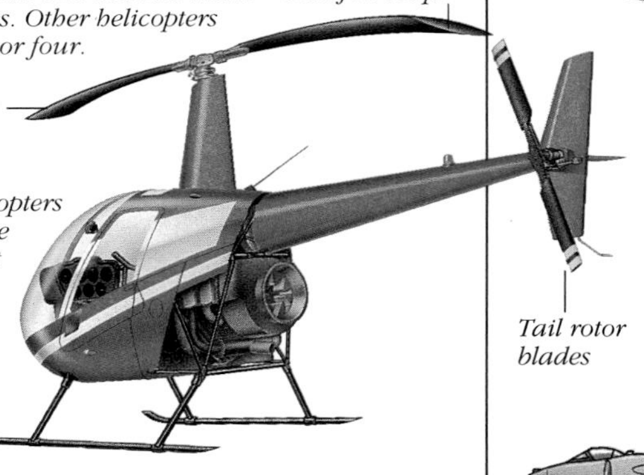

HOW HELICOPTERS FLY

Helicopters can travel in any direction, or just hover in the air without moving. Their rotor blades are aerofoils and provide lift as they spin around rapidly. To provide thrust, the blades are tilted forwards. They push the air behind them and this moves the helicopter forwards.

This Robinson R22 has two main rotor blades. Other helicopters have three or four.

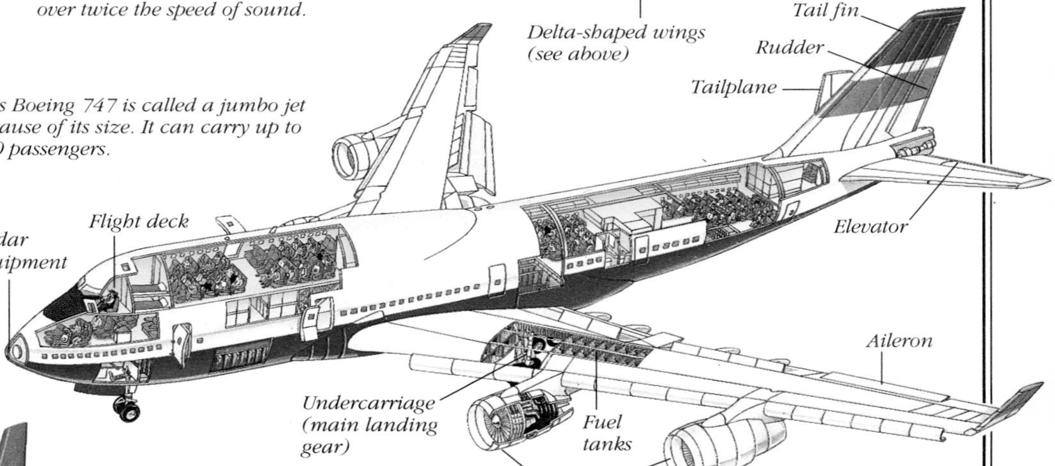

Aerofoil shape

Main rotor blades

Some helicopters do not have wheels, but rest on the ground on flat blades called skids.

Without the small rotor blades on the tail, helicopters would spin around very fast under their main blades. As well as keeping the helicopter stable, the tail rotor blades are used for turning.

This Boeing 747 is called a jumbo jet because of its size. It can carry up to 500 passengers.

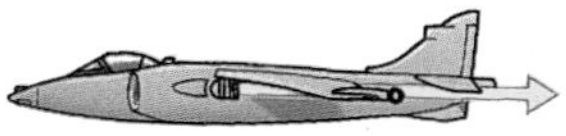

Flight deck

Radar equipment

Delta-shaped wings (see above)

Tail fin

Rudder

Tailplane

Elevator

Aileron

Undercarriage (main landing gear)

Fuel tanks

Jet engines*

Tail rotor blades

The Harrier is a VTOL plane. VTOL stands for Vertical Take Off and Landing. The plane does not need a runway to take off.

This Harrier is taking off. Its thrusters point down at the ground, pushing the plane upwards.

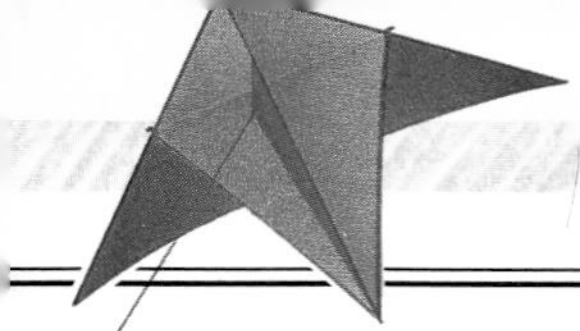

A VTOL plane has thrusters which direct the power from its jet engines. *In normal flight, the thrusters point to the back. This pushes the plane forwards.*

Thruster

*Jet Engines, 29

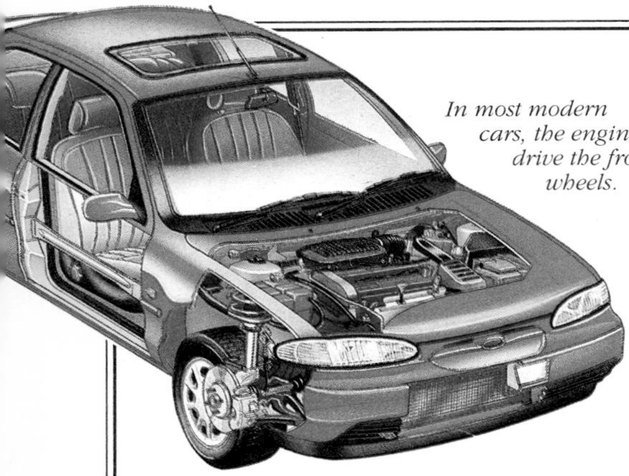

ENGINES

Engines are machines that convert the energy stored in fuel into movement. They provide the power for transportation and industry. Without them, there would be no cars, planes, nor many other machines. Engines release the energy in fuel by burning it. The most efficient way to do this is by burning the fuel inside the engine itself. This is called internal combustion.

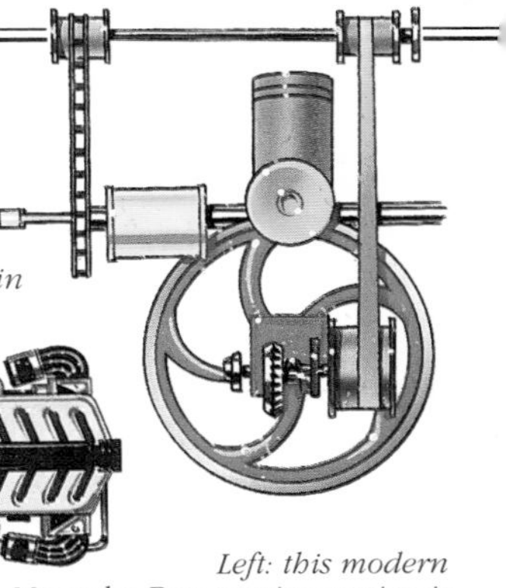

In most modern cars, the engines drive the front wheels.

Right: early internal combustion engine built by Karl Benz in the 1880s.

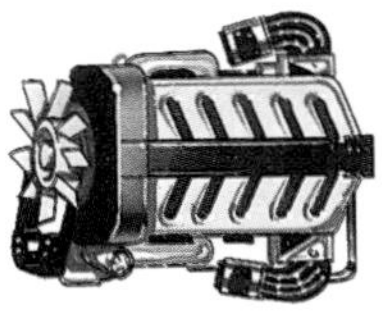

Left: this modern Mercedes-Benz racing engine is over 300 times as powerful as the early Benz engine shown above.

INTERNAL COMBUSTION

The term combustion* means burning, and internal combustion engines burn a mixture of fuel and air inside the engine itself. This produces hot gases. The hot gases take up much more space than the fuel and air they come from, and are used to create movement. For example, in jet planes, the hot gases shoot out of the back of the engine at high speed, pushing the plane forward.

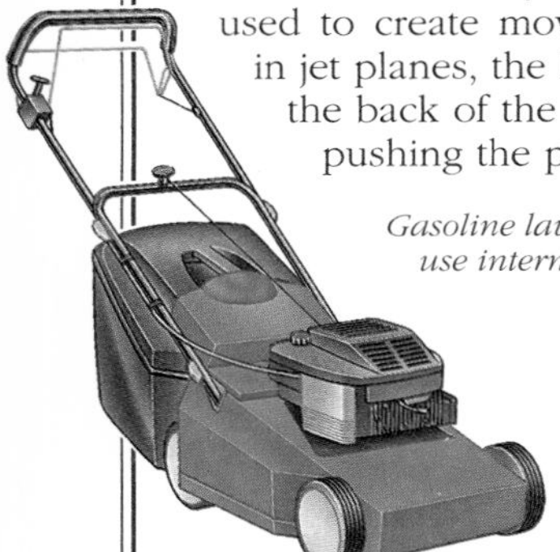

Gasoline lawn mowers and chainsaws use internal combustion engines.

The engines in these small machines use just one piston (see right). The fewer pistons an engine has, the noisier it is.

EXHAUST FUMES

Some of the gases produced by combustion are poisonous. They leave the engine in the form of exhaust fumes. Carbon monoxide is a health threat, as it prevents the blood from carrying oxygen around the body, and nitrogen oxides add to the problem of acid rain.*

Many cyclists wear masks to keep out tiny particles of soot in exhaust fumes.

To reduce pollution,* new car engines are connected to catalytic converters. These contain catalysts,* substances that can alter the speed of chemical reactions. The converter changes the poisonous exhaust fumes into less poisonous gases.

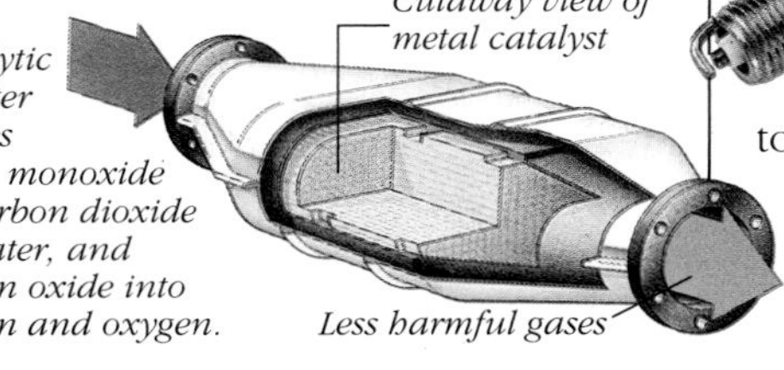

A catalytic converter changes carbon monoxide into carbon dioxide and water, and nitrogen oxide into nitrogen and oxygen.

Cutaway view of metal catalyst

Less harmful gases

GASOLINE AND DIESEL ENGINES

Most car engines burn gasoline. Diesel is used mainly by larger vehicles and by some trains. Both gasoline and diesel engines use internal combustion to drive pistons up and down in hollow cylinders. Each piston works in four stages, shown below, called a four-stroke combustion cycle.

In gasoline engines, air and fuel enter through here.

Cylinder

Piston

(1)

Stroke one
The piston goes down, sucking a mixture of air and fuel into the cylinder from the air and fuel pipes.

Piston rises.

(2)

Stroke two
The piston goes up, compressing the mixture of fuel and air. This heats the mixture.

Spark plug

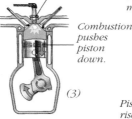

Combustion pushes piston down.

(3)

Stroke three
A spark from the spark plug ignites the mixture. The gases expand and force the piston down. It is this stroke that creates the engine's power.

Exhaust fumes

Piston rises.

(4)

Stroke four
The piston rises again, pushing out the remains of the burned gases as exhaust fumes.

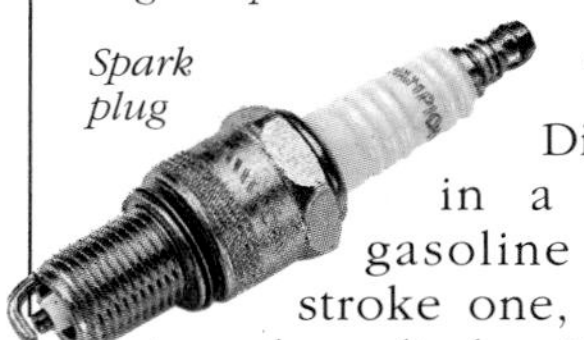

Spark plug

Diesel engines work in a similar way to gasoline engines, but at stroke one, only air is taken into the cylinder. This is compressed to a very high temperature at stroke two. Diesel fuel is forced into the cylinder at stroke three, where it is so hot that the fuel burns without a spark.

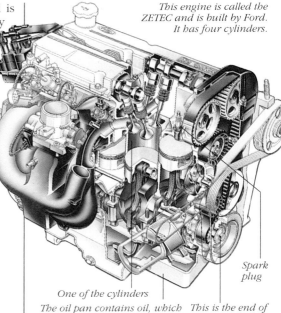

This engine is called the ZETEC and is built by Ford. It has four cylinders.

Spark plug

One of the cylinders

The oil pan contains oil, which reduces friction between the engine's moving parts.*

This is the end of the crankshaft (see below).

Modern car engines often have four cylinders, although larger cars may have six. The four-stroke combustion cycle (see left) takes place in each cylinder. The movement of the pistons is used to turn the wheels of the car. A series of shafts and gears, called the transmission* system, converts the up-and-down motion of the pistons into a rotating motion. The transmission system of a rear wheel drive car is shown below.

The up-and-down movement of the pistons (1) turns the crankshaft (2). The gears (3) connect the crankshaft to the drive shaft (4).

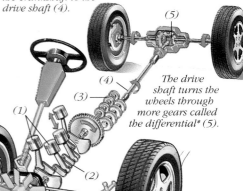

The drive shaft turns the wheels through more gears called the differential (5).*

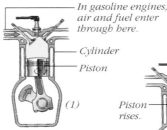

*Combustion, 72; Acid Rain, 63; Air Pollution, 63; Catalysts, 70

*Transmission, 31; Differential, see Transmission, 31

*Friction, 17

JET ENGINES

Jet engines are very powerful internal combustion engines used by aircraft. The hot gases they produce are forced out of the back of the engine at high speed. This pushes the plane through the air.

Jet engines are also known as gas turbine engines because the hot gases turn a series of blades called turbines in the engine. The turbines suck air into the engine, and compress the air before it is mixed with fuel and burned.

A cutaway view of a turbojet engine

Air enters the front of the engine (1). Turbines in the compression chamber (2) compress the air. The compressed air is channeled into the combustion chamber (3) and mixed with kerosene, a fuel for jet engines. The mixture burns explosively and produces hot expanding gases.

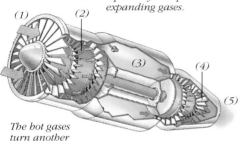

The hot gases turn another turbine (4) as they pass through the back of the engine. This helps drive the compression turbines near the front. The gases are forced out of the exhaust tailpipe (5) at high speed, pushing the plane through the air.

The turbojet engine above is the simplest and fastest type of jet engine. All early jet engines were turbojets, but they are very noisy and less efficient with fuel than turbofan engines (see right). Today, turbojet engines are really only used for high speed jet planes, such as fighter aircraft and the supersonic plane, Concorde.*

ROCKET ENGINES

Rocket engines are a simple form of engine. Like jet engines, they produce hot gases which are forced out behind them at high speed. Instead of using a very complicated mechanism to suck in enough air for combustion, rocket engines carry their own tank of liquid oxygen. This means that they can travel in space, where there is no air.

Rocket fuel

Liquid oxygen

Rocket fuel and oxygen burn in the combustion chamber.

Today's space rockets were developed from rocket missiles. This V-2 missile was launched in 1942.*

Hot gases shoot out of the exhaust.

Turbofan engines are not as fast as turbojets, but are quieter and use less fuel. They are used on commercial jets.

A cutaway view of a turbofan engine

An extra large fan at the front (1) sucks in huge amounts of air. Some of the air goes through the compression and the combustion chambers (2), as in a turbojet, producing hot expanding gases which are forced out of the back (3).

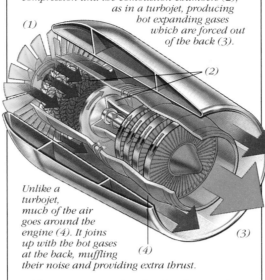

Unlike a turbojet, much of the air goes around the engine (4). It joins up with the hot gases at the back, muffling their noise and providing extra thrust.

There are two other kinds of gas turbine engine: the turboprop and the turboshaft.

Left: the power from a turboprop's engine turns propellers that pull the plane through the air.

Right: turboshaft engines are usually used by helicopters. The engine powers both the main rotor blades and the tail rotor blades.

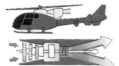

SEE FOR YOURSELF

This experiment shows how jet and rocket engines work. You need a balloon, a piece of string, some sticky tape and a straw.

Tape   Balloon

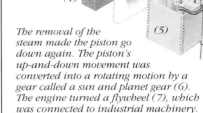

Thread a piece of string through a straw and tie the string tightly between two pieces of furniture. Blow up a balloon and hold the end so that it does not deflate. Ask a friend to tape the balloon to the straw.

Straw

String

When you let go of the balloon, the air inside it rushes out very fast, pushing the balloon forward in the opposite direction.

STEAM ENGINES

The first engines were steam engines. They were invented about 300 years ago, and used external combustion. In a chamber outside the engine, wood or coal was burned to boil water. This produced steam. Because steam expands to take up to 2,000 times more space than water, it could be used to move a piston.

This early steam engine, built by Thomas Newcomen (1663-1729), pumped water from flooded mines.

Piston

Cylinder

The earliest steam engines were not very reliable or efficient, but by the 19th century they were being used to drive trains and power machinery in factories. James Watt (1736-1819) designed the widely used steam engine shown below.

Coal was burned in a furnace (1) to heat water in the boiler (2). A pipe (3) carried steam from the boiler to the cylinder (4). Steam pushed a piston up the cylinder. The condenser (5) took the used steam from the cylinder and turned it back into water.

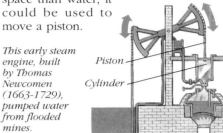

The removal of the steam made the piston go down again. The piston's up-and-down movement was converted into a rotating motion by a gear called a sun and planet gear (6). The engine turned a flywheel (7), which was connected to industrial machinery.

Modern power stations use a type of steam engine called a steam turbine. Pressurized steam turns huge turbines which are used to generate electricity.*

KEY TERMS

Combustion The scientific term for all forms of burning.
Cylinder In an engine, it is the container in which the piston moves up and down.
Piston A short cylinder that moves up and down in a longer cylinder.
Turbine A set of blades that turn when a fluid such as water or gas passes through them.

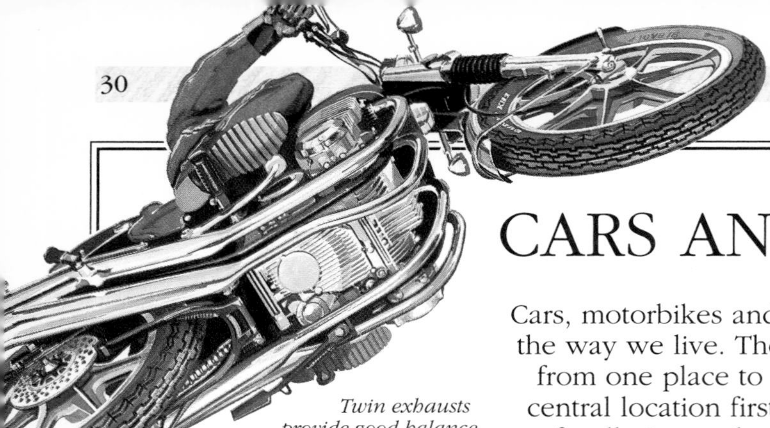

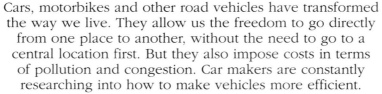

CARS AND MOTORBIKES

Cars, motorbikes and other road vehicles have transformed the way we live. They allow us the freedom to go directly from one place to another, without the need to go to a central location first. But they also impose costs in terms of pollution and congestion. Car makers are constantly researching into how to make vehicles more efficient.

Twin exhausts provide good balance and an even airflow around each side of this motorbike.

The Ford Ka uses fuel more efficiently than most cars.

EARLY VEHICLES

The first vehicle to move on land by its own power was the steam tractor, built by Nicolas-Joseph Cugnot of France in 1769. But despite many experiments with steam, the history of modern road transport does not begin until the development of the internal combustion engine* at the end of the 19th century.

The steam tractor could only travel for 15 minutes.

The internal combustion engine was much lighter and more efficient than the steam engine. By the early years of the 20th century, cars and motorbikes had become quite fast and reliable machines.

Right: this car, built in 1885 by Karl Benz, had a top speed of 14.5kph (9mph).

Only twenty years later, the Rolls Royce Silver Ghost could go nearly nine times faster.

The Ford Model T is probably the most important car ever built. Henry Ford (1863-1947) used an assembly line to build the cars. By 1913, he was producing 1,000 cars a day. This enabled ordinary people to own a car for the first time.

The Ford Model T Assembly Line

1. The body and chassis were assembled separately.
2. The body and chassis moved along the line to be bolted together.
3. All the accessories, such as lights and mudguards, were attached.
4. The Ford Model T was finished in as little as an hour.

MODERN CARS

The aerodynamic cars of today look very different to earlier vehicles. Numerous advances in technology have transformed suspension, braking, materials, safety and efficiency, but the basic mechanical structure of the car is still much the same as at the beginning of the century. This is because the internal combustion engine* is still the only viable form of power. The cutaway picture below identifies some of the main features of a modern family car.

Electric cars like this solar-powered SunRayer are still experimental.

Aerodynamic shape

Solar panels

The spark plugs are inside the engine block.

This car's cylinders are arranged in a line in the engine block.

Air filter

Laminated shatterproof glass

Steering column

The hydraulic reservoir contains brake fluid (see right).

Engine block

The dipstick is used for checking the oil level.

The distributor helps to time the firing of the pistons.

The radiator contains a fan to keep the engine cool.

Most modern cars have their chassis and body combined. This method of construction is called monocoque (one shell).

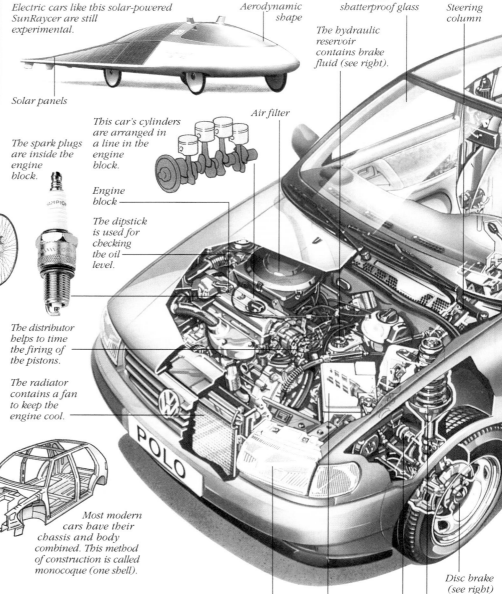

Headlight

The battery stores electricity to power the electrical system.*

Disc brake (see right)

Suspension (see right)

*The steering wheel turns this rack and pinion gear.**

BRAKES

Cars and motorbikes rely on disc brakes or drum brakes. In each case, when the brake pedal or lever is pressed, brake fluid is pushed down tubes (see Pressure*) forcing brake pads to press against a disc in the wheel. The friction causes the wheel to slow down.

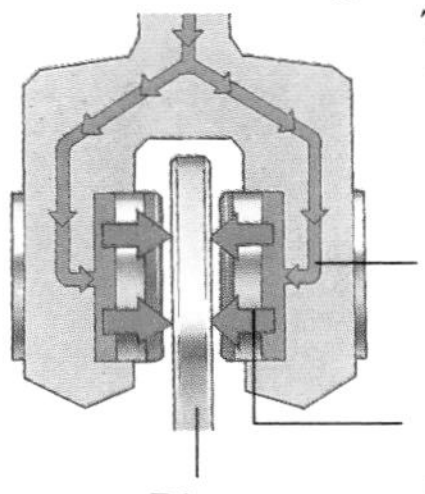

This is a disc brake.

The brake fluid is forced down pipes on both sides of the disc.

The fluid pushes the brake pads against the disc.

Disc

Rear suspension

The silencer muffles the noise of the exhaust.

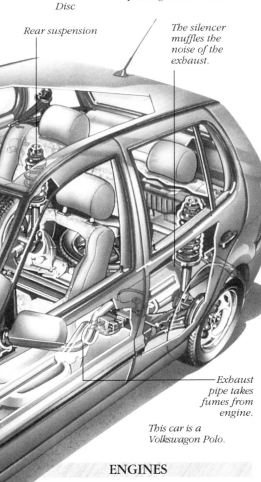

Exhaust pipe takes fumes from engine.

This car is a Volkswagon Polo.

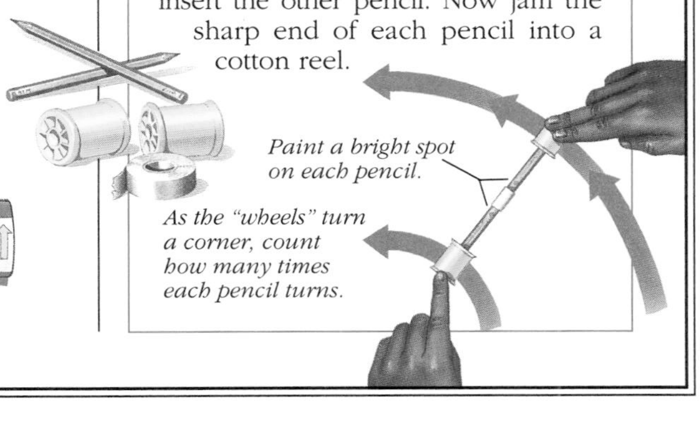

ENGINES

In an internal combustion engine,* petrol or diesel is burned, creating gases that push pistons up and down in a cylinder. This up-and-down motion creates the engine's power. Engines can be two-stroke or four-stroke, depending on whether the pistons move up and down twice or four times in each cycle.

This is a cylinder.

Cylinders are measured in cc (cubic centimetres). A 1000cc motorbike has cylinders measuring 1000 cubic centimetres in volume.

Expanding gases

Spark plug

Piston

Cylinder casing

MOTORBIKES

Motorbikes and cars share many features, although motorbikes do not need a differential (see Transmission). Because they are relatively light, motorbikes can have engines as small as 50cc (see Engines). Bikes with very large engines are incredibly powerful and can accelerate much faster than cars. The picture below shows the main parts of a modern motorbike.

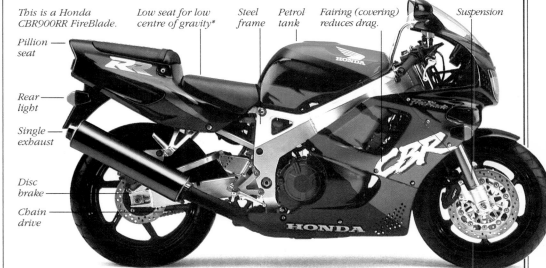

This is a Honda CBR900RR FireBlade.

Pillion seat

Rear light

Single exhaust

Disc brake

Chain drive

Low seat for low centre of gravity*

Steel frame

Petrol tank

Fairing (covering) reduces drag.

Suspension

TRANSMISSION

The transmission is a system of gears* that transmits the engine's power to its wheels. Gears are toothed wheels that turn other gears. The engine turns a shaft called the input shaft that has different sized gears on it. This shaft turns another shaft, called the output shaft, which is connected to the wheels.

Engine powers the input shaft.

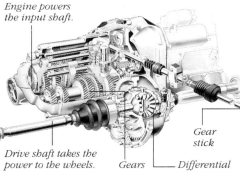

Drive shaft takes the power to the wheels.

Gears

Gear stick

Differential

As well as the main gears which take power to the wheels, the differential is a vital part of a car's transmission. The differential is a system of gears on the axles which allows the wheels to go at different speeds. This is necessary for corners, when the outer wheels turn farther and faster than the inner ones.

The inner wheel travels a shorter distance.

SUSPENSION

Suspension is a system of springs to absorb the effect of bumps and ruts in the road. The suspension on motorbikes is typical of modern suspension. It comprises two parts, a spring and a damper. The spring compresses and expands as the wheel goes over a bump. The damper delays the spring's action, so that the ride is not too bouncy.

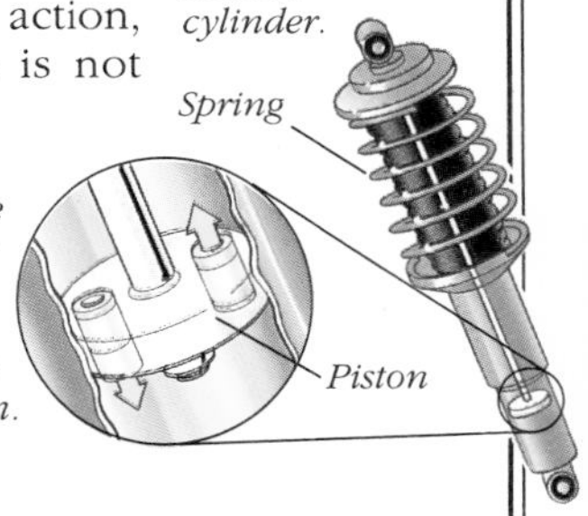

The spring expands and contracts, moving a piston up and down a cylinder.

Spring

Oil in the cylinder is forced through valves, slowing the piston down.

Piston

SEE FOR YOURSELF

Use two pencils, two cotton reels, a strip of paper and some tape to see how a differential works. Roll the paper around one pencil and tape it down. Slide it to the blunt end and insert the other pencil. Now jam the sharp end of each pencil into a cotton reel.

Paint a bright spot on each pencil.

As the "wheels" turn a corner, count how many times each pencil turns.

ASTRONOMY

Our Earth is part of the solar system, the system of planets that revolves around the Sun. However, the Sun itself is just a star, and the solar system is just one tiny part of a huge cluster of stars called a galaxy. This galaxy is just one of the millions that make up the Universe. Astronomy is the scientific study of all the stars, planets and other bodies in the Universe.

Comets are frozen bodies of gas, ice, dust and rock that orbit the Sun.

The Magellan space probe has mapped Venus, revealing a surface covered by solidified lava.

STARS

Stars are globes of very hot gas many times larger than the Earth. Depending on their age and how hot they are, they may shine blue, yellow or red. They are so far away - much farther than the farthest planet - that they can only be seen as points of light in the sky.

Left: stars twinkle because their light passes through the Earth's atmosphere.

Right: millions of stars make up the Milky Way Galaxy.

The patterns made by the stars are called asterisms. Asterisms are parts of large groups of stars that are known as constellations. These are often named after animals, people or objects.

The Plow (also known as the Big Dipper), shown in blue, is an asterism. It is part of a constellation called Ursa Major, or The Great Bear.

These constellations are seen in the southern hemisphere in summer, looking north.

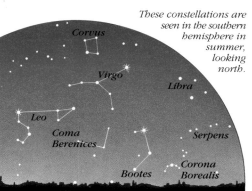

Corvus
Virgo
Libra
Leo
Coma Berenices
Serpens
Bootes
Corona Borealis

LIGHT YEARS

Space distances are so staggeringly huge that ordinary measures are impractical. Astronomers use light years instead. Light* is the fastest thing in the Universe, traveling at 300,000 kilometers (186,000 miles) per second. One light year is the distance light travels in a year: 9.46 million million kilometers (5.88 million million miles). Our galaxy (see right) is 100,000 light years across.

GALAXIES

The Sun, with all the stars that can be seen from Earth, and hundreds of millions of others, are part of a huge system of stars called a galaxy. This galaxy is called the Milky Way.

This is a picture of what the Milky Way might look like. Millions of stars form arms which curve away from its center.

At the very core of the galaxy there may be a black hole, a collapsed star which is so dense that even light cannot escape its gravity.

The Milky Way is only one galaxy among millions and millions of others. They are scattered throughout the Universe, separated by vast gulfs of empty space. Galaxies can be in the shape of a spiral, like the Milky Way, or have one of two other shapes.

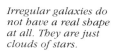

Elliptical galaxies are lens-shaped masses of old, red stars that contain little gas or dust.

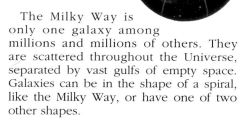

Irregular galaxies do not have a real shape at all. They are just clouds of stars.

Just as stars group in clusters, galaxies form clusters too. Our galaxy is a member of a cluster called the Local Group. It contains around 30 galaxies, and ours is one of the two largest.

THE SUN

Like all stars, the Sun is a massive ball of glowing gas. Inside, atoms of hydrogen are continually joined together in nuclear fusion reactions (see Nuclear Energy and Radioactivity*). These reactions generate the huge amounts of energy that the Sun gives off as heat and light.

The Sun and its solar system is enormous, but compared to the Milky Way it is tiny. It occupies only a small part of the galaxy.

Below: this is a cutaway picture of the Sun. The core is 27 times the diameter of the Earth, and it has a temperature of approximately 15 million°C (27 million°F).

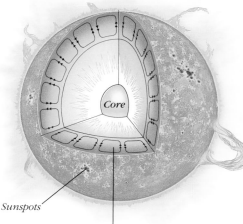

Core

Sunspots

This is the convective zone, which carries the Sun's energy to the surface. The arrows show how the energy moves around in a churning motion.

The Sun looks as if it is marked with small, dark patches. These are called sunspots and they are parts of the surface that are slightly cooler than their surroundings.

Sunspots can form into large groups. The largest group yet seen covered an area of 18,130 million square km (6,969 million square miles).

Solar flares are violent explosions that often occur above sunspots. They send large amounts of radiation out into space.

*Light, 38; Nuclear Energy and Radioactivity, 10

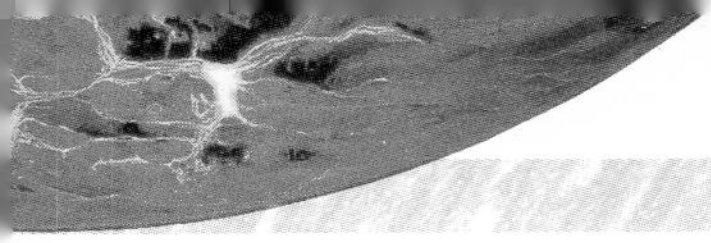

THE SOLAR SYSTEM

The solar system is the system of planets, comets and asteroids which orbits the Sun. Earth is one of the nine known planets in the solar system. Mercury and Venus are closer to the Sun than the Earth, and are called by astronomers the inferior planets. The other planets - Mars, Jupiter, Saturn, Uranus, Neptune and Pluto - are farther away from the Sun than the Earth. They are known as the superior planets.

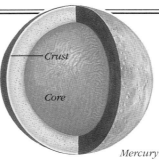

Mercury

Mercury is the smallest planet, and the closest to the Sun. Seventy percent of its mass is made up of a huge metal core. The surface is a thin crust of rock.

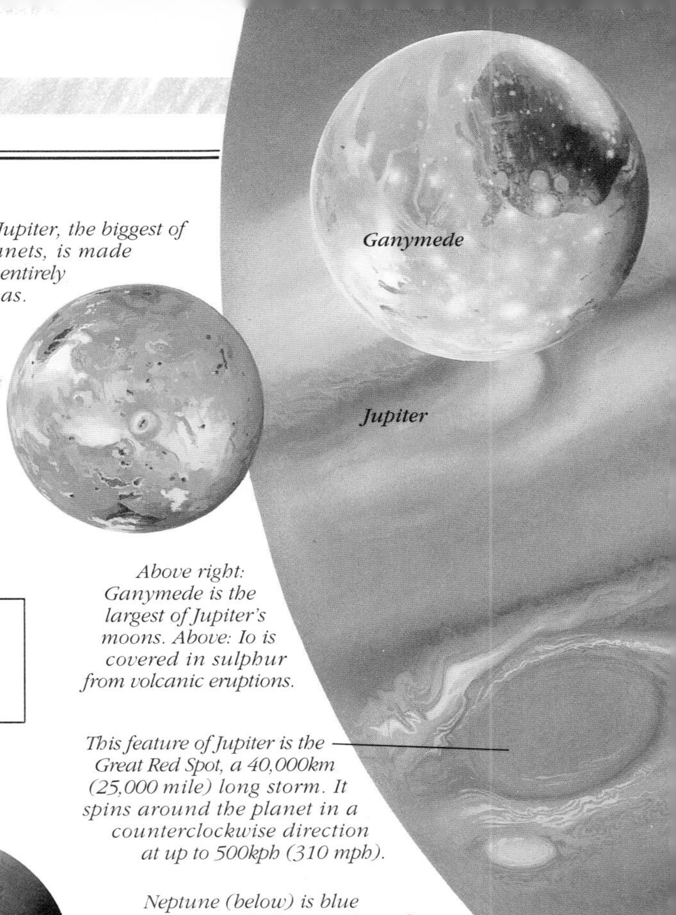

Right: Jupiter, the biggest of the planets, is made almost entirely from gas.

Ganymede

Io

Jupiter

Above right: Ganymede is the largest of Jupiter's moons. Above: Io is covered in sulphur from volcanic eruptions.

This picture shows the relative sizes of the planets.

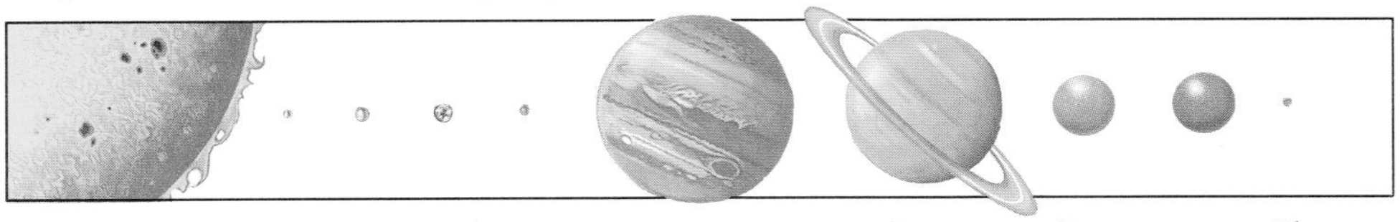

| The Sun | Mercury | Earth | Jupiter | Saturn | Uranus | Pluto |
| | Venus | Mars | | | Neptune | |

This feature of Jupiter is the Great Red Spot, a 40,000km (25,000 mile) long storm. It spins around the planet in a counterclockwise direction at up to 500kph (310 mph).

The Earth is unique in the solar system because it sustains life. Its temperature allows water to exist in its liquid state. The other planets are too hot or too cold.

Pluto (right) was discovered in 1930. Scientists are unsure whether it really is a planet or just a comet.

Neptune (below) is blue because its thick atmosphere of methane reflects blue light.

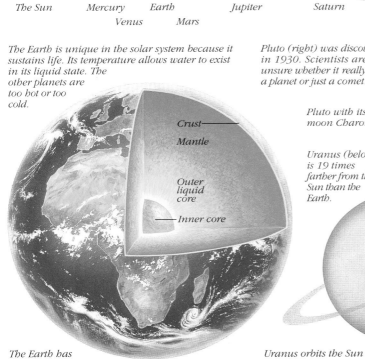

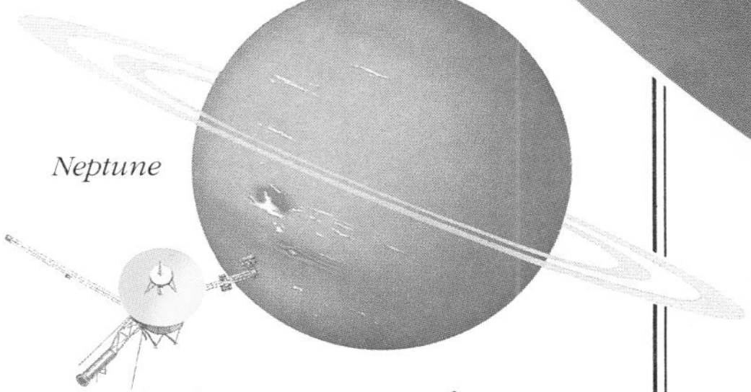

Crust — Mantle — Outer liquid core — Inner core

Pluto with its moon Charon.

Uranus (below) is 19 times farther from the Sun than the Earth.

Neptune

Uranus

The planet Neptune was first observed in detail by the Voyager 2 space probe in the 1980s.

Mars

The Earth has an inner core, an outer liquid core, a partly liquid layer called the mantle, and a crust.

The shifting outer liquid core produces the Earth's magnetic field.

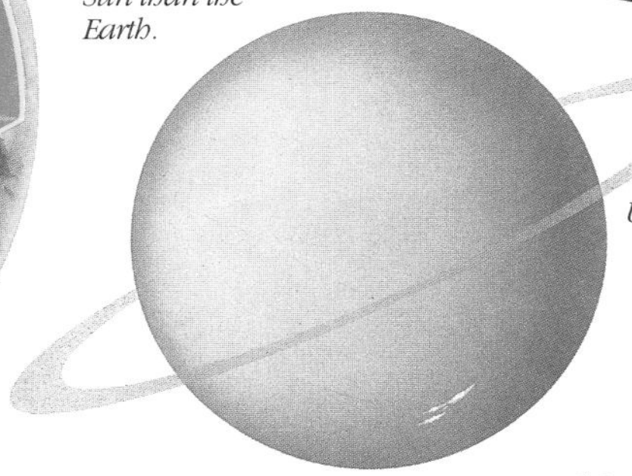

Uranus orbits the Sun on its side, rolling like a wheel. It is thought a huge comet struck it millions of years ago, tipping it sideways.

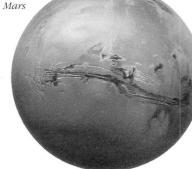

Saturn, like Jupiter, is made almost entirely from gas.

Saturn

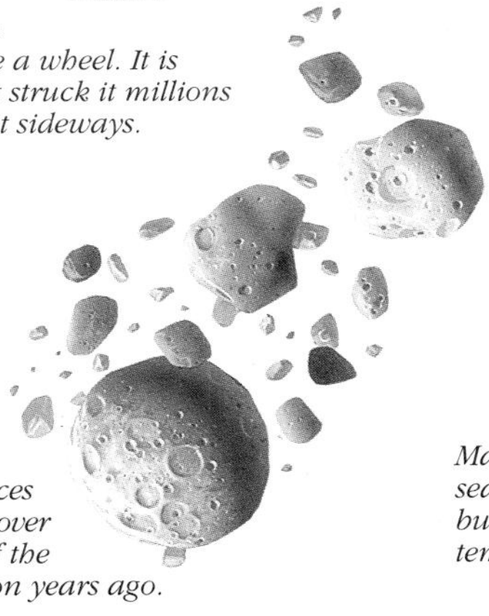

Asteroids are large pieces of rock and metal left over from the formation of the solar system five billion years ago.

Mars, like Earth, has seasons, and its day is only half an hour longer, but because it is farther away from the Sun, its temperature averages -28°C (-18°F).

Mars is covered in volcanoes and craters.

Dried-up river beds show that Mars was once warm enough to have water.

Saturn is encircled by a system of beautiful rings almost five times as wide as the planet itself. They are made up of dust and millions of rocks.

This is the landscape on Mars. Iron makes it a rusty-red color.

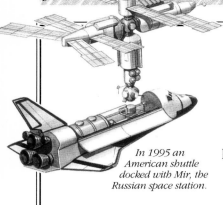

ROCKETS AND SPACECRAFT

The exploration of our solar system - the system of planets and other bodies revolving around the Sun - began in 1957 when a Russian satellite, Sputnik 1, was launched into space. Since then, rockets have landed people on the moon, and unmanned space probes have visited all the planets except Pluto. Satellites which orbit the Earth are part of everyday life, sending television signals into millions of homes.

In 1995 an American shuttle docked with Mir, the Russian space station.

Parachutes are used to return some rocket parts to Earth.

ROCKETS

The history of space travel began with rockets. Rockets were first used to launch bombs in the Second World War, but in 1957 it was a rocket that sent the Russian satellite Sputnik 1 into space. Most of a rocket is made up of fuel tanks. Only the top part, called the payload, survives the voyage intact.

This is the payload of Ariane 4, the European Space Agency's unmanned launch rocket.

This is the third stage of the rocket. Its engine is fueled by liquid hydrogen and oxygen, which burns for approximately twelve minutes.

The second stage is discarded when the rocket has reached a height of 135km (76 miles).

Ariane 4 has three separate fuel tanks. A rocket's fuel tanks are called its stages. Each stage propels the craft a certain distance before dropping off when it is empty. Eventually, only the payload is left.

The first stage carries 226 tonnes (221 tons) of liquid fuel. Together with the two strap-on boosters, it provides the enormous amount of thrust that is needed for take off.

Booster

This picture shows when each stage is jettisoned.

In the 1950s and 60s, Russia and America competed to explore space. The main rockets of this era are shown below. Vostok was the first manned rocket, while Saturn 5 was the first to take people to the moon.

Left: Sputnik was the rocket that launched the first satellite, Sputnik 1.

The Russian rockets are green.

CRITICAL VELOCITIES

A rocket has to leave Earth's atmosphere to get into space. If it is not going fast enough the Earth's gravitational pull drags it back. The speed needed for a successful exit is called escape velocity. Escape velocity is 40,000kph (29,000mph). Once in space, it needs to go at orbital velocity in order to circle the Earth. Orbital velocity depends on the distance of the craft from the Earth.

Below are orbital velocities at different distances.

Distance from Earth		Orbital velocities	
160km	99 miles	27,950kph	17,329mph
800	496	26,650	16,523
16,000	9,920	15,050	9,331
35,880*	22,246*	11,070	6,863

*This is the geostationary orbit (see Satellites, right).

When a rocket is at orbital velocity, it is actually just falling. The reason it does not fall back to Earth is that it loses height at the same rate as the planet's surface curves away underneath it.

Rockets of the 1950s and 60s:

1. Sputnik
2. Vanguard
3. Juno I
4. Vostok
5. Mercury-Atlas
6. Gemini-Titan 2
7. Soyuz
8. Saturn 1B
9. Saturn 5

Right: Saturn 5 was the first rocket to take people to the Moon.

SPACE PROBES

Space probes are unmanned spacecraft that are sent into distant space. They have been sent to every planet except Pluto. They can take years to get to their destination. When they reach it, they orbit it, transmitting data back to Earth.

This is a picture of Mariner 10, the only space probe that has visited Mars.

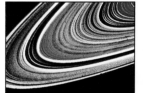

Mariner 10 was launched in 1973 and took many photographs.

These photos of Saturn's rings were taken by the Voyager space probe in 1981.

Pioneer 10 is the first space probe that has left the solar system. It will take more than a million years to reach the nearest star.

Some space probes are designed to land on the surface of other planets, or carry machines called landers that can do the same. Landers can collect samples of rock that are then transported back to Earth for scientists to analyze.

In 1966, a probe called Luna 9 was the first mechanical object to land on the Moon. After landing, it opened like a flower and took television pictures.

1957   1958   1958   1961   1962   1965   1967   1968   1968

SATELLITES

A satellite is an unmanned spacecraft that orbits a planet, usually Earth, in order to perform a particular task - for example, monitoring the weather, transmitting telecommunications, spying, or searching for mineral deposits. Satellites travel at orbital velocity (see left).

This modern communications satellite sends and receives messages.

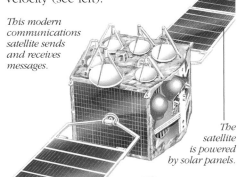

The satellite is powered by solar panels.

Right: Landsat is an Earth resources satellite.

Sensory rings hold instruments for collecting data about the Earth's surface.

Below: this picture of the Humber Estuary in England was taken by a Landsat satellite orbiting the Earth far out in space.

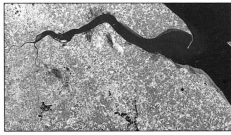

The Landsat satellite can pinpoint an area on the Earth's surface one meter (3.28 ft) square.

A satellite can orbit directly above the equator, or pass over the poles, or at any angle between the two, depending on the task it has been designed to perform. A satellite in orbit above the equator at a height of 35,880km (22,300 miles) takes exactly 24 hours to complete one orbit. This is called a geostationary orbit, because the satellite always stays in the same position in relation to the Earth.

Right: telecommunications satellites often use a geostationary orbit.

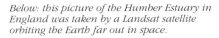

Equator

Left: polar orbits are useful for satellites monitoring the weather. They circle the Earth slowly, viewing a different part of its surface all the time.

THE SPACE SHUTTLE

The Space Shuttle is a manned spacecraft that is reusable, giving it a major advantage over rockets. At lift-off it has two rocket boosters. These help the shuttle reach a speed of 1.4km (0.9 miles) per second. At a height of 43km (27 miles), the rocket boosters are jettisoned. They land in the ocean by parachute and are recovered.

This is a picture of the shuttle with its fuel tank and boosters attached.

Boosters ———

Parachutes ———

The external fuel tank is the only part which is lost.

Flight deck ———

Cargo bay ———

Engines ———

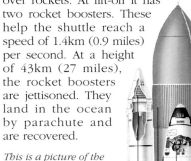

Once in space, the shuttle can orbit the Earth for up to thirty days. It can be used to launch satellites, or to repair broken satellites which are already in orbit. Alternatively, it can be fitted with a space lab for doing experiments.

In 1993, a shuttle made a special journey to repair the Hubble Space Telescope, a telescope that orbits the Earth and can see far out into the Universe.

Because space has no gravity,* a space lab can be used for experiments that would not be possible on Earth.

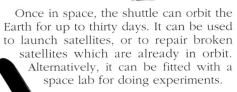

After the Space Shuttle has completed its mission, it returns to Earth without power. It reduces its speed, which causes the Earth's gravity to pull it down in a spiral motion. Once in the Earth's atmosphere, it glides down to the ground.

The shuttle re-enters Earth's atmosphere at very high speeds.

Friction* with the air makes the shuttle red hot. It is protected by a heat shield, which is a layer of special tiles that can withstand the very high temperatures.

SPACE STATIONS

A space station is like a manned satellite. It orbits the Earth for years at a time. Other spacecraft can dock with it, bringing a fresh crew and supplies. The American Skylab and the Russian Salyut and Mir are the only long-term space stations that have gone into orbit so far.

Skylab went into orbit in 1973. Three separate crews visited it. It broke up in orbit in 1979.

Solar tracking equipment

This Apollo spacecraft is docking with the space station.

Skylab had two-story accommodations, with a workshop on the top and living quarters below.

Workshop ———

Living quarters ———

Solar panels convert sunlight into electricity.

Space stations have been very important in increasing scientists' understanding of what happens to the human body in space. Future space stations, such as Freedom, a new American station being built with help from Europe, Japan and Canada, will be used for very long-term projects, or to manufacture products in space.

Astronauts wear a special suit when they go outside a space station or other spacecraft.

A space suit is pressurized inside, to resemble the Earth's pressure.

Layers of nylon and airtight rubber.

Inner clothes are liquid cooled.

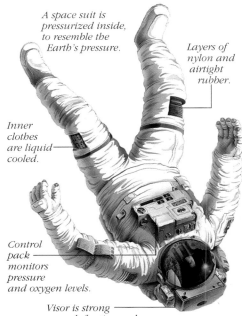

Control pack monitors pressure and oxygen levels.

Visor is strong enough for tiny rocks called micrometeoroids to bounce off.

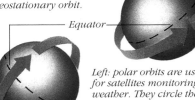

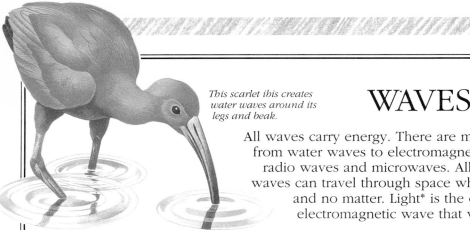

This scarlet ibis creates water waves around its legs and beak.

WAVES

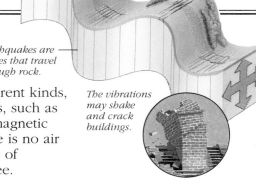

Earthquakes are waves that travel through rock.

The vibrations may shake and crack buildings.

All waves carry energy. There are many different kinds, from water waves to electromagnetic waves, such as radio waves and microwaves. All electromagnetic waves can travel through space where there is no air and no matter. Light* is the only type of electromagnetic wave that we can see.

WHAT IS A WAVE?

Waves occur in different forms and in different substances, called mediums. Water, glass and air are all mediums. A wave carries energy* through a medium by causing the particles of the medium to vibrate.

When a droplet falls in liquid, waves spread out in a circle, transporting energy away from the disturbed area.

The waves get smaller as they move away.

A wave does not permanently disturb the medium through which it travels. The waves around the water droplet above are caused by the liquid's particles vibrating up and down. As the particles gradually stop vibrating and settle in their original positions, the liquid will eventually become calm. Because the liquid particles vibrate up and down, they do not travel with the wave.

Like the water particles themselves, a bird is not moved forward by a passing wave.

Depending on the direction of the vibrations that make them, waves are described as either transverse or longitudinal. Transverse waves, such as water waves, are waves in which the vibrations move at right angles to the direction of travel.

The rope moves up and down.

The transverse wave travels in this direction.

A rope attached to a wall and vibrated up and down shows how transverse wave particles vibrate at right angles to the direction in which the wave is traveling.

Waves where the particles vibrate in the same direction as the wave are called longitudinal waves. The particles of the medium move forward and backward, acting like the coils in a spring as they squash up and spread out.

The coils in a moving spring show how longitudinal waves move.

Direction in which the wave travels.

Coil vibrates back and forth.

Sound waves* are longitudinal waves. They carry vibrations away from the source of the sound, for example, a musical instrument.

Air vibrations inside a saxophone produce sound waves.

MEASURING WAVES

Transverse waves create a repeating pattern of high points, called peaks and low points, called troughs. A complete wave has one peak and one trough and is measured by its frequency, wavelength and height from rest position to peak, called its amplitude. Amplitude decreases as a wave moves away from its source and loses energy. Frequency is the number of complete waves that pass a point in one second.

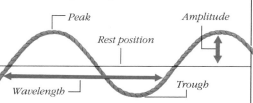

Peak — Amplitude
Rest position
Wavelength — Trough

Frequency is measured in hertz (Hz) after the German scientist, Heinrich Hertz (1857-1894), who was the first person to discover and use radio waves.*

WAVE BEHAVIOR

When a wave meets an obstacle, whether a barrier or a different medium, it alters its behavior. Deep and shallow water act as different mediums.

Tsunami are giant waves that slow down and increase in height rapidly as they enter shallow water.

Waves are reflected* (bounced) on hitting a barrier, refracted* (bent) on passing into a new medium at an angle and diffracted (spread out and bent) on passing through a gap. Before the change, the wave is called the incident wave.

Reflection

The angle at which incident waves hit a barrier is equal to the angle at which they are reflected.

Refraction

The first part of a wave to pass into a new medium is slowed down and this makes the wave bend.

Diffraction

Waves with a long wavelength are diffracted more by small gaps than waves with a short wavelength.

If two peaks arrive in the same place at the same time, they combine to form a peak twice as large. This is constructive interference. If a peak meets a trough, they cancel each other out and the wave disappears. This is destructive interference.

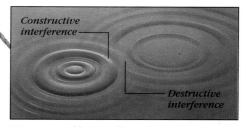

Constructive interference

Destructive interference

Waves caused by two objects dropped in water show constructive and destructive interference.

*Energy, 6-7   *Light, 38, Sound Waves, 44; Radio Waves, 42   *Reflection and Refraction, 38

ELECTROMAGNETIC WAVES

Electromagnetic waves are made up of vibrations in ever-changing electric and magnetic fields.* Apart from those that make up light, all electromagnetic waves are invisible. Depending on their wavelength and frequency, they are used in different ways, from X-rays, which let us see inside our bodies, to radio waves.*

Electromagnetic waves can be placed in order of wavelength and frequency in the electromagnetic spectrum. This starts with short-wave, high-frequency waves and finishes with waves with a long wavelength and low frequency. They all travel at the speed of light, which is 300,000km (186,000 miles) per second.

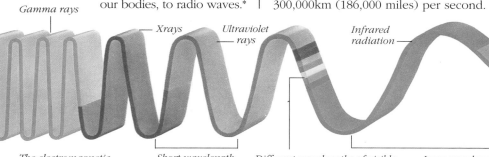

Gamma rays

Xrays   *Ultraviolet rays*

Infrared radiation

Microwaves

*Radio waves**

The electromagnetic spectrum arranges waves in order of wavelength and frequency.

Short wavelength, high frequency

*Different wavelengths of visible light produce different colors.**

Long wavelength, low frequency

Gamma rays (see Radioactivity) can kill living cells. They are used to sterilize medical equipment by killing any bacteria that may be forming.*

X-RAYS

X-rays travel through most soft objects but not hard, dense substances. They are used in hospitals to obtain shadow pictures of parts of the body as they can travel through soft tissue but not through bone or an accidentally swallowed object.

X-rays have been passed through this hand to project a clear image of the bones onto a photographic plate.

X-rays are also used for security at airports to check what may be hidden in people's bags and suitcases.

KEY TERMS

Diffraction The way a wave bends around a barrier or spreads out after passing through a gap.
Frequency The number of waves per second, measured in hertz (Hz).
Medium The substance or space in which objects exist and phenomena, such as waves, occur.
Reflection The way a wave bounces off a different medium.
Refraction The way a wave bends as it passes into a medium in which its speed is different.
Wavelength Length of a wave, between two similar points.

ULTRAVIOLET RADIATION

Ultraviolet (UV) radiation lies just beyond the violet end of the visible color spectrum. It has more energy than light* and can cause chemical reactions to take place. UV rays from the Sun tan skin by producing a brown chemical, called melanin. Too much UV produces high levels of melanin, which can cause skin cancer.

Sunscreens protect skin by blocking out harmful UV rays.

A layer of gas in the atmosphere, called the ozone layer, absorbs UV and stops too much from reaching the Earth.

INFRARED RADIATION

Infrared radiation is given out by anything hot, including the Sun. It carries the Sun's heat to the Earth, or the heat of a fire to you. Infrared cameras on board satellites take pictures that provide experts with vital weather information.

This infrared hurricane image shows the heat reflected from different surfaces, including the freezing tops of clouds.

Rattlesnakes have heat sensors in pits near their eyes that can detect infrared radiation.

Heat sensors enable rattlesnakes to catch prey at night.

MICROWAVES

Microwaves are short-wave radio waves that have many different applications in communications and technology because they are easy to control and direct.

Microwave ovens work by making food molecules vibrate vigorously. Because the radiation penetrates through to the middle of the food, all the molecules vibrate at the same time, which heats and cooks the food more quickly than in an ordinary oven.

A fan spreads the waves around the oven.

Microwave generator tube

Microwaves are used for international telephone calls. Beams of microwaves are sent up to satellites* and back down to receivers in other countries.

One microwave beam can carry more telephone conversations than a wire.

RADAR

Radar uses microwaves to locate distant objects, such as aircraft and ships. A transmitter sends out a beam of microwaves that is reflected off a solid object and picked up again by a receiver. This information is transformed into a screen image that shows where the object is and how fast it is moving.

Bats emit high squeaks that work like echo radar. The sounds bounce off prey, enabling the bats to track it down.

Microwaves bounce off raindrops, which makes radar a vital tool for weather experts, letting them track the bands of rain in large storms.

This radar can spot a tornado 20 minutes before its funnel hits the ground.

*Magnetism, 48; Radio Waves, 42; Radioactivity, 10

*Light and Color, 38; Radio Waves, 42; Satellites, 35

LIGHT AND COLOR

Light is a form of energy. It travels in waves and can be reflected (bounced) or refracted (bent) just like waves* in water. Over 300 years ago, the English scientist, Isaac Newton, discovered that white light can be split up into the colors of the rainbow.

Diamonds are cut so that most of the light emerges from one face, making it sparkle.

A solar eclipse occurs when the Moon lies between the Sun and Earth. The Moon blocks out sunlight and casts its shadow on the Earth.

LIGHT

Any object that gives off light, whether the Sun or a light bulb, is said to be luminous. Most objects are nonluminous and can be seen only because they are reflecting the light from something that is luminous.

The light bouncing off this baseball bat makes it visible.

Some objects give off more light than others. The level of brightness is called intensity. The farther you are from a source of light, the less intense light is, because light waves* spread out as they travel.

Light from a flashlight is more intense than candlelight.

Like other waves, light waves transport energy from a source to its surroundings. The Sun is the Earth's biggest light source. Light waves are called transverse waves.* They are made up of vibrations that change direction millions of times a second, but are always at right angles to the direction of the light beam.

Light fades because the vibrations of the waves become gradually smaller.

Sunlight takes about eight minutes to reach Earth.

The substance light travels through, for example, air, water or glass, is called the medium. The medium is not altered when light passes through it. When passing through space, where there is no air and no matter, light travels at 300,000km (186,000 miles) per second.

REFLECTION AND REFRACTION

Light travels in a straight line through space, but when its medium (the substance it is traveling through) changes, the light waves can change direction. Some substances reflect light, so that it bounces off the surface. Light bounces off a smooth, shiny surface at the same angle that it strikes it. Rougher surfaces reflect light in many directions, scattering it widely.

Light waves bounce off a smooth surface like a ball off the ground.

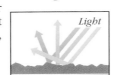

Rough surface

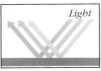

Smooth surface

An image made by a reflection in a surface is called a virtual image because the image is not real, but formed only by the light reflected off it into the eye.

The reflection of the clock is a virtual image.

Reflecting surfaces are called reflectors.

Refraction occurs when light bends as it passes from one medium to another. For example, air is less dense than water, and when light passes from one to the other, it changes speed, which makes it bend. This causes objects lying in the water to appear distorted or bent.

Refraction makes the end of this straw appear bent in the water.

The straw is at point Y, but it appears to be at X.

SHADOWS

Light cannot pass through most solid objects, so shadow falls on the side light does not reach. Shadows help us to judge shapes and distances. Some animals are marked so that light and shadow act as camouflage.

Shadows tend to form at the base of solid objects.

These gazelles have light patches below and dark patches above. This creates the impression they have no shadow, which helps to camouflage them.

Substances that only let some light through are said to be translucent. Those through which light passes fully are called transparent. Solid objects, which let no light through, are said to be opaque. Opaque objects cast two types of shadow. The dark shadow, where no light reaches, is called umbra. The grey shadow, where some light reaches, is called penumbra. The smaller the light source, the more umbra and less penumbra it creates.

These sunglasses are translucent. Only some light can pass through.

Above: general light makes the shadow under these sunglasses all penumbra.
Right: this medium-sized light creates both umbra and penumbra.

Penumbra
Umbra

KEY TERMS

Dispersion The splitting up of light into the colors of the spectrum.
Luminous Used to describe any object that gives out light.
Medium The substance or space in which an object exists and phenomena, such as waves, occur.

*What is a wave? 36   *Waves, 36   *Wave Behavior, 36

COLOR

White light is made up of seven colors: red, orange, yellow, green, blue, indigo and violet. Normally the colors merge and cannot be seen separately. Each color has a different wavelength* and frequency,* and when light passes through a different medium, the colors refract by different amounts. This splits the light up into the color spectrum.

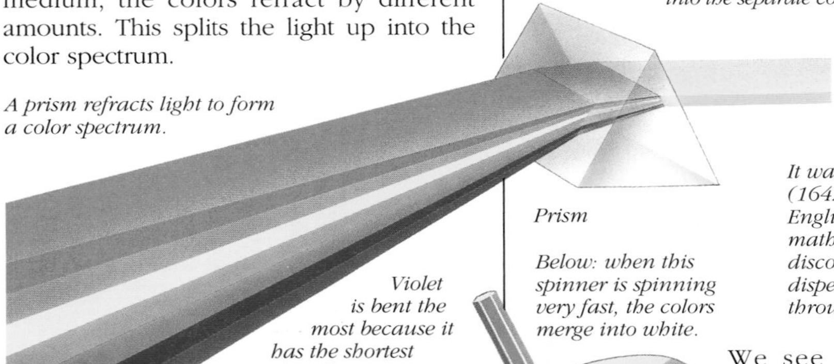

A prism refracts light to form a color spectrum.

Violet is bent the most because it has the shortest wavelength.

The sky appears blue due to the scattering of light by specks of dust in the atmosphere. The dust refracts and reflects the light, with blue light being dispersed most. At sunset, light has to pass through more atmosphere, and the blue end of the spectrum is scattered so much that, in a wide area of sky around the Sun, the blue light cannot be seen. *Warning: never look directly at the sun.*

At sunset, sunlight passes through more of the Earth's atmosphere.

Midday sunlight
Light at sunset

Rainbows (right) form when light is refracted through tiny drops of rain still present in the air after a shower. Each drop acts like a tiny prism (below), dispersing light into the separate colors.

White light enters prism.

Prism

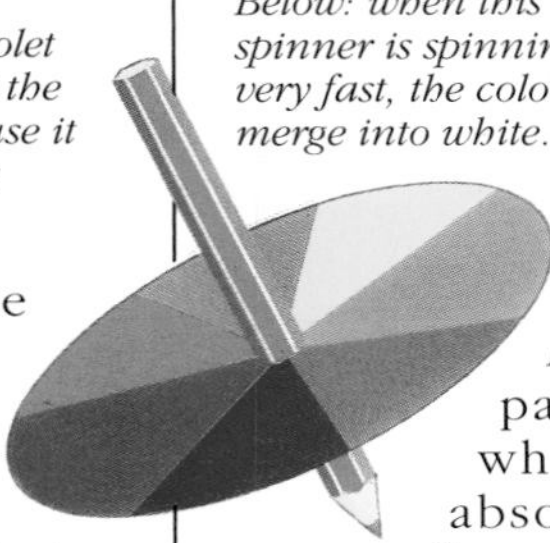

Below: when this spinner is spinning very fast, the colors merge into white.

It was Isaac Newton* (1642-1727), the English scientist and mathematician, who discovered that light disperses when passed through a prism.

We see an object as colored because it only reflects that color of light. All colored objects and paints contain pigments which are substances that absorb certain colors and reflect others. A red flower looks red because it reflects red light and absorbs all the other colors of the spectrum. White objects reflect all the colors of light equally, while black ones reflect hardly any light.

White reflects light and heat better than black, so white clothes show up better than black clothes and also keep the body cooler.*

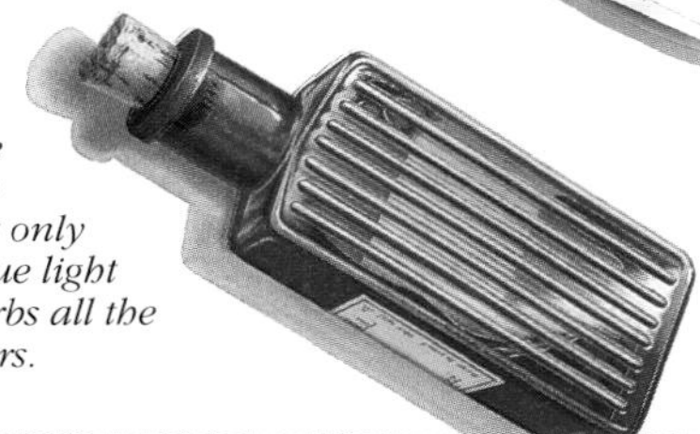

This bottle looks blue because it only reflects blue light and absorbs all the other colors.

PRIMARY COLORS

Primary colors are colors that can be mixed to make up almost any other color. They are different for light and for paints. Red, green and blue are the primary colors for light. When you mix two together, the color of light they make is called a secondary color.

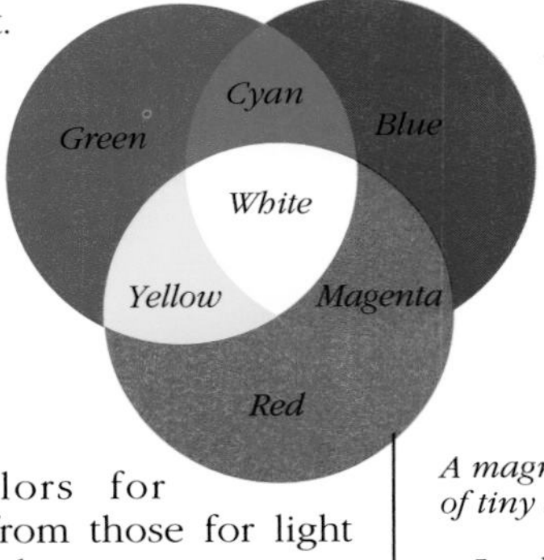

All the colors on a television are made by mixing the three primary colors of light.*

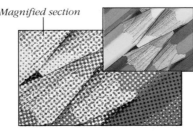

Layers of magenta, yellow and cyan dots of ink are used to print the colors in books, along with black to make pictures darker. This is called four-color printing.

Magnified section

A magnified printed picture shows it is made up of tiny dots of magenta, yellow, cyan and black.

The primary colors for paints are different from those for light because, unlike light, they are never pure color. They are magenta (a red color), yellow and cyan (a bright blue).

Look through a magnifying glass at any picture on this page and you will see the dots which make up the color images.

LASERS

Lasers are narrow beams of pure color. Unlike ordinary light, they do not spread out from their source, but remain parallel and focused.

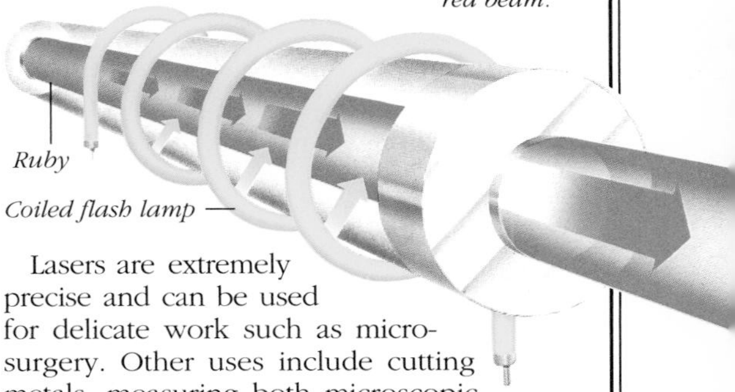

In this laser, a rod of ruby absorbs light from a coiled flash lamp.

The ruby re-emits the light as a concentrated red beam.

Ruby

Coiled flash lamp

Lasers are extremely precise and can be used for delicate work such as micro-surgery. Other uses include cutting metals, measuring both microscopic and vast distances, carrying phone calls, aligning underground pipes, and also "reading" bar codes.

Lasers can cut through metal.

FLUORESCENCE

Fluorescent substances absorb energy, such as electricity* or UV radiation,* and give it out as bright light. They are widely used in advertising and paints as they make colors seem to glow.

Some laundry detergents contain fluorescent substances that convert UV rays into blue light which makes white clothes look whiter.

Fluorescent lights consist of a tube filled with a gas such as neon. Electricity is passed through the tube, giving energy to electrons in the gas, which give off their new energy as light. Different kinds of gases give off different colors.

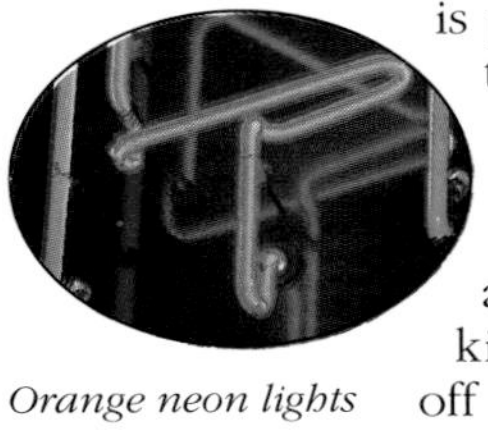

Orange neon lights

SEE FOR YOURSELF

You can split up white light into the color spectrum with a clear plastic ruler.

Put the ruler on its side on a sunny table and tilt it until you see colors on the table. Put white paper down at that spot to reveal the full spectrum.

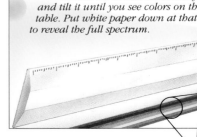

LENSES AND MIRRORS

Contact lenses are worn directly over the eye.

A magnifying glass is a converging lens. It makes objects look bigger than they really are.

A lens is a piece of transparent substance with curved surfaces. Lenses bend light in a certain way. Both lenses and mirrors are used in optical instruments, from simple magnifying glasses to sophisticated telescopes, to let us study objects in more detail than with the naked eye.

Binoculars use lenses to magnify objects.

LENSES

Lenses are shaped so that light passing through them bends. This is called refraction.* There are two main types of lens: converging and diverging. Converging lenses curve outward. Parallel rays of light pass through and converge to a point called the focus. A converging lens will produce an upside-down image beyond the focus of an object placed in front of the lens.

Below: parallel rays pass through a converging lens to meet at the focus.

Focus

Right: light waves bounce off this vase and refract as they pass through the converging lens of a human eye.

A diverging lens curves inward, making parallel rays of light spread out, so that the rays appear to have come from a focus behind the lens.

Refracted rays spread out as they pass through a diverging lens.

Focus

Single lenses suffer from defects and can transmit blurred images. Some images may have a colored "halo" because the colors that make up white light separate as they pass through the lens (see Color*). Optical instruments use two or more lenses stuck together, called compound lenses, to correct any distortion that may occur.

A simple microscope

Focusing controls

Compound lenses on revolving triple nosepiece

In a compound lens, the second lens corrects any distortion caused by the first.

Glass slide

Mirror directs light through object on slide

EYES AND EYESIGHT

The eye is a highly developed optical instrument that turns light reflected from an object (see Light*) into an image the brain recognizes. A converging lens focuses the light rays and an image is formed on the retina, at the back of the eye. Because the retina lies beyond the focus of the lens, the image is upside down (see left).

This insect's eye is made up of hundreds of lenses.

Human eye

Pupil

Retina

A hole called the pupil lets the light in.

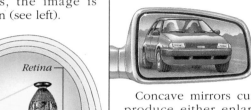

Lens

The retina sends signals through the optic nerve to the brain.

Optic nerve

Distant objects are blurred for nearsighted people because the image forms in front of the retina. Farsighted people cannot see nearby objects well because the rays focus behind the retina.

Diverging lens

Nearsightedness is corrected by a diverging lens.

Converging lens

Farsightedness is corrected by a converging lens.

MIRRORS

When light hits a flat mirror straight on, it bounces straight back (see Reflection and Refraction*). Curved mirrors bounce light off at an angle, producing different kinds of images. A convex mirror curves outward and creates small, wide-angled images.

Light reflected off a convex mirror.

Car wing mirrors are convex to give drivers a wide view of the traffic behind them.

Concave mirrors curve inward and produce either enlarged images or small, upside-down images, depending on the distance between the mirror and the object.

Concave mirror

Light reflected off a concave mirror

The bowl of a spoon is a concave mirror. The image is big when the spoon is near your face, but small and upside-down when it is farther away.

PRISMS

Prisms* are glass shapes that can change the direction in which light is traveling. When light hits the boundary between the prism and air at an angle beyond a certain value, the light is all reflected back into the prism instead of passing into the air. This is called total internal reflection.

This refractor telescope uses a prism to redirect light.

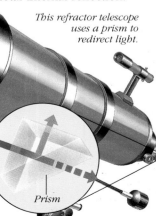

Lens

Incoming light is redirected by a prism through a 90° angle to send it through the eyepiece.

Prism

KEY TERMS

Concave An inward-curving surface on a lens or mirror.
Converging lens A lens that bends parallel rays of light inward.
Convex An outward-curving surface on a lens or mirror.
Diverging lens A lens that bends parallel rays of light outward.
Total internal reflection The way all the light hitting a glass/air boundary beyond a certain angle is reflected.

CAMERAS AND PHOTOGRAPHY

Cameras are optical instruments that produce permanent photographic representations of real life. Before they were invented, the only way to record a scene was by drawing or painting it. Cameras use lenses to focus light onto a photographic film and form an image. The film is then developed and set before being used to make prints.

This is an early polaroid camera. Polaroid cameras develop and print the image.

Slide photographs can be projected onto screens.

Right: a short sequence from an early film.

CAMERAS

A camera works in a similar way to an eye (see left). Light enters the camera through a lens to form an upside-down image on photographic film at the back of the camera. The amount of light that enters is called the exposure and is controlled by a hole called an aperture and a flap called a shutter. The image is brought into focus by moving the lens nearer or farther away from the film.

Single-lens reflex (SLR) camera

Viewfinder *Pentaprism*

Film wind-on lever *Shutter release button* *Aperture adjuster*

The take-up film spool is in here. *The shutter is behind this mirror.* *Rear lens* *Front lens*

Camera lenses are described in terms of their focal length, which is the shortest distance of the lens from the film. A standard lens has a focal length of about 50mm. Shorter focal lengths give a wider angle of view, making objects seem smaller. Wide angle lenses, typically 28mm or 35mm, are often used for landscape photos. Telephoto lenses have focal lengths of 80mm or more and make objects seem nearer than they are. Macro lenses are used for very close-up shots.

The longer a telephoto lens, the nearer the subject appears.

Focus ring moves lenses

This close-up photograph of a needle with cotton thread in it was taken with a macro lens.

PHOTOGRAPHIC FILM

Photographic film has a coating of silver nitrate, a chemical that is sensitive to light. How each film reacts depends on the amount of light that reaches it. Fast films react quickly to small amounts of light and slow films need a lot of light.

Left: a strip of photographic color film

Some cameras recognize film speed by reading metallic squares, called a DX code, on the film cassette.

The exposed film is made into a strip of negatives by dipping it in chemicals which develop and set the image. Negatives show dark things as light and light things as dark. In order to make an actual photograph, light is shone through the negative onto light-sensitive photographic paper.

Slides are photographs printed onto a transparent base.

Left: a light-proof cartridge protects the film from further exposure.

MOVING PICTURES

Movie cameras use cine film, which has to be developed just like photographic film. The moving pictures in films are made up of lots of individual photos, called frames. The frames move so fast that you see the next frame before the last one fades in your brain. This is called persistent vision.

The first films showed simple actions.

TELEVISION CAMERAS

TV cameras do not use film or tape, but turn the light bounced off people and objects into a series of electrical signals. The signals are sent down a cable and either transmitted immediately for a "live" broadcast, or sent to a video recorder* to be transmitted later.

This is a TV studio camera.

Lens

The viewfinder is a miniature TV screen.

The cable carries the electronic signals to the control room.

A camcorder is a TV camera and a video recorder.* Lenses create an image on a tiny light-sensitive electronic part called a charge-coupled device (CCD). The CCD produces electrical signals which create a magnetic field that records the picture as a pattern of magnetic particles on the videotape.

Cable

Light goes through lens.

Light hits CCD.

Magnetic pattern forms on videotape.

*Video, 43

RADIO

A Marconiphone, one of Marconi's early radio transmitting machines

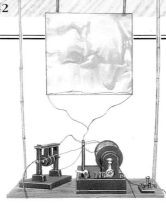

Some galaxies give out radio signals.

Radio waves can travel through air, objects and even empty space at the speed of light, without wires or cables. They are used to carry signals for radio and television programs, to carry phone calls, and to communicate with astronauts in spacecraft. Radio messages have even been sent into outer space to tell alien lifeforms (if there are any) about human existence.

Space probes send radio information back to Earth.

RADIO WAVES

Radio waves are part of the electromagnetic spectrum.* They are made up of a combination of electrical and magnetic fields, and can be produced by an electric current that oscillates (changes direction) rapidly.

Radio waves are the longest of the waves that make up the electromagnetic spectrum.

Electromagnetic spectrum

Radio waves

Radio waves are measured by their wavelength or their frequency. The wavelength is the distance from the top of one wave to the top of the next. The frequency is the number of waves per second and is measured in hertz (Hz).

Very High Frequency (VHF) or Ultra High Frequency (UHF) waves are the shortest waves of all.

Short waves (SW)

Medium waves (MW)

Long waves (LW)

Radio transmitters send radio waves in all directions. Some go directly to people's houses.

To carry messages, such as sounds, radio waves are altered, or modulated, so that their shape represents the messages. There are two types of modulation: frequency modulation (FM) varies the wave frequency and amplitude modulation (AM) varies the wave's amplitude (strength).

Carrier signal

The basic radio wave, called the carrier signal, is mixed with the sound wave.

Sound wave

Modulated wave

After modulation, the shape of the carrier wave is altered to represent the sound wave.

RADIO BROADCASTING

Radio waves were first used to send messages in 1896 by Guglielmo Marconi. Now, radio programs are sent from the radio station where they are made to a large transmitter. This sends out radio waves that are picked up by radios in people's homes. Each station uses a specific wavelength. The radio waves may travel directly, or be sent up to a satellite* to be beamed down to another part of the world.

VHF and UHF (very short) radio waves pass through a part of the Earth's atmosphere called the ionosphere. They are used for transmitting to satellites and space stations.

Radio satellite

VHF or UHF waves

Short waves

Medium waves

Long waves

Ionosphere

Long-wave, medium-wave and short-wave radio waves travel around the Earth, bouncing off the ionosphere.

A radio set receives the modulated radio waves through its antenna, which converts the wave signals back into very weak electrical signals.

A radio's antenna receives many radio signals of different wavelengths. The tuner can be adjusted so that a particular wavelength is selected. The selected signal is strengthened (amplified) and then translated back into a sound signal.

Antenna

Plastic casing

The loudspeaker turns the sound signal into a sound that can be heard.

Volume is adjusted with a variable resistor.*

Tuner

RADIO COMMUNICATIONS

Radio is often used as a form of two-way communication, for example in walkie-talkies and mobile phones.

Antenna

This mobile phone has a waterproof carrying case.

Buttons for dialing

Two-way radios, for example police walkie-talkies and CB (Citizen's Band) radios used by truck drivers, send radio signals directly to each other. Radios in buses, trains, planes, and ships allow them to communicate with a base station, or radio for help.

A handset makes it easier to use the radio while driving.

Right: walkie-talkies

Far right: two-way car radio

Handset

Animals are studied using radio tracking. A radio collar is attached to the animal and it is released. Radio signals from the collar allow scientists to track the animal's movements.

Black-footed ferrets have been tracked by radio.

Black-footed ferret wearing a radio collar.

KEY TERMS

Wavelength Length of a complete wave, from peak to peak.
Frequency Number of waves per second, measured in hertz (Hz).
Broadcast To send out radio signals over a wide area.
Aerial or **antenna** A device that picks up radio waves and converts them into electrical signals.
Transmitter A device that broadcasts (sends) radio waves.

*Electromagnetic Waves, 37

*Satellites, 35; Space Stations, 35; Variable Resistor, see Electronic Components, 50

TELEVISION AND VIDEO

Television is a way of carrying picture signals over long distances. The signals are usually carried by radio waves (see opposite), but television signals can be sent along cables too. Usually, a sound signal is carried as well, so films, news and many other kinds of programs can be broadcast to television sets in people's homes.

A TV antenna receives radio waves carrying television signals and sends them to a TV set.

Pocket televisions have liquid crystal display* screens.

Speaker

HOW A TELEVISION SET WORKS

A television set converts radio signals into sound and pictures. The sound is converted in the same way as in a radio set (see opposite). The pictures are converted by a cathode ray tube.

Cutaway television cathode ray tube

Screen

The electrical signals are converted into three cathode rays, or beams of electrons (tiny atomic particles).

There is one beam for each primary color (red, blue and green). The beams are fired down the tube at the screen.

The electron beams sweep very quickly across the whole screen, varying in strength.

The screen is covered in pixels, tiny areas made up of chemicals called phosphors. They glow red, blue and green when they are hit by an electron beam, making up a picture.

Extra large high-definition televisions (HDTVs) have more pixels than ordinary TVs, so the picture is sharper.

Pixels

A computer monitor (below) works in the same way as a cathode ray tube television.

Some televisions can receive extra information such as weather forecasts, news and timetables, in the form of text on the screen. The system is interactive - the viewer can choose what to see using a hand-held control pad.

TV information services use pixellated pictures. This plane illustrates holiday information.

THE HISTORY OF TELEVISION

A German scientist called Paul Nipkow (1860-1940) first discovered how to convert pictures into electrical signals in 1884. His invention, the Nipkow disc, converted a picture into a pattern of light flashes that could be sent along a wire.

The Nipkow disc (1) spins around and the holes in the disc (2) break up an image (3) into a pattern of light flashes. A photoelectric cell (4) turns the light into electric signals, which are sent along a wire (5).

The electric signals make a light bulb (6) flash the same light patterns.

Another Nipkow disc (7) spinning at the same speed as the first turns the light patterns back into a picture (8).

John Logie Baird (1888-1946), a Scottish inventor, was the first to combine Nipkow disc technology with radio waves. In 1926, he used radio waves to transmit a television picture across the Atlantic.

John Logie Baird's 1926 television transmitting equipment

Motor for spinning the disc

Object

Nipkow disc

KEY TERMS

Electron A negatively charged particle that exists around the nucleus of an atom.
Pixel Short for "picture element". A dot that forms part of a picture.
Radio waves The longest of all the waves that make up the electromagnetic spectrum.

SATELLITE AND CABLE TV

Satellite television stations transmit radio signals to a satellite* orbiting the Earth. This means they can transmit programs from all around the world. The signals are picked up by satellite TV dishes.

Satellite TV dish

The dish collects radio signals beamed down from a satellite and focuses them onto a receiver.

Receiver

The signals travel along a cable to a television set.

Cable

Cable TV is another way of transmitting television signals. Instead of using radio waves, the signals are sent along buried cables. Fiber-optic cables are often used.

Fiber-optic cables contain tiny glass fibers less than 1mm (0.04in) thick.

VIDEO

A video cassette recorder (VCR) records moving television pictures and sounds onto tapes called videotapes, so that they can be played back later.

A VCR records signals straight from the transmitter, so the television does not need to be switched on.

Video cassette recorder

Videotape cut away to show tape inside.

Sounds and pictures are recorded as patterns of magnetic particles on the tape.

Plastic flap

Close-up view of particles

CDs* can be used instead of videotapes to store moving pictures. They are played on a special CD player which plugs into a TV.

Compact Discs, 45; Liquid Crystal Displays, 77; Satellites, 35

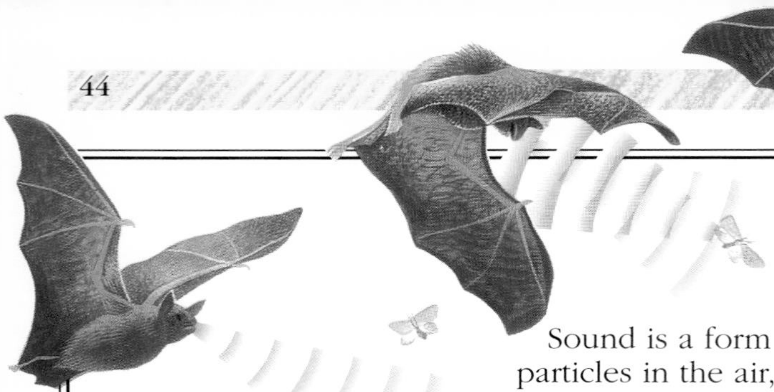

Bass clarinet

Clarinet

SOUND

Sound is a form of energy* that is carried by waves of vibrating particles in the air, or other medium. Sound can only travel through a medium, such as air, water or glass. In space, there is no medium, so there are no sounds. By converting sound energy into other forms of energy, such as electricity* or radio waves,* sound can be recorded or transmitted over long distances.

Bats emit very high-pitched squeaks which they use for echo-location.

Wind instruments make a column of air vibrate inside the instrument.

SOUND WAVES

Sounds are made by objects vibrating and causing vibrations in the air or other medium around them. The vibrations make the particles in the medium move backward and forward, forming waves that travel through the medium.

The vibrations from an alarm clock or a jet plane make particles in the air vibrate.

Sound waves are longitudinal waves.* The particles of the medium vibrate backward and forward, rather than up and down as in transverse waves. Waves are usually drawn as diagrams showing their frequency (the number of waves per second, measured in hertz) and their amplitude (the strength of the waves).

Diagram of sound waves. In fact, sound waves move backward and forward, not up and down, but this diagram shows their measurements more clearly.

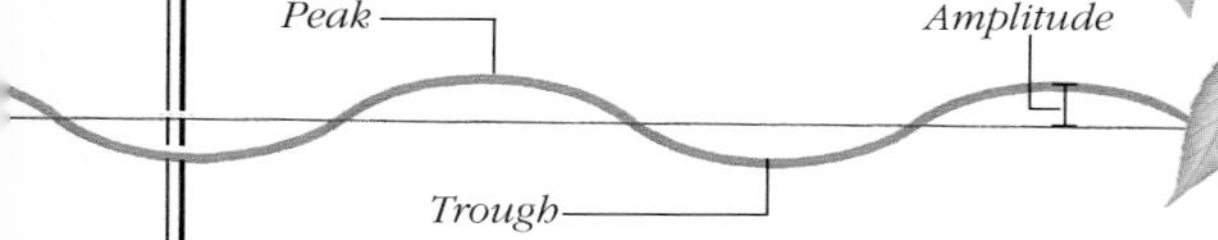

Peak

Amplitude

Trough

High-pitched sounds produce high-frequency waves and low-pitched sounds make low-frequency waves. Sounds above 20,000 hertz are called ultrasound. Loud sounds produce waves with a large amplitude and soft sounds produce small-amplitude waves. As sounds travel farther from their source, their amplitude becomes smaller and the sounds become quieter.

High-pitched sounds, such as birdsong, make high-frequency waves.

Low-pitched sounds, such as those made by the engine of a heavy truck, make low-frequency waves.

Sound waves travel at different speeds in different mediums. In dry air at 20°C (68°F), the speed of sound is 343m (1,125ft) per second. Supersonic speed is a speed greater than the speed of sound. Sonic booms are shock waves produced by aircraft traveling faster than the speed of sound. Supersonic speed is measured in units called Mach and Mach 1 is the speed of sound.

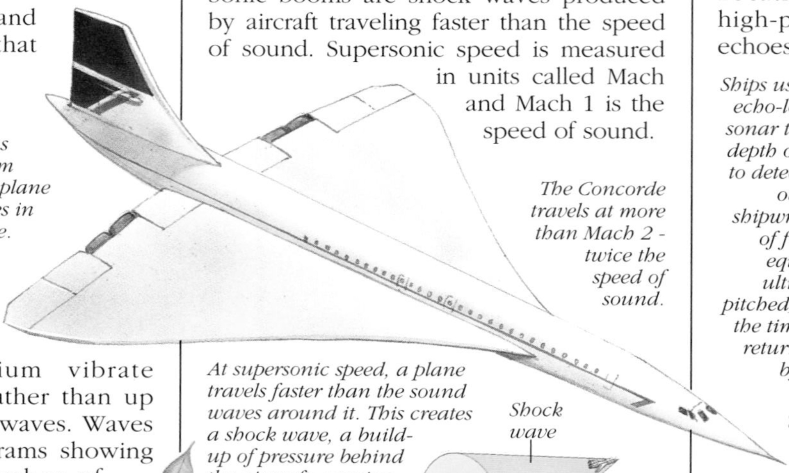

The Concorde travels at more than Mach 2 - twice the speed of sound.

At supersonic speed, a plane travels faster than the sound waves around it. This creates a shock wave, a build-up of pressure behind the aircraft, causing a sonic boom.

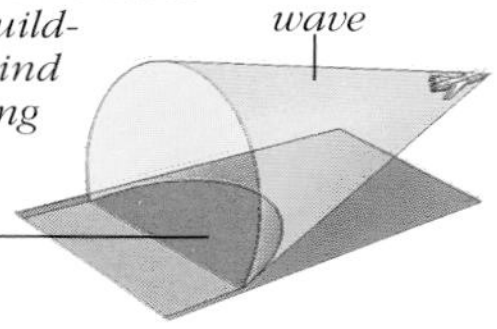

Shock wave

Area where boom is heard

Noise is sound that is thought to be unpleasant. The loudness of noise is measured in decibels (dB) and sounds over 120dB can be painful.

The sound of falling leaves measures 10dB and an airplane taking off measures 110dB.

The loudest animal in the world is the blue whale. It makes sounds of 188dB that can be detected 850km (530 miles) away.

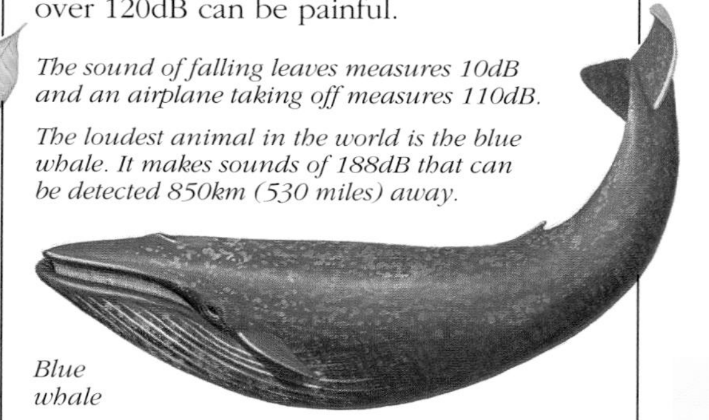

Blue whale

SEE FOR YOURSELF

You can feel sound vibrations with a balloon and a radio.

Turn on a radio and hold a balloon about 10cm (4in) away from the loudspeaker.

The vibrations of the sounds make the air in the balloon vibrate.

ECHOES AND ECHO-LOCATION

Echoes are sound waves that have reflected* (bounced) off a surface and are heard shortly after the original sound. Locating objects by timing how long high-pitched sounds take to return as echoes is called echo-location.

Ships use a method of echo-location called sonar to measure the depth of seawater, or to detect underwater objects, such as shipwrecks or shoals of fish. The sonar equipment emits ultrasonic (high-pitched) sounds, and the time they take to return is measured by a computer.

Several different species of animals, such as bats and dolphins, use echo-location to find their way around and locate prey.

Dolphins send out streams of over 700 ultrasonic clicks a second. They use these to find their prey by echo-location.

Echoes are also used in ultrasound scanning to see inside the body - for example to monitor the growth of a baby. As the sounds pass from one substance to another, some of the sound is reflected as echoes and the computer makes an "echo picture" from this information.

KEY TERMS

Amplitude The height of a wave from its rest position to its peak.
Frequency The number of waves per second, measured in hertz (Hz).
Medium The substance or space in which objects exist and phenomena, such as waves, take place.
Pitch The highness or lowness of a musical note or other sound.
Ultrasound Very high-pitched sounds above 20,000Hz.

*Waves, 36   *Energy, 6; Electricity, 46; Radio Waves, 42   *Reflection, see Wave Behavior, 36

MUSICAL INSTRUMENTS

Musical instruments work by making air particles vibrate. They do this in various ways. The shape of the instrument and the material of which it is made also affect the sound. Some instruments have a soundbox that resonates (vibrates at the same frequency as the original sound), making the sound fuller and richer.

The strings on a stringed instrument vibrate when they are plucked or bowed. The thicker, longer or looser the string, the lower the sound.

Covering a hole in the tube of a wind instrument makes the column of air inside longer and the note lower.

Soundbox

Bridge

The bridge carries vibrations from the strings into the soundbox.

A piano has strings that are hit and vibrate when you press a key. Strings of different lengths make different notes.

The vibrations of a drum skin echo inside the drum and are amplified (strengthened).

Most instruments produce complex sound waves that have higher, quieter sounds mixed in. These are called harmonics and they give an instrument its individual sound.

On a sound wave diagram, harmonics look like extra little waves.

A sound synthesizer is an instrument that stores the wave measurements of sounds as binary code* in its electronic memory. Pulses of electricity that represent the code for a particular sound are converted to an electric current and sent to a loudspeaker (see above right).

A keyboard synthesizer contains binary code for the sound waves of many different instruments.

Sound effects, such as footsteps or dogs barking, can also be stored as binary code and reproduced by a synthesizer.

MICROPHONES AND LOUDSPEAKERS

A microphone converts sound into an electric current whose varying strength represents the shape of the sound waves. A loudspeaker turns the varying electric current back into sounds. A microphone contains a thin metal disk, called a diaphragm, attached to a coil of wire between the poles of a magnet.

When sound waves hit the diaphragm, it vibrates at the same frequency. The diaphragm makes the wire coil vibrate. When the wire moves near the magnet, an electric current flows in the wire.

Diaphragm
Coil
Magnet

The strength of the current produced by a microphone varies according to the size and frequency of the sound waves. The current can be sent to a loudspeaker, used to record sounds on a cassette, or sent along telephone wires.

A telephone has a microphone that turns sounds into electric current. This is sent along wires to another phone, or converted into radio waves* and sent by satellite. A telephone also has a loudspeaker in the earpiece.

In the first gramophone, made in 1895, grooves on a disk made a needle vibrate and created sound waves that were amplified by the horn.

Horn

Inside a loudspeaker there is a magnet and an electromagnet (a coil of wire around an iron bar). When an electric current passes through the coil, it becomes magnetized (see Electromagnetism*). The coil is attached to a diaphragm shaped like a cone.

The parts that make up a loudspeaker

Magnet

Electromagnet and coil

When an electric current representing a sound wave flows through the coil, the force of the coil's magnetic field and that of the magnet make the coil and the diaphragm vibrate. The air in front of the diaphragm vibrates at the same frequency as the sound.

Diaphragm

CASSETTE RECORDERS

In a cassette recorder, sounds are recorded as a pattern of magnetized particles of iron or chromium oxide on plastic tape. The recording head is an electromagnet - a piece of metal with a coil of wire around it that becomes magnetized when an electric current flows through it.*

A cassette recorder records sound on tape by creating a changing magnetic field in the recording head. This arranges the magnetic particles on the tape in patterns representing sounds.

Recording head

Tape

The patterns of particles on the tape can be read by the playback head. It produces a varying current which is converted into sound by a loudspeaker.

Tape

Cutaway cassette

COMPACT DISCS

A compact disc, or CD, stores sound waves (or other information) as binary code* represented by tiny holes, called pits, and flat areas, called lands, on the surface of the disc.

Inside a CD player, a laser beam scans the disc's surface. Light that hits a pit is scattered, but light that hits a land is reflected back to a light-sensitive detector.

Light that strikes the detector generates a pulse of current. The pulses represent the sound in binary code.

Land   Pit

The pulses of electricity representing the sound in binary code are converted to sound by a loudspeaker (see above).

Close-up of disc's surface

Compact disc

A motor spins the disc while it is being scanned.

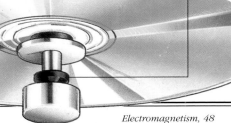

Binary code, see Digital Electronics, 51; Radio Waves, 42   Laser beam   Electromagnetism, 48

ELECTRICITY

When rubbed, a piece of amber has an electric charge and tissue paper clings to it.

Electricity is a very useful form of energy.* It can easily be converted to other forms of energy, such as heat or light, and it flows along cables so it is easy to transport. People have known about static electricity since ancient times, but scientists only discovered how to generate an electric current about two hundred years ago. Electricity is now used to power machines and provide heat and light, and even, in computers and calculators, to do calculations.

The word "electricity" comes from the Greek word "electron", which means "amber".

Lamps, such as this string of lights, convert electrical energy to light energy.

WHAT IS ELECTRICITY?

Electricity is the effect caused by electrically charged particles. All matter contains charge - the nuclei of atoms* contain positive charge and negatively charged electrons exist around the nuclei.

Left: an electric current is a flow of electric charge, for example, electrons.
Right: diagram of an atom

Normally, an atom is electrically neutral, but if it loses electrons to other atoms, it becomes positively charged, while the atoms that gained electrons have a negative charge. It is possible to give an object an electrical charge, called static electricity, by rubbing it.

If you rub a balloon on a woolen sweater, some of the sweater's electrons rub onto the balloon and give the balloon a negative charge.

The sweater has a positive charge and the balloon will cling to the sweater because objects with opposite charges are attracted to each other.

Electrical forces exist between charged objects and objects with opposite charges (positive and negative) attract each other. Objects with the same type of charge, for example, two positive charges, repel each other.

A van de Graaff generator builds up a very large static charge by rubbing a rubber belt against two rollers. When you touch the dome, the charge makes your hair stand on end.

In certain substances, for example, metals,* the electrons are free to move and when they are made to move, they create a flow of electric charge called a current. Substances through which an electric current can flow are called conductors.

Substances that do not conduct an electric current are called insulators.

Electric switches have plastic cases to insulate them.

Aluminum foil is a conductor.

Electrons

Wood and plastic are insulators.

Electricity wires are usually made of copper covered with plastic to insulate them.

Electrons cannot flow.

Electrons can flow and make a current.

Static electricity was first observed over 2,000 years ago in Ancient Greece. Today, equipment such as photocopiers, facsimile machines and laser printers use static electricity as part of their printing process.

In a laser printer, a laser beam reflected by a mirror makes dots of static electricity on a drum. Toner clings to the dots of static and is pressed onto the paper.

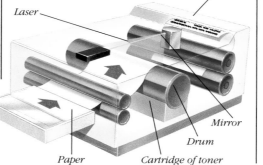
Printed copy
Laser
Mirror
Drum
Paper
Cartridge of toner

LIGHTNING

Lightning is caused by static electricity that builds up as water droplets and ice crystals rub against each other in storm clouds.

Water droplets and ice crystals become charged as they rub against each other and the air.

Positively charged droplets gather at the top of the cloud and a negative charge builds up at the base. A giant spark, called the leader stroke, leaps out toward a point with an opposite charge on the ground.

Before the leader stroke, the electrical potential difference between the top and the bottom of the cloud may be as much as 100 million volts.

The leader stroke is followed by a return stroke that shoots back to the cloud along the same path. The air inside the return lightning stroke is five times hotter than the surface of the Sun (over 33,000°C or 86,000°F).

The air heated by the flashes of lightning expands very rapidly and creates shock waves in the air. These make the noise that we hear as thunder.

KEY TERMS

Ampere The unit for measuring the strength of an electric current.
Conductor A substance through which an electric current can flow.
Electron A negatively charged particle that exists around the nucleus of an atom.
Insulator A substance that cannot conduct a current of electricity.
Potential difference The energy needed to push a certain amount of electric charge along a conducting pathway between two points.
Volt The unit for measuring the potential difference between two points in an electrical circuit.

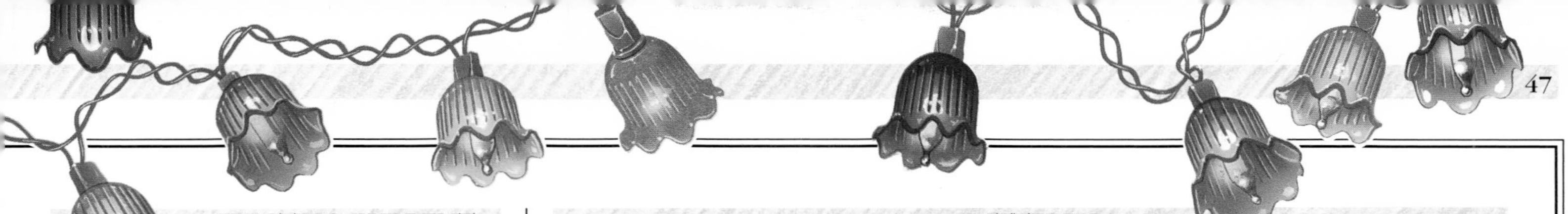

ELECTRIC CURRENT

An electric current is a flow of electrically charged particles from an area at high electrical potential to an area at low potential. The difference of electrical potential makes the particles move. For a current to flow, there must be a continuous pathway called a circuit. The potential difference is measured in volts.

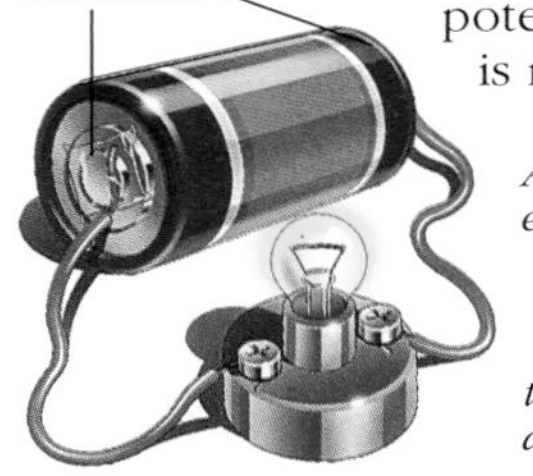

Terminals

A potential difference exists between the two terminals of a battery and when they are joined to form a circuit, a current flows.

The size of the current depends on the strength of the potential difference and the resistance* of the components in the circuit. All substances, even conductors, resist the current to a certain extent, and this reduces the size of the current. Current is measured in units called amperes (amps), after the French scientist André-Marie Ampère (1775-1836).

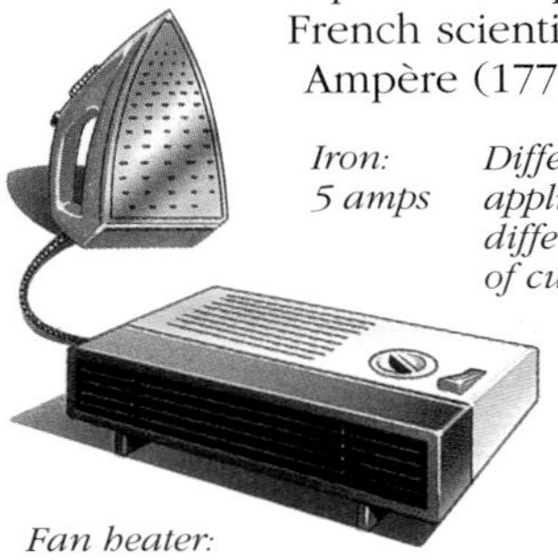

Iron: 5 amps

Different appliances need different amounts of current.

Calculator: 1/100 amp

Fan heater: 10 amps

Components, such as bulbs, convert the electrical energy carried by the current into other forms of energy such as heat and light. They do not use up the current itself. The components in a circuit can be arranged in two ways: in series and in parallel.

Left: this is a circuit diagram of the series circuit shown below.

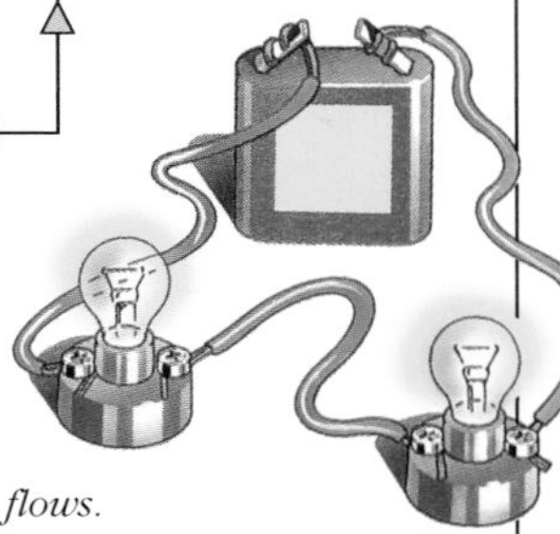

Battery

Bulbs

In a series circuit, the current passes through the components one after the other. If one component is not working, it breaks the circuit and no current flows.

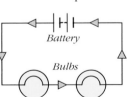

Battery

Bulbs

A parallel circuit (left) has more than one path for the current. If a component in one path does not work, current continues to flow through the other path.

BATTERIES

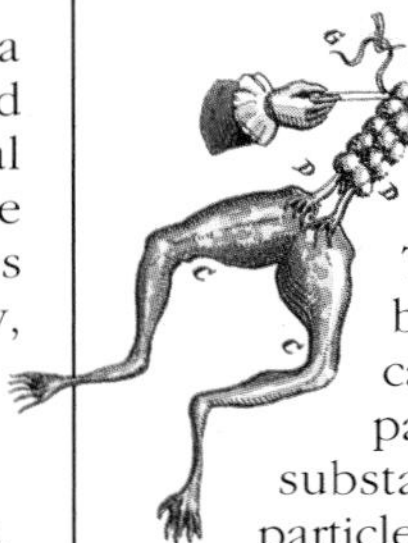

A battery is a storage of chemical energy that is converted to electrical energy. The most common type of battery used at home is called a dry cell. It contains a paste that is an electrolyte (a substance that contains charged particles that can move). Chemical reactions make the charges separate and positive charges go to one terminal and negative to the other.

Early experiments showed that fluids in a dead frog act as an electrolyte and carry current between two pieces of metal.

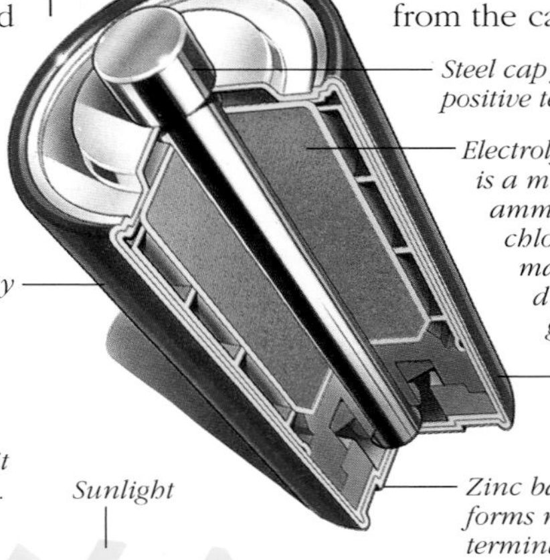

A dry cell with side cut away

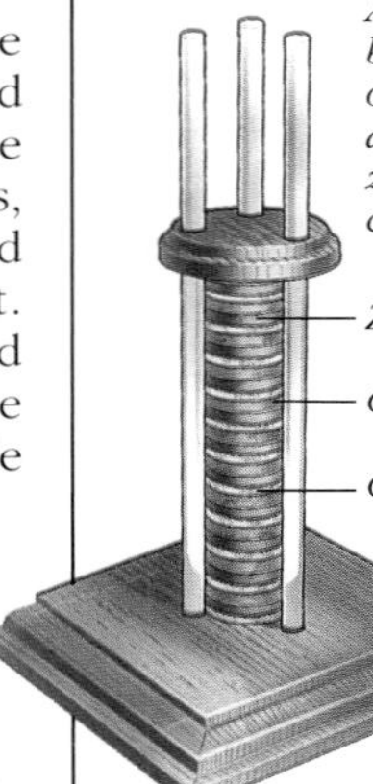

Alessandro Volta (1745-1827) built the first battery from a "pile" of cardboard disks soaked in acid and sandwiched between disks of zinc and copper. The electrical unit called the volt is named after Volta.

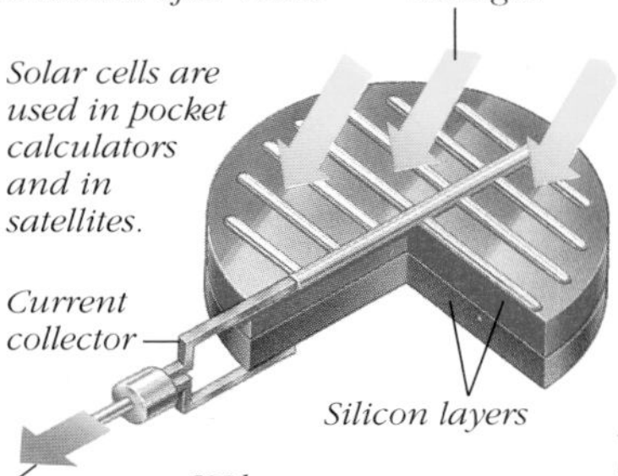

Zinc disk

Copper disk

Cardboard

Solar cells are used in pocket calculators and in satellites.

Current collector

Sunlight

Electricity

Silicon layers

9V battery contains 6 single cells

A 1.5V battery is called a single cell. Larger batteries are made up of several single cells.

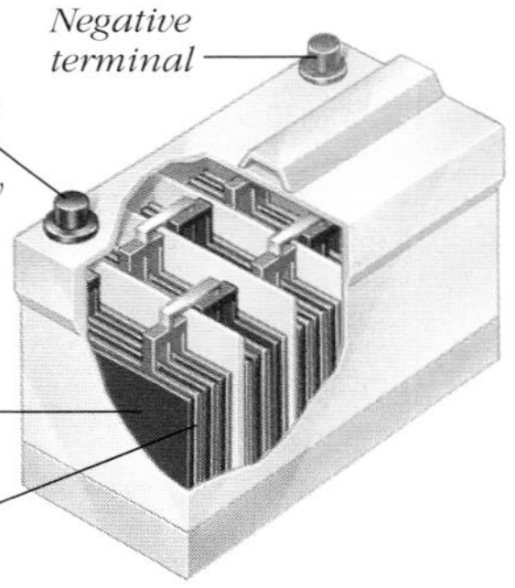

Single cell

Dry cells are also called primary cells. When the chemicals in the electrolyte run out, the battery is finished. Secondary cells, or accumulators, are batteries that can be recharged. A car battery is a type of secondary cell. It is continually recharged with electric current from the car.

Steel cap forms positive terminal.

Electrolyte which is a mixture of ammonium chloride, manganese dioxide and graphite.

Plastic or paper cover

Zinc battery case forms negative terminal.

A solar cell (left) converts the Sun's energy into electricity. Sunlight falling on the layers of silicon makes the electrons move, creating a potential difference (see Electric Current) between the two layers.

Negative terminal

Positive terminal

Right: cutaway view of a car battery

Accumulators containing dilute sulphuric acid as the electrolyte.

Lead and lead oxide electrodes

ELECTRICITY AT HOME

Household electricity is 240 volts in some countries and 110 volts in others. This is a large voltage that can give you a deadly electric shock. Parallel circuits (see left) carry the electricity around the house. In some countries, appliances are protected by fuses that contain very thin pieces of wire that melt and cut off the current if it is too large.

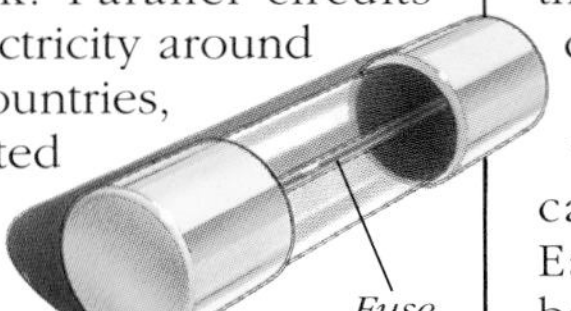

Fuse wire

Above: fuse with part of cover removed

This fuse box contains fuses to protect each circuit, and a meter to measure how much energy is used.

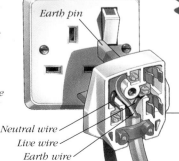

Main fuse

Fuse box

Incoming cable

Meter

Each parallel circuit usually contains three wires called the live, neutral and earth. The live and neutral wires carry the current and the earth wire is a safety device. It provides a path to the ground through which electric current can escape into the Earth if the plug becomes live.

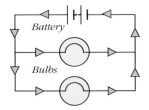

Earth pin

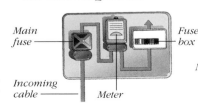

Above: some countries use two-pin plugs with no earth pin.

When a plug is put into a socket, the pins connect with the live and neutral points in the circuit.

Neutral wire

Live wire

Earth wire

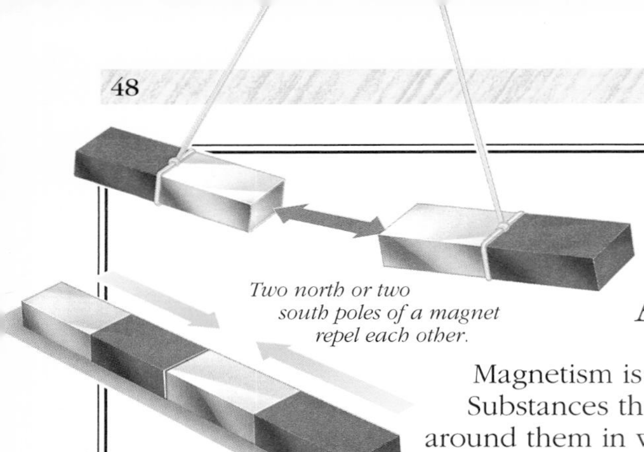

MAGNETISM
AND ELECTROMAGNETISM

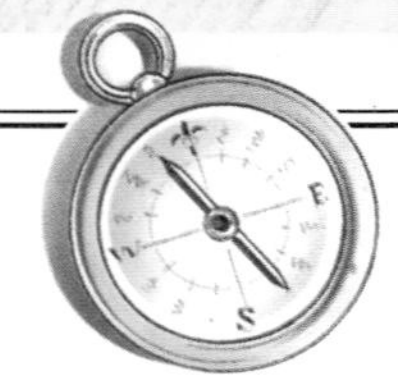

Two north or two south poles of a magnet repel each other.

The north and south poles of a magnet attract each other.

19th century compass

Marine compass

Magnetism is an invisible force* that attracts or repels iron and steel. Substances that create this force are said to be magnetic and the area around them in which the force operates is called the magnetic field. When an electric current flows through a wire, it produces a magnetic field and this effect is called electromagnetism. It can be used to make powerful magnets, called electromagnets, and to produce motion from an electric current.

A compass needle is a magnet that points to the Earth's magnetic north pole.

MAGNETISM

Magnetism takes its name from a place called Magnesia, in Turkey, where over 2,000 years ago, the Ancient Greeks found pieces of rock that attracted metals. The rock was a form of iron ore called magnetite.

North

South

A piece of magnetite hanging on a thread rotates to point north/south. Long, thin pieces of magnetite, called lodestones, were once used as compasses.

A magnet is a substance, usually a metal such as iron or steel, that has been magnetized and behaves like magnetite. A magnet has two poles, called the north and the south poles.

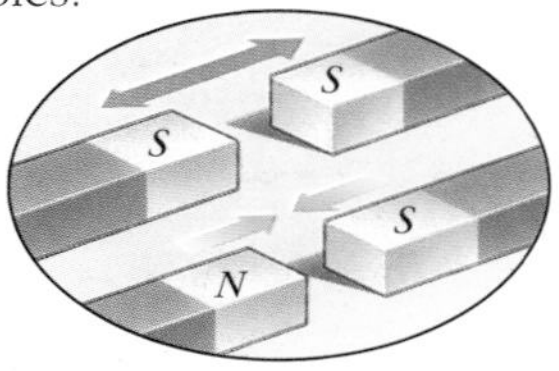

Two north or two south poles will repel each other, while a north and a south pole will pull toward, or attract, each other.

Metals that can be magnetized are said to be ferromagnetic. "Soft" ferromagnetic metals, such as iron, quickly lose their magnetic properties. Steel is a "hard" ferromagnetic material and it retains its magnetic properties for much longer.

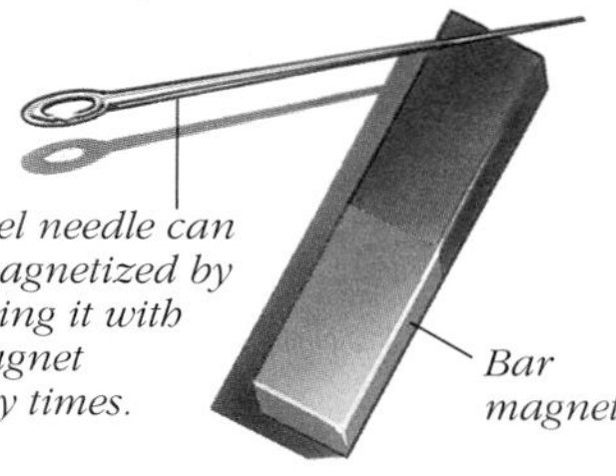

A steel needle can be magnetized by stroking it with a magnet many times.

Bar magnet

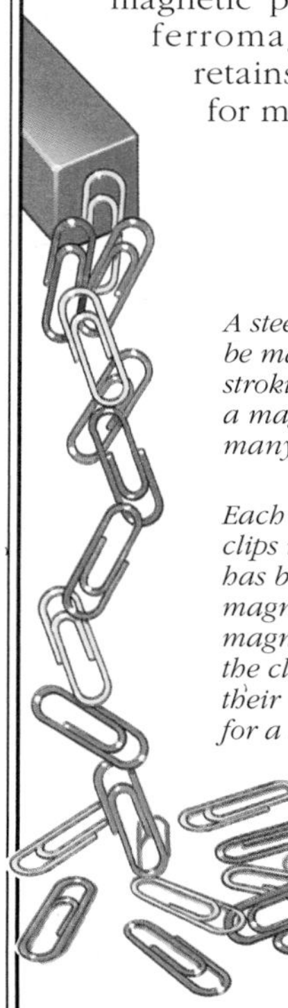

Each of the paper clips in this chain has become magnetized. If the magnet is removed, the clips will retain their magnetism for a short while.

Ring magnet

Round magnet

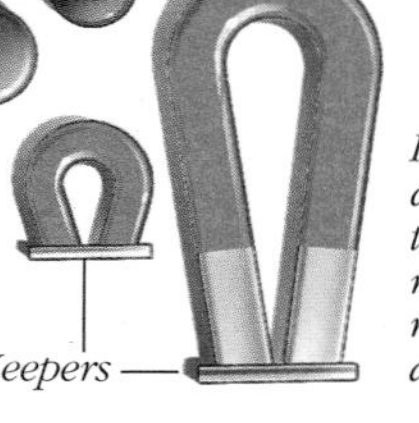

A "keeper" across the end of a horseshoe magnet helps it to retain its magnetism.

Keepers

Magnetic substances contain groups of molecules called domains that behave like tiny magnets. When the domains all point the same way, the material is magnetized, but if it is heated, or hit very hard, the domains become jumbled up.

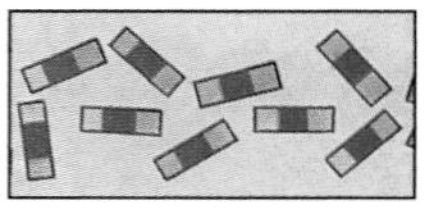

When magnetic material is in a non-magnetized state, the domains are jumbled up.

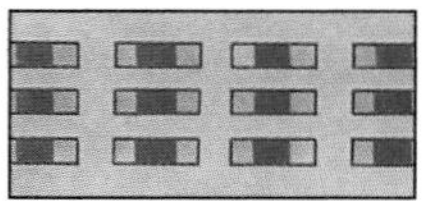

When it is magnetized, the domains line up with their poles all pointing the same way.

A magnetic field is the region around a magnet in which objects are affected by its magnetic force. The strength and direction of the magnetic field can be shown by magnetic flux lines. The Earth itself has a magnetic field around it. As the Earth rotates on its axis, the molten metal in its outer core moves around very slowly, producing a magnetic field around the Earth.

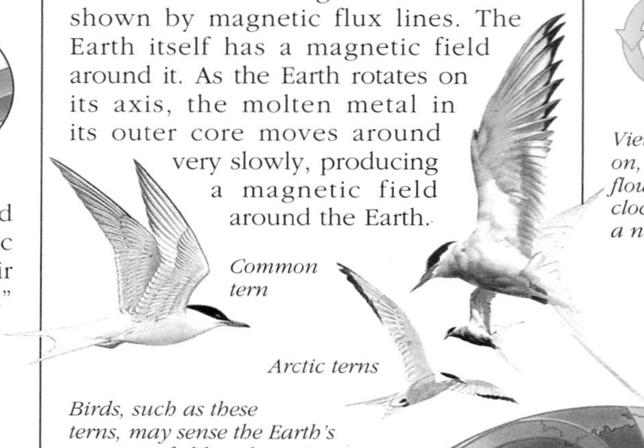

Common tern

Arctic terns

Birds, such as these terns, may sense the Earth's magnetic field and use it to guide them when they are migrating.

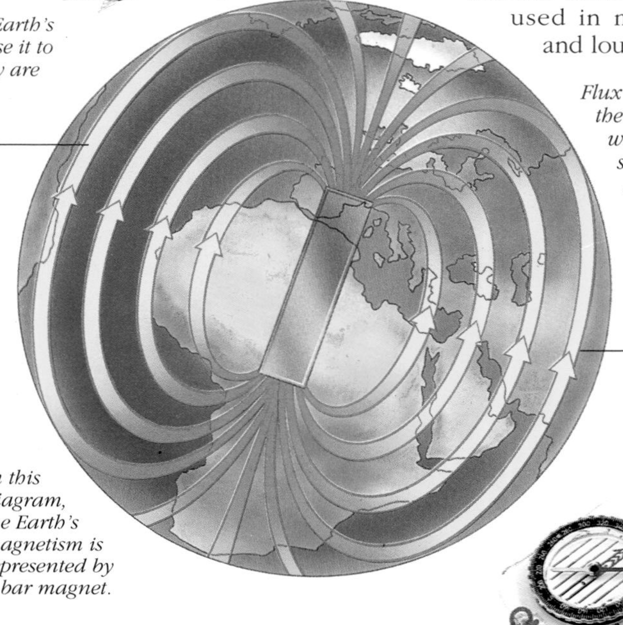

Flux line showing the direction of the magnetic field around the Earth. The lines are closest near the poles where the field is strongest.

In this diagram, the Earth's magnetism is represented by a bar magnet.

ELECTROMAGNETISM

An electric current flowing through a wire produces a magnetic field. This effect is called electromagnetism. A length of wire wrapped around an iron bar behaves like a bar magnet when a current is passed through it. The wire is called a solenoid.

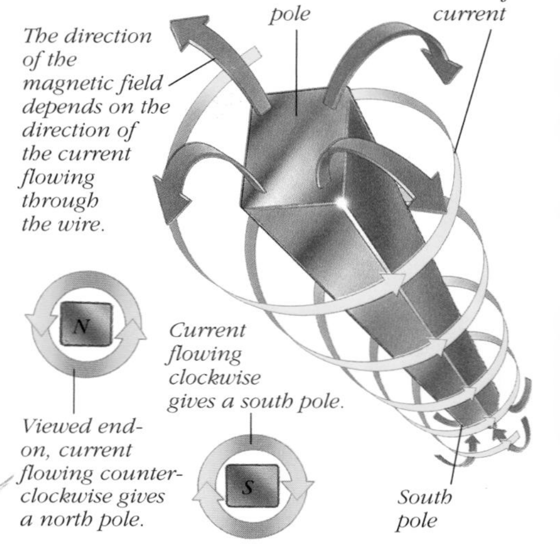

North pole

Direction of current

The direction of the magnetic field depends on the direction of the current flowing through the wire.

Current flowing clockwise gives a south pole.

Viewed end-on, current flowing counter-clockwise gives a north pole.

South pole

A solenoid can be used to make a device called an electromagnet (see right) whose magnetic field can be switched off and on with the current. Solenoids are also used in microphones and loudspeakers.*

Flux lines show the direction in which the north-seeking pole of a compass, such as the orienteering compass shown below, would point.

Flux line

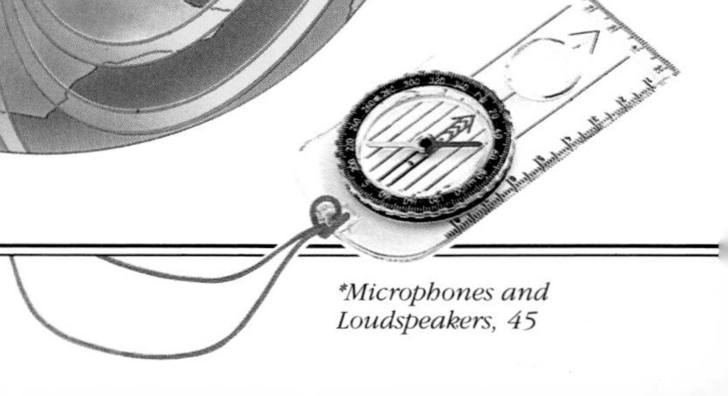

Orienteering compass

ELECTROMAGNETS

An electromagnet is a magnet that can be switched on and off by an electric current. To make an electromagnet, a length of iron is placed inside a coil of wire called a solenoid (see Electromagnetism).

Section through coil

Very powerful electromagnets are used in steelworks to lift heavy loads.

A simple electro-magnet

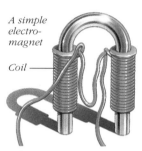

Coil

When current flows through the coil of wire, the iron becomes magnetized.

Iron is a soft ferromagnetic material (see Magnetism) so it loses its magnetic properties when the current is switched off. Relay switches, and electric bells and buzzers, rely on electromagnetism to make them work.

When you press an electric bell (1), current flows through the coils of an electromagnet (2) which attracts a metal arm (3) and breaks the circuit (4). A spring (5) pulls the arm back so it hits the bell and the cycle repeats.

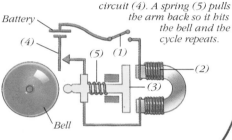

Battery

(4)

(5) (1)

(2)

(3)

Bell

Magnetic levitation ("maglev") trains have electromagnets on the track and bottom of the train. The magnets repel each other, so the train hovers just above the track. This reduces friction so the train can travel faster.

Japanese "maglev" train

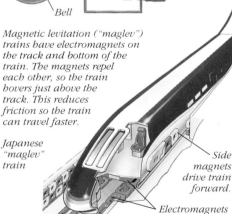

Side magnets drive train forward.

Electromagnets

KEY TERMS

Alternating current Current that changes direction many times a second.
Direct current Current that flows in only one direction.
Magnetic field The area around a magnet in which the magnetic force operates.
Solenoid or ***coil*** A coil of wire that creates an electromagnetic field when a current passes through it.

ELECTRIC MOTORS

Electric motors use electromagnetism to convert electrical energy into movement. A simple electric motor contains a flat coil of wire called an armature between two magnets. When current flows through the armature, the combination of the electromagnetic field of the armature and the magnetic fields of the magnets push one side of the armature up and the other side down.

Below: a simple electric motor. When the armature is in a vertical position, a device called a commutator causes the direction of the electric current to be reversed, so the magnetic field is reversed. The side of the armature that was pushed up is now pulled down and the armature completes its circle and the cycle begins again.

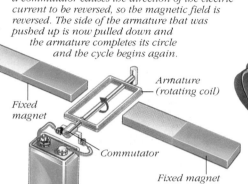

Armature (rotating coil)

Fixed magnet

Commutator

Fixed magnet

Electric motors are used in all kinds of equipment, from washing machines and hairdryers to battery-driven toy cars and model trains. Tiny micromotors (see below, right) are being developed for use in microsurgery and space research.

Exploded view of a powerful electric motor

Electromagnet creates fixed magnetic field.

Armature turns inside field.

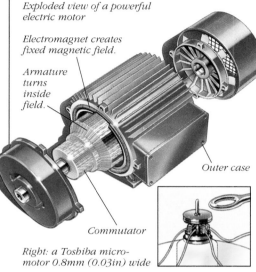

Outer case

Commutator

Right: a Toshiba micro-motor 0.8mm (0.03in) wide

GENERATING ELECTRICITY

The English scientist, Michael Faraday (1791-1867), discovered that if a wire is moved in a magnetic field, a current of electricity will flow through the wire.

Faraday produced an electric current by rotating a disk near a magnet, using this device called a disk dynamo.

A dynamo or generator is a machine for converting the energy of movement into electricity. It works somewhat like an electric motor in reverse.

Generator containing coils

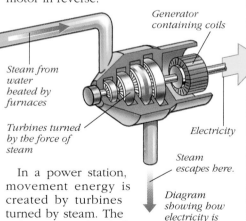

Steam from water heated by furnaces

Turbines turned by the force of steam

Electricity

Steam escapes here.

Diagram showing how electricity is generated

In a power station, movement energy is created by turbines turned by steam. The turbines turn the shaft of a generator that has coils of wire that turn between two magnets. Turning the coils between the magnets induces a current that changes direction every half-turn. This type of current is called alternating current and it is explained in the diagrams above right.

Diagrams to show how a generator works

South pole

Armature

North pole

Direction of current for first half-turn

South pole

North pole

Direction of current for second half-turn

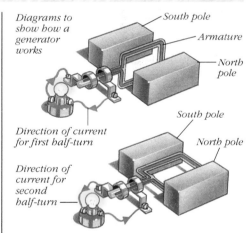

Above: these diagrams show how a generator produces alternating current. Turning the armature (a type of coil) between the two magnets induces a current. As the armature passes through its vertical position, the direction of the current changes (see Electromagnetism).

Fixed magnet

Coil

A bicycle dynamo is a type of generator. It uses movement energy from the moving wheel to produce electric current for a lamp.

A bicycle dynamo contains a coil of wire that spins between two magnets.

ELECTRONICS

Electronics is the use of devices called electronic components to control the way electricity flows around circuits. Electronic components, such as resistors, capacitors and transistors, can be so tiny that a complicated circuit containing thousands of components can be fitted onto a chip the size of your fingernail. Circuits like these are used in all sorts of machines, such as televisions, robots and computers.

Robot arms controlled by electronic circuits can carry out very precise movements.

This part of the arm can move in three ways.

Capacitor

LED

Resistor

Components can be fitted together in different ways. Metal tracks underneath this board link them together.

ELECTRONIC CIRCUITS

An electronic circuit is a type of electric circuit. In an electronic circuit, the flow of electricity is controlled using electronic devices, or components, to make the circuit do particular tasks.

This simple electronic circuit contains a resistor which reduces the current.

Electronic circuits can be made by fitting components into circuits printed on boards called PCBs, or printed circuit boards. Integrated circuits (see opposite) are tiny circuits engraved onto small slices of silicon.

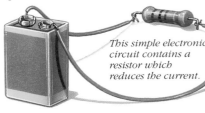

Resistor

Battery

Bulb

This electronic circuit is the same as the one above, but drawn using circuit symbols.*

RESISTANCE

Resistance is the ability of a substance to resist the flow of electric current. All the parts of an electric circuit have a certain amount of resistance, and this reduces the amount of current that is able to flow around the circuit.

The filament inside a light bulb is a thin, coiled-up piece of wire. Its resistance to electric current makes it glow.

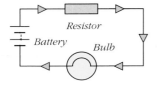

Close-up of filament

When a substance resists an electric current, it converts some of the electrical energy into heat or light. Resistance is measured in units called ohms, after Georg Ohm, a 19th-century physicist.

Ω

The Greek letter omega is used as a symbol for ohms.

ELECTRONIC COMPONENTS

There are several types of electronic components, each designed to do a different job in an electronic circuit, such as storing electricity, or switching the current on and off. For example, a resistor reduces current in a circuit.

Resistors cut down the current in a circuit. The larger the resistance, the less current will flow.

The colored stripes on a resistor are a code showing how much resistance it provides.

Resistors

The stripes on this resistor show that it provides 55 ohms of resistance.

A variable resistor, or rheostat (below), can be adjusted to give different amounts of resistance.

The volume control on a radio uses a variable resistor to change the amount of current.

A thermistor is a heat-sensitive resistor. Its resistance falls as the temperature rises and vice versa.

Thermistor

Diodes allow the current to flow through them in only one direction. A light-emitting diode, or LED, glows when current flows through it.

This TV remote control has an LED light on it to show it is in use.

LED

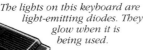

The lights on this keyboard are light-emitting diodes. They glow when it is being used.

Transistors

Transistors are electronic switches. A transistor has three legs, called the base, the collector and the emitter. When a small current flows into the base leg, the transistor allows a current to flow between the collector and the emitter.

Base

Emitter

Collector

A radio uses transistors to amplify (strengthen) the signals picked up by the antenna.

Below: cutaway pocket radio

Loudspeaker

Resistor

Integrated circuit may also contain transistors.

Circuit board

Tuning control

Volume control

Capacitors

Battery case

There are several kinds of capacitors.

Capacitors store up electrical energy and release it when it is needed.

A television uses capacitors to build up and store very high voltages.

Capacitors

Number display made up of LEDs

LEDs

Right: a printed circuit board from a computer

*Circuit Symbols, 84

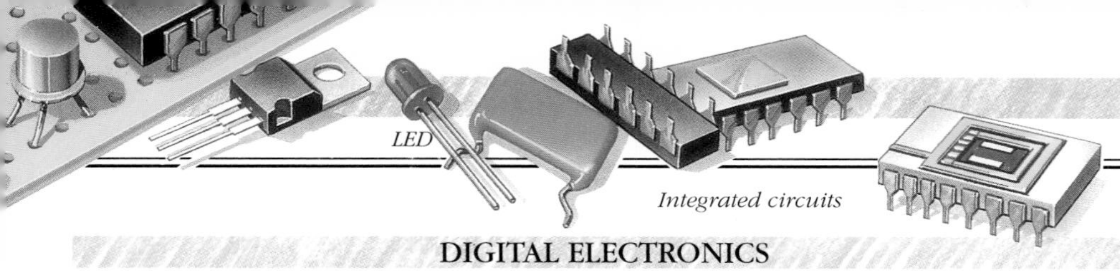

LED

Integrated circuits

DIGITAL ELECTRONICS

Digital electronics uses pulses of electricity instead of continuously flowing, or analogue, electricity. In a digital circuit, the current exists in pulses of either high or low current. Digital electronics is used in integrated circuits (see right) and in electronic equipment such as calculators and digital watches.

In a digital circuit, the current is broken up into a series of pulses.

In an analogue circuit, the current flows continuously.

The pulses of electricity in a digital circuit can be used to represent information using binary code. This is a way of expressing information using only the numbers 0 and 1. Words, sounds and pictures can be translated into binary too.

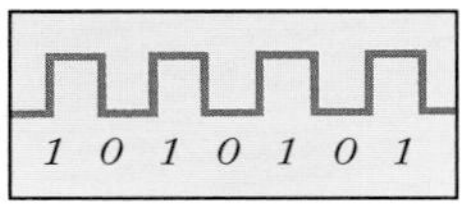

1 0 1 0 1 0 1

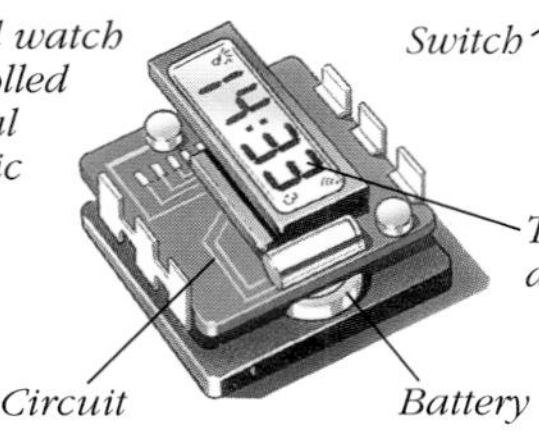

A digital watch is controlled by digital electronic circuits.

In digital electronics, a pulse of high current represents a 1 and a pulse of low current represents a 0.

Circuit   *Battery*

Electronic components (see opposite) change and redirect pulses of current that flow around digital circuits. Arrangements of components, such as logic gates (see below), can do calculations with numbers.

A pocket calculator contains complicated digital electronic circuits that can store numbers and do calculations with them. When you press the buttons, electronic signals are sent to the circuits.

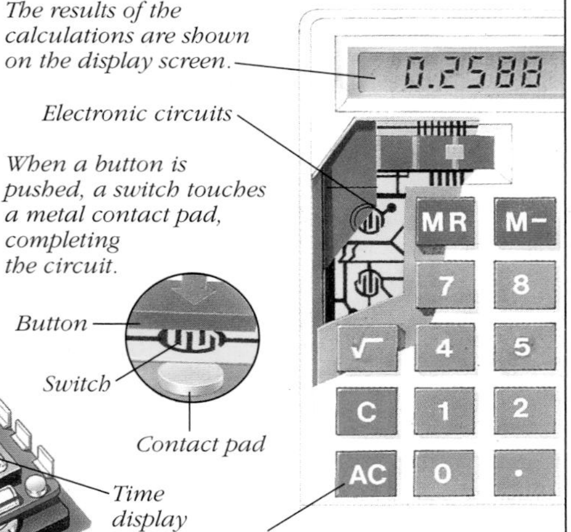

The results of the calculations are shown on the display screen.

`0.2588`

Electronic circuits

When a button is pushed, a switch touches a metal contact pad, completing the circuit.

Button
Switch
Contact pad
Time display

MR M–
7 8
√ 4 5
C 1 2
AC 0 .

Button   *Cutaway view of a pocket calculator, showing circuits*

LOGIC GATES

A logic gate is an arrangement of transistors (see Electronic Components) for carrying out calculations in digital electronic circuits. Logic gates change or redirect the pulses of current that flow through them. Most logic gates have two inputs, which receive signals, and one output, which gives out a signal. Logic gates can be represented by circuit symbols* such as those shown on the right.

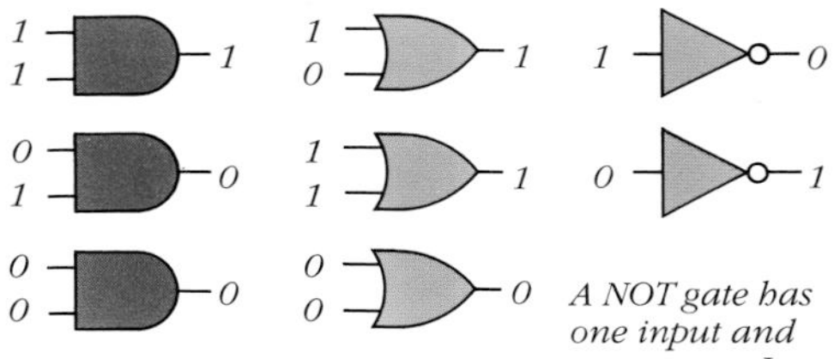

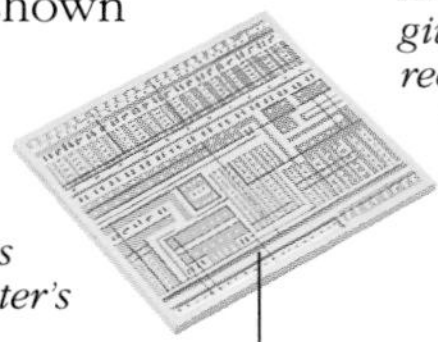

Right: an integrated circuit contains millions of tiny logic gates. There are many chips like this on a computer's circuit board (below).

Tiny electronic components

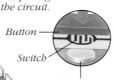

1,1 → 1
0,1 → 0
0,0 → 0

1,0 → 1
1,1 → 1
0,0 → 0

1 → 0
0 → 1

An AND gate gives out a 1 if it receives two 1s. Otherwise, it gives out a 0.

An OR gate gives out a 1 if it receives a 1 in either of its inputs.

A NOT gate has one input and one output. It always reverses the signal it receives. It changes a 1 to a 0 and a 0 to a 1.

Combinations of different types of logic gates make up devices called flip-flops. Arrangements of flip-flops can store information and do complex calculations.

A JK-type flip-flop contains two logic gates which affect each other. This flip-flop can store a small piece of data.

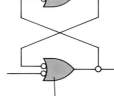

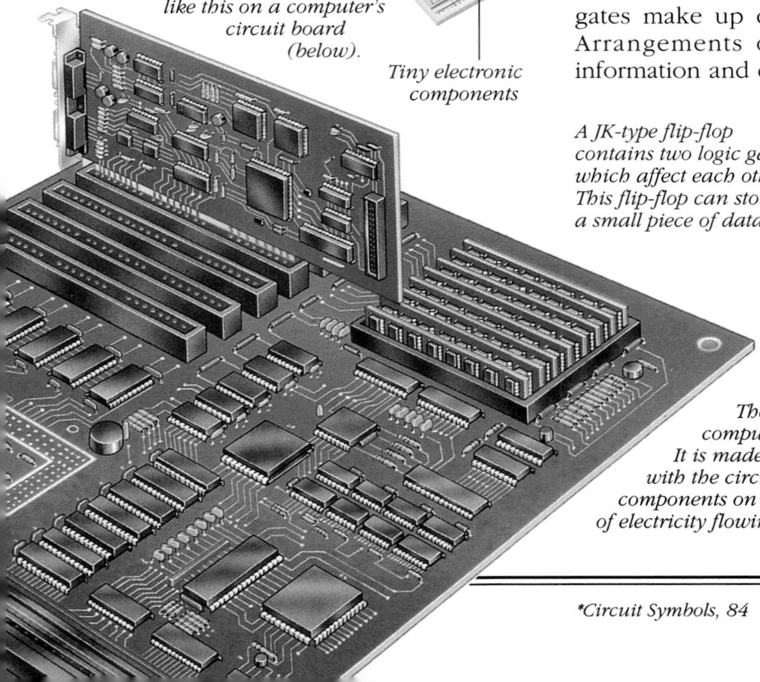

One of the logic gates making up the flip-flop

The main circuit board in a computer is called the motherboard. It is made up of a large piece of plastic with the circuits printed on it. The components on the board control the amount of electricity flowing through the chips.

INTEGRATED CIRCUITS

An integrated circuit, also known as a chip or silicon chip, is a complete electronic circuit containing thousands of tiny components printed on a very small piece of an element called silicon.

Wire foot

Above: wire feet link chips to other components.

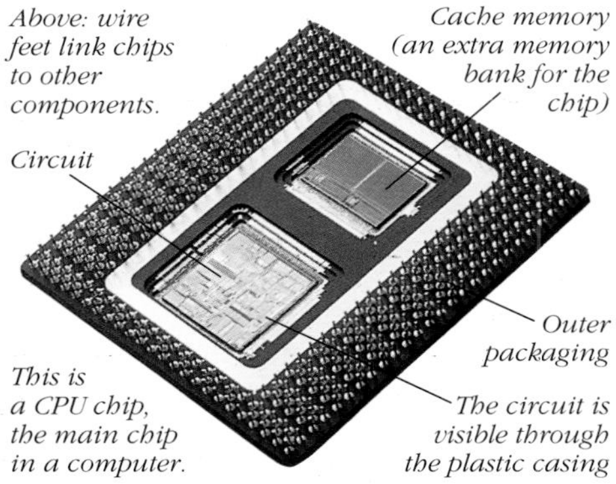

Circuit

Cache memory (an extra memory bank for the chip)

This is a CPU chip, the main chip in a computer.

Outer packaging

The circuit is visible through the plastic casing

Impurities are added to the silicon to make semiconductors. These are substances that vary in how well they conduct electricity, depending on conditions such as temperature.

This picture shows how a transistor is made up of layers of semiconductors and aluminum.

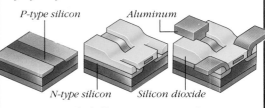

P-type silicon   *Aluminum*

N-type silicon   *Silicon dioxide*

Layers of different types of semi-conductors are printed onto a piece of silicon, called a wafer, in specially designed patterns. These make up the whole integrated circuit, including all its tiny components.

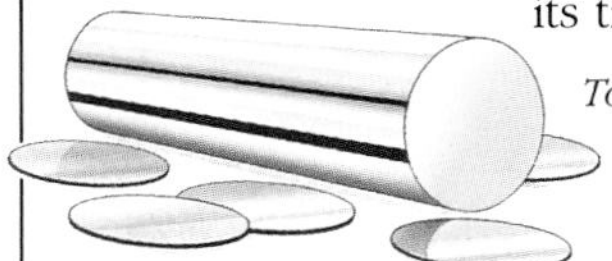

To make chips, silicon is sliced into very thin wafers.

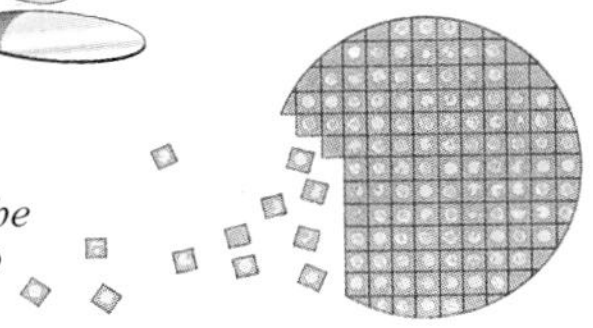

Many circuits are printed onto each wafer. Then the wafer is cut up into individual chips.

KEY TERMS

Binary A code consisting of only 0s and 1s which is used in electronic circuits to represent information.

Digital A word used to describe something that flows in separate pulses that can be used to represent the 0s and 1s of binary code.

Semiconductor A substance that conducts electricity better than an insulator, but not as well as a good conductor.

*Circuit Symbols, 84

COMPUTER TECHNOLOGY

Computer-controlled robot dinosaurs are used in museum exhibitions.

With computer technology, people can do things not thought possible before. We can crash-test cars and planes before they are even built, create computerized special effects for science fiction films, explore imaginary 3-D worlds with virtual reality and link up to data all over the world on the Internet. Computers also help with millions of everyday tasks, such as writing letters, diagnosing diseases and reserving a seat on a train.

The Analytical Engine, an early mechanical computer designed by Charles Babbage (1792-1871). Modern computers are electronic.

WHAT IS A COMPUTER?

A computer is a machine that computes, or does calculations. All computers need software - instructions that tell them how to do particular jobs. A piece of software is called a program.

Data that is put into a computer is called input.

The work a computer does is called processing.

The results that come out of a computer are called output.

Computers come in many shapes and sizes. They usually have several parts, which are known as hardware. The processing unit is the main part of a computer.

A keyboard is an input device. It is used to type letters and numbers into a computer.

A personal computer or PC is one of the most common types of computers used in homes, schools and offices. It normally has a processing unit, a keyboard, a monitor and a mouse.

A mouse is an input device. It moves a pointer around on the monitor screen.

Mouse ball

The mouse ball rolls when you push the mouse across a desk, sending signals to the computer.

A monitor is an output device that displays data on a screen.

The processing unit contains electronic circuits and chips which do the calculations.*

Keyboard

Mouse

Extra pieces of computer equipment, such as a joystick used in computer games, are called peripherals.

MEMORY AND STORAGE

A computer has memory chips to hold data and instructions. RAM (Random-Access Memory) holds data while the computer is working on it. ROM (Read-Only Memory) is where the computer stores the instructions it needs to start working when it is switched on. Disks, such as the hard disk, store data when the computer is switched off.

The hard "disk" contains several disks

The hard disk usually stays permanently inside the hard disk drive in the computer. It is often used to keep data organized.

Floppy disks are made of flexible plastic. They store data in the form of arrangements of millions of magnetic particles.

Pit
Land

On compact discs (CDs), data is recorded as a pattern of holes ("pits") and flat areas ("lands") on the disk's surface.*

The hard disk is usually kept permanently inside the computer. Other storage devices, such as floppy disks and compact discs (CDs),* can be taken out of the computer. Computers write data onto, and read data from, disks using devices called disk drives.

Floppy disk drives and compact disc drives usually fit into a space in the front of the processing unit. The disks can be fitted into the drives and then taken out and stored safely.

HOW COMPUTERS WORK

Most computers do calculations using a code of only two numbers: 0 and 1. This is known as binary code. Each 0 or 1 is called a bit. Groups of eight bits, called bytes, are used to represent letters, numbers and other data.

One byte

$$0\ 0\ 1\ 1\ 1\ 0\ 0\ 1$$

A bus is an electronic pathway that carries data in the form of 0 signals and 1 signals.

Inside the computer, pulses of current representing 0s and 1s travel around along electronic pathways, called buses, to and from the integrated circuits* that do the calculations. The results are then translated back into a form the user can understand, and sent back to the user as output - for example, as a display on a screen.

Inside the processing unit of a PC

Power supply converts electricity from a socket into power for the computer.

Integrated circuits and other electronic components

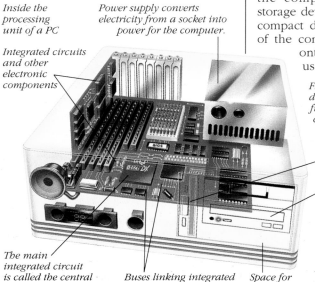

The main integrated circuit is called the central processing unit or CPU.

Buses linking integrated circuits together

Space for hard drive

Space for floppy disk drive

Space for compact disk drive

Punched cards used by Charles Babbage

Before electronic computers were invented, data and instructions were stored as patterns of holes punched in cards.

*Integrated Circuits, 51   *Electronic Circuits, 50   *Electronics, 50; Compact Discs, 45

THE INTERNET

The Internet is a worldwide computer network that links together millions of computers all around the world. An Internet connection can be used to send letters to a friend in another country in a few seconds, using e-mail (electronic mail), to look up information in a foreign library by linking up to its computers, or to spread information over a wide area.

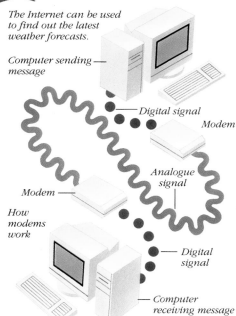

The Internet can be used to find out the latest weather forecasts.

Computer sending message

Digital signal

Modem

Analogue signal

Modem

How modems work

Digital signal

Computer receiving message

Computers are usually connected to networks such as the Internet by cables or telephone wires. A machine called a modem is used to translate digital signals (pulses) from the computer into analogue signals (waves) which can travel down the telephone line.

KEY TERMS

Data Information, especially information that is being processed or stored by a computer.
Hardware Computer equipment, such as the keyboard, the monitor and the processing unit.
Input Data that is put into a computer to be processed.
Output Processed data that comes out of a computer.
Processing Any kind of work that a computer does on data.
Program A set of software instructions that allow a computer to do a task.
Software Instructions a computer needs in order to do tasks.

USING COMPUTERS

Computer technology affects almost every area of life, from education and training to medical treatment, and from going shopping to going on vacation. This display shows some of the varied uses, or applications, of computer technology, and some of the types of computers and software used.

CAD "wire frame" design

Above: CAD design for a machine part

Left: CAD design for a bicycle

CAD, or Computer-Aided Design, is used to design airplanes, cars, buildings and many other things. Designs can be tested using computers before they are even built.

CAD design for an airplane

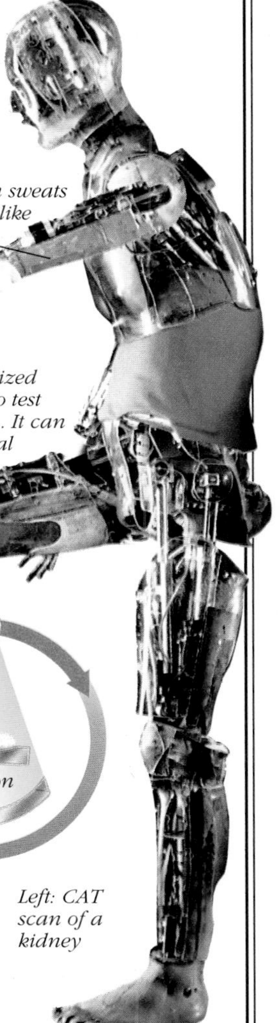

The robot's imitation skin sweats and stretches like real skin.

Tickets and cards can store information that can be read by a computer.

This train ticket holds information in a magnetic strip.

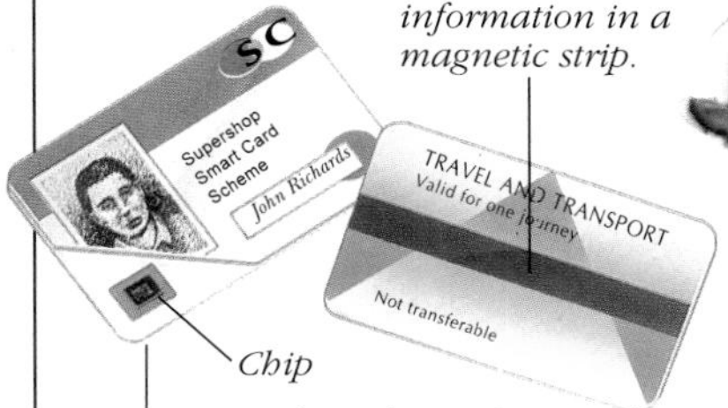

The robot can perform very precise movements.

This computerized robot is used to test safety clothing. It can move like a real person.

Supershop Smart Card Scheme
John Richards

TRAVEL AND TRANSPORT
Valid for one journey

Not transferable

Chip

A smart card can be used to pay for goods. Here, it is cut away to show the chip inside, where data is stored.*

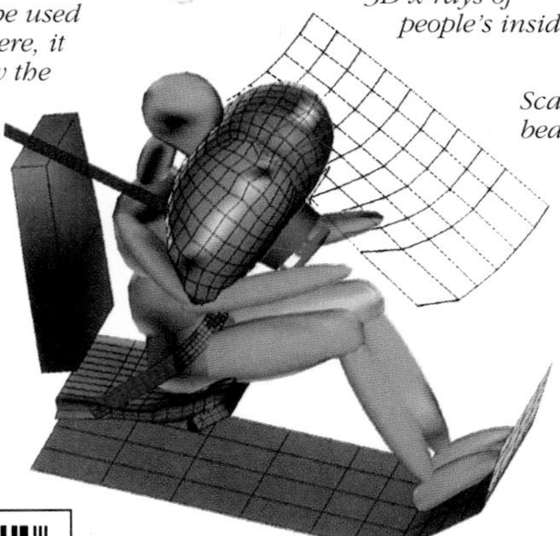

Right: a car crash test simulated using computer graphics

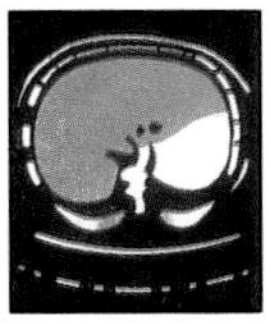

Below: computerized supermarket checkouts scan items for prices.

Above: satellites are controlled by computer.

Right: Computerized Axial Tomography (CAT) scanners take 3D x-rays of people's insides.

Person

Scanner beam

Left: CAT scan of a kidney

7 80746 016510

Each item is marked with a bar code.

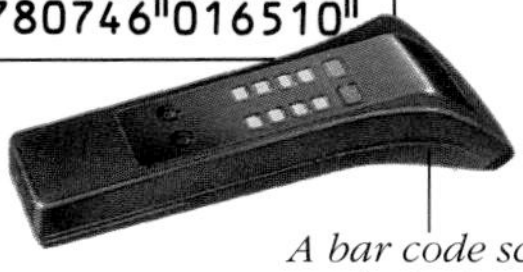

A bar code scanner reads the bar codes.

Computerized robots are used for security patrols, and to do dangerous jobs such as bomb disposal.

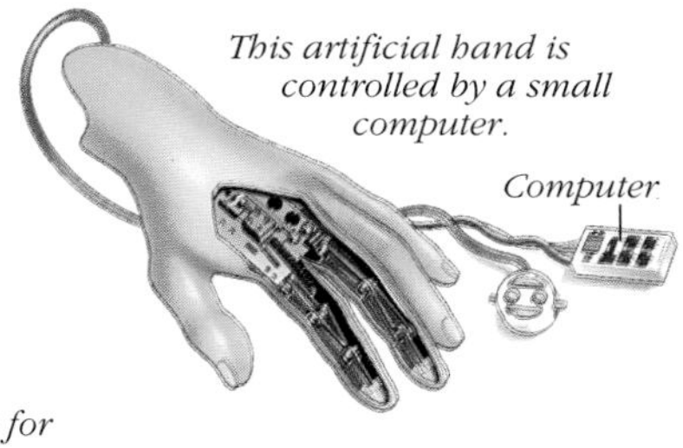

This artificial hand is controlled by a small computer.

Computer

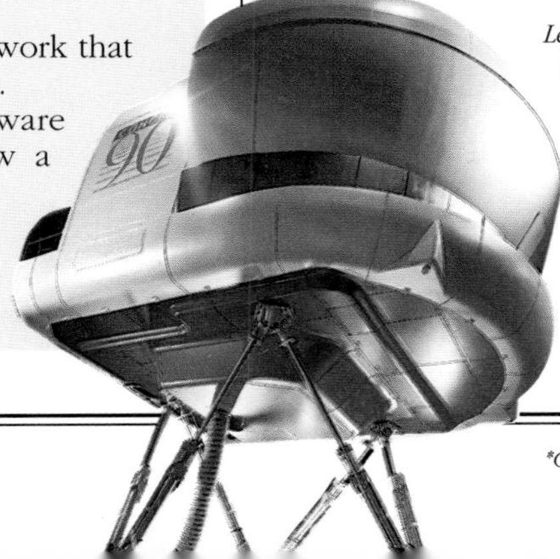

Left: this machine for training pilots uses VR (virtual reality) to imitate the inside of a plane's cockpit.

Computer graphics software is used to make animated cartoons and special effects for films. Animated monsters like this one can be added to films alongside human actors.

*Chip, see Integrated Circuits, 51

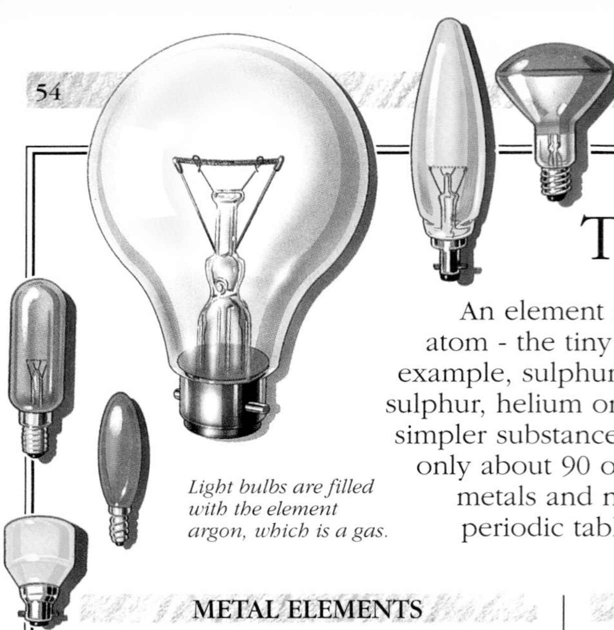

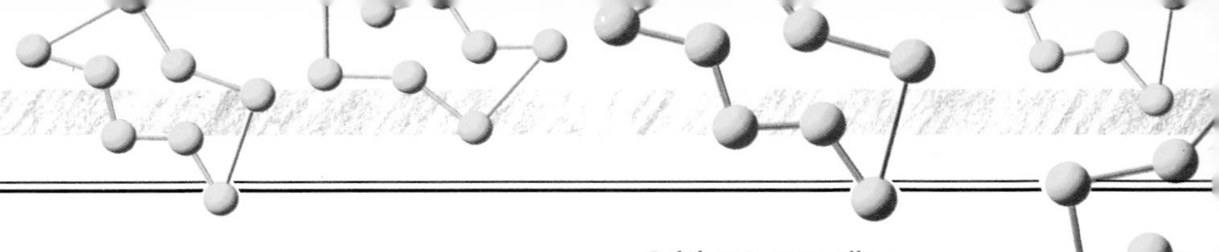

THE ELEMENTS

An element is a substance that contains only one kind of atom - the tiny particles of which all substances are made. For example, sulphur, helium and iron are elements: they contain only sulphur, helium or iron atoms and they cannot be broken down into simpler substances. So far, 109 elements have been discovered, but only about 90 occur naturally on Earth. They can be sorted into metals and nonmetals, and arranged in a table, called the periodic table, according to the structure of their atoms.*

Light bulbs are filled with the element argon, which is a gas.

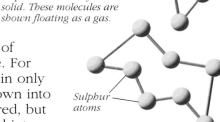

Sulphur is normally a solid. These molecules are shown floating as a gas.

Sulphur atoms

Sulphur is a nonmetal element. Atoms of sulphur group together in rings of eight to form molecules.

METAL ELEMENTS

Over three-quarters of all the elements are metals.* Most of the metal elements are dense and shiny and they have many uses as they are strong, but can be easily shaped. Metals are usually found combined with other elements in the Earth's crust.

Metals are strong, but can be easily shaped to form spacecraft, aircraft, vehicles and machines.

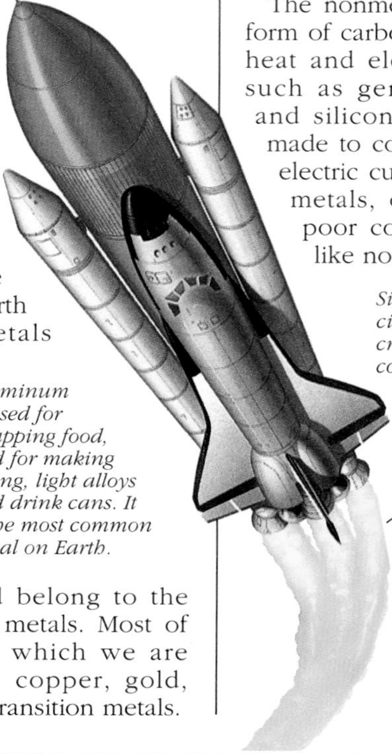

Metals are colored blue in the periodic table shown on the opposite page. They are in groups called the alkali metals, alkaline earth metals, transition metals and poor metals.*

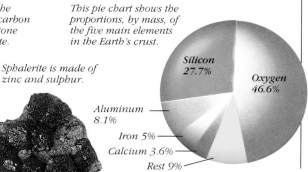

Aluminum is used for wrapping food, and for making strong, light alloys and drink cans. It is the most common metal on Earth.

Tin and lead belong to the group called poor metals. Most of the other metals with which we are familiar, such as iron, copper, gold, platinum and silver, are transition metals.

NONMETALS

There are only 25 elements that are not metals, including the semi-metals which can be made to act like a metal or a non-metal. Nonmetals are colored yellow in the periodic table shown on the right, and the semi-metals are orange.

The nonmetals, apart from graphite (a form of carbon*), are poor conductors of heat and electricity. But semi-metals, such as germanium and silicon, can be made to conduct an electric current like metals, or act as poor conductors like nonmetals.

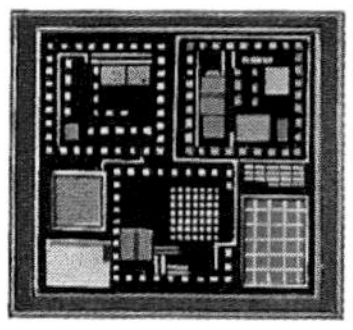

Silicon is used to make integrated circuits ("chips"). It is treated to create microscopic pathways that conduct electricity through the chip.*

Liquid hydrogen (made by compressing hydrogen gas) is used as a fuel for rockets and other spacecraft.*

At room temperature, 11 of the nonmetals are gases (for example, hydrogen, nitrogen and chlorine). Phosphorus, carbon, sulphur and iodine are solids and bromine is a liquid.

ATOMS AND ELEMENTS

The atoms* of which elements are made are themselves made up of even smaller, subatomic particles.

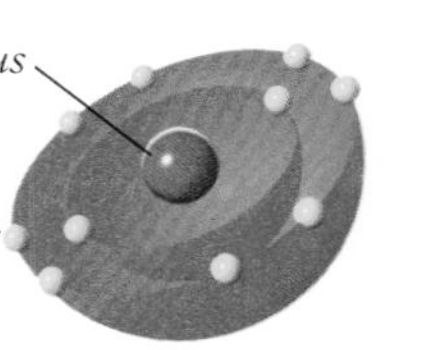

An atom consists of a nucleus with electrons moving around it.

Nucleus

Electron

The nucleus is made up of subatomic particles called protons and neutrons. The atoms of different elements have different numbers of protons and the number of protons is called the atomic number. An atom usually has an equal number of protons and electrons.

Argon has 18 protons so its atomic number is 18. It also has 18 electrons.

The hydrogen atom has only one proton, so its atomic number is 1.

The electrons move around the nucleus in different energy levels, or shells. The first shell can hold two electrons, the second can hold eight and the third can hold up to 18, but usually holds up to eight.

KEY TERMS

Atom The smallest particle of an element that still has the chemical properties of that element.

Atomic number The number of protons in the nucleus of an atom.

Isotope An atom that has a different number of neutrons and so has a different mass number from the other atoms in an element.

Mass number The total number of protons and neutrons in the nucleus of a particular atom.

Relative Atomic Mass (RAM) The average mass number of all the atoms in a sample of an element.

Shell A region in which a certain number of electrons can exist around the nucleus of an atom.

ELEMENTS IN THE EARTH'S CRUST

Most of the Earth's crust is made up of only eight elements. The elements rarely occur alone and they combine together to form minerals, the substances of which the rocks are made.

Calcite is made of the elements calcium, carbon and oxygen. Limestone rock contains calcite.

Pyrolusite is made of manganese, a metal element, and oxygen.

Sphalerite is made of zinc and sulphur.

Oxygen is the most common element in the Earth's crust. It often occurs combined with silicon, the second most common element, and with iron and aluminum, the most common metals.

This pie chart shows the proportions, by mass, of the five main elements in the Earth's crust.

Silicon 27.7%

Oxygen 46.6%

Aluminum 8.1%

Iron 5%

Calcium 3.6%

Rest 9%

*Metals, 56-57

*Atomic Structure, 4; Carbon, 61; Integrated Circuits, 51; Hydrogen, 60

*Atoms and Molecules, 4

THE PERIODIC TABLE

The periodic table is a chart of the elements arranged in order of their atomic numbers. Each element is represented by a rectangle containing its chemical symbol, name, atomic number and relative atomic mass (see Key Terms).

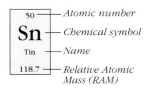

50	— Atomic number
Sn	— Chemical symbol
Tin	— Name
118.7	— Relative Atomic Mass (RAM)

Hydrogen is the lightest element. It has an atomic number of 1, but it does not belong with the metals so it is placed separately.

The rows across the chart are called periods. All the elements in one period have the same number of electron shells. Elements in period 2 have two and those in period 3 have three and so on.

The vertical columns are called groups and are numbered from 1 to 8, with the transition metals forming a block between groups 2 and 3. For elements with atomic numbers of less than 20 (but not the transition metals), the group number shows the number of electrons in their outer shells.

The change in the number of electrons leads to a regular pattern of change in the chemical behavior of the elements along each period. For example, along period 2, the melting and boiling points of the solid elements (lithium, beryllium, boron and carbon) increase.

All the elements in one group have similar chemical properties and some of the groups have names. For example, the metals in group 1 are all alkali metals* and group 2 are akaline earth metals.* The elements in group 7 are halogens* and group 8 are called the noble gases.*

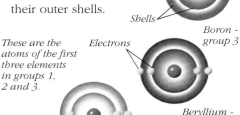

Shells

Boron - group 3

Beryllium - group 2

Lithium - group 1

These are the atoms of the first three elements in groups 1, 2 and 3.

Electrons

Metals

Nonmetals

Semi-metals

Transition metals

The RAMs for unstable, radioactive elements are shown in brackets.

The elements with atomic numbers 58 to 71 belong to period 6 and the elements with atomic numbers 90 to 103 belong to period 7. Little is known about elements with atomic numbers greater than 103 and they are not shown in the chart.

Periodic Table:

Period	1	2	3	4	5	6	7				3	4	5	6	7	8
1	1 **H** Hydrogen 1.0															2 **He** Helium 4.0
2	3 **Li** Lithium 6.9	4 **Be** Beryllium 9.0									5 **B** Boron 10.8	6 **C** Carbon 12.0	7 **N** Nitrogen 14.0	8 **O** Oxygen 16.0	9 **F** Fluorine 19.0	10 **Ne** Neon 20.2
3	11 **Na** Sodium 23.0	12 **Mg** Magnesium 24.3									13 **Al** Aluminum 27	14 **Si** Silicon 28.1	15 **P** Phosphorus 31.0	16 **S** Sulphur 32.1	17 **Cl** Chlorine 35.5	18 **Ar** Argon 39.9

Transition metals (periods 4-6):

	21	22	23	24	25	26	27	28	29	30
4	**Sc** Scandium 45.0	**Ti** Titanium 47.9	**V** Vanadium 50.9	**Cr** Chromium 52.0	**Mn** Manganese 54.9	**Fe** Iron 55.9	**Co** Cobalt 58.9	**Ni** Nickel 58.7	**Cu** Copper 63.5	**Zn** Zinc 65.4

Period 4: 19 **K** Potassium 39.1 | 20 **Ca** Calcium 40.1 | ... | 31 **Ga** Gallium 69.7 | 32 **Ge** Germanium 72.6 | 33 **As** Arsenic 74.9 | 34 **Se** Selenium 79 | 35 **Br** Bromine 79.9 | 36 **Kr** Krypton 83.8

Period 5: 37 **Rb** Rubidium 85.5 | 38 **Sr** Strontium 87.6 | 39 **Y** Yttrium 88.9 | 40 **Zr** Zirconium 91.2 | 41 **Nb** Niobium 92.9 | 42 **Mo** Molybdenum 95.9 | 43 **Tc** Technetium 97.9 | 44 **Ru** Ruthenium 101.1 | 45 **Rh** Rhodium 102.9 | 46 **Pd** Palladium 106.4 | 47 **Ag** Silver 107.9 | 48 **Cd** Cadmium 112.4 | 49 **In** Indium 114.8 | 50 **Sn** Tin 118.7 | 51 **Sb** Antimony 121.8 | 52 **Te** Tellurium 127.6 | 53 **I** Iodine 126.9 | 54 **Xe** Xenon 131.3

Period 6: 55 **Cs** Caesium 132.9 | 56 **Ba** Barium 137.3 | 57 **La** Lanthanum 138.9 | 72 **Hf** Hafnium 178.5 | 73 **Ta** Tantalum 181.0 | 74 **W** Tungsten 183.9 | 75 **Re** Rhenium 186.2 | 76 **Os** Osmium 190.2 | 77 **Ir** Iridium 192.2 | 78 **Pt** Platinum 195.1 | 79 **Au** Gold 197.0 | 80 **Hg** Mercury 200.6 | 81 **Tl** Thallium 204.4 | 82 **Pb** Lead 207.2 | 83 **Bi** Bismuth 209.0 | 84 **Po** Polonium (210) | 85 **At** Astatine (210) | 86 **Rn** Radon (222)

Period 7: 87 **Fr** Francium (223) | 88 **Ra** Radium (226) | 89 **Ac** Actinium (227)

Lanthanides:

58	59	60	61	62	63	64	65	66	67	68	69	70	71
Ce Cerium 140.1	**Pr** Praseody-mium 140.9	**Nd** Neodymium 144.2	**Pm** Promethium (147)	**Sm** Samarium 150.4	**Eu** Europium 152.0	**Gd** Gadolinium 157.3	**Tb** Terbium 158.9	**Dy** Dysprosium 162.5	**Ho** Holmium 164.9	**Er** Erbium 167.3	**Tm** Thulium 168.9	**Yb** Ytterbium 173.0	**Lu** Lutetium 175.0

Actinides:

90	91	92	93	94	95	96	97	98	99	100	101	102	103
Th Thorium 232.0	**Pa** Protactinium (231)	**U** Uranium 238.1	**Np** Neptunium (237)	**Pu** Plutonium (242)	**Am** Americium (243)	**Cm** Curium (247)	**Bk** Berkelium (245)	**Cf** Californium (251)	**Es** Einsteinium (254)	**Fm** Fermium (253)	**Md** Mendelev-ium (256)	**No** Nobelium (254)	**Lr** Lawrencium (257)

Group numbers

The mineral galena is made of the elements lead and sulphur.

This rock contains specks of pure gold, one of the few elements that can be found in its pure state.

Turquoise is made of aluminum, phosphorus, copper, oxygen and hydrogen.

Chalcopyrite, or copper pyrites, is made of copper, iron and sulphur.

Beryl is made of the elements silicon, oxygen, aluminum and beryllium.

METALS

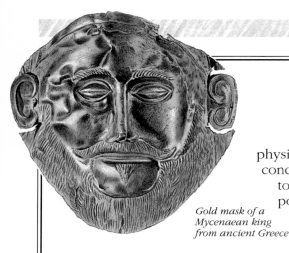

Gold mask of a Mycenaean king from ancient Greece

Although all the metal elements share certain physical properties, for example, they are shiny and they conduct electricity, they can also be grouped according to the way they behave chemically. Some, such as potassium and sodium, are very reactive and react violently with water and air, while others, for example gold, do not react at all.

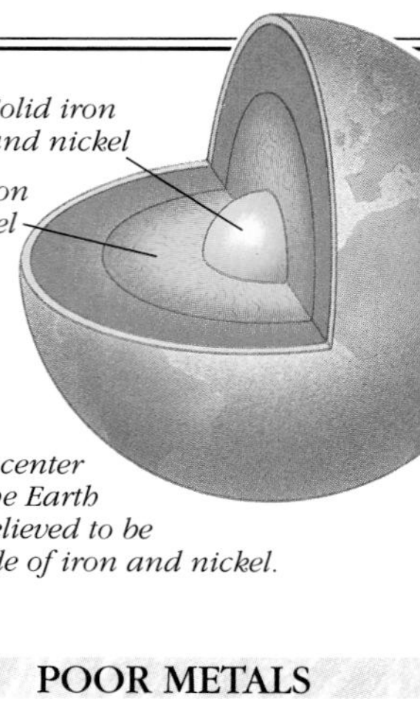

Solid iron and nickel

Molten iron and nickel

The center of the Earth is believed to be made of iron and nickel.

PROPERTIES OF METALS

All metals, except for mercury, are solid at room temperature (20°C or 68°F) and they are good conductors of electricity and heat. They are shiny when cut, and some, such as iron and nickel, are magnetic. Metals that can be pulled out to make wire are described as ductile, and those that can be beaten flat are malleable.

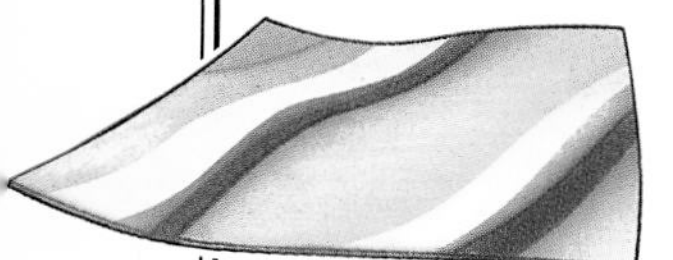

Flat panel of malleable metal

Metal wire

NOBLE METALS

Noble metals are those that can be found as pure metals rather than as part of compounds in the Earth's crust. Copper, silver, gold and platinum are noble metals. They are all very unreactive (see Reactivity Series) and do not easily combine with other elements to form compounds.

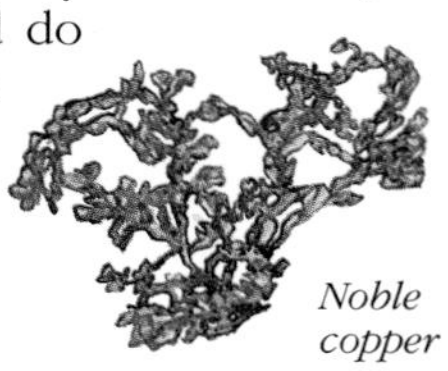

Noble copper

Gold is one of the most unreactive elements.

Because they are unreactive, noble metals do not easily corrode (see right) and they are used for jewelry and coins. Gold is very unreactive and ancient gold objects are still shiny.

ALKALI METALS

These are six very reactive metals, including sodium and potassium, that form group 1 of the periodic table.* They have low melting points - potassium melts at 64°C (147°F) - and they are soft and can be cut with a knife. They form alkaline* solutions when they react with water and this is why they are called alkali metals.

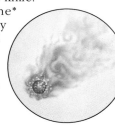

Potassium reacts violently with water, giving off hydrogen that bursts into lilac colored flames.

ALKALINE EARTH METALS

The alkaline earth metals are the six metals, including magnesium, calcium and barium, that form group 2 of the periodic table.* These metals are found in many different minerals in the Earth's crust. For example, calcium is found in calcite, which forms veins in limestone and chalk. Alkaline earth metals are not as reactive as the alkali metals and they are harder and have higher melting points.

Calcium is found in shells, bones and teeth.

Magnesium is found in chlorophyll, the green pigment needed for photosynthesis.

POOR METALS

The poor metals are the group of seven metals, including aluminum, tin and lead, to the right of the transition metals in the periodic table.*

Aluminum alloys are used to make aircraft and bicycle frames.

Aluminum is one of the least dense metals, so it is very light. Lead is very dense and is used as a barrier against radiation from X-rays in hospitals. In general, the poor metals have low melting points and they are quite soft. Many are used in alloys* (mixtures of metals) to make metals that have properties suitable for particular tasks.

TRANSITION METALS

The transition metals have the properties of typical metals. They are strong, hard and shiny and have high melting points. They are less reactive than the alkali and alkaline earth metals. Iron, gold, silver, chromium, nickel and copper are all transition metals. They are easy to shape and have many different industrial uses, both on their own and as alloys (see Main Metals and Alloys*).

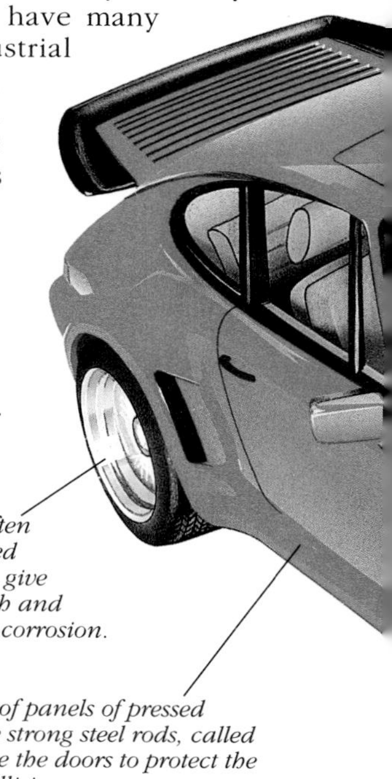

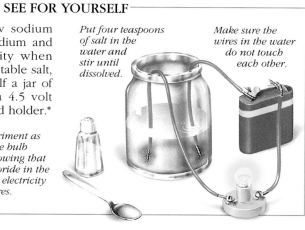

About 77 percent of a car, such as this Porsche, is made of metals, mostly steel* - an alloy of iron and carbon.

Wheel hubs are often made of steel plated with chromium to give them a shiny finish and protect them from corrosion.

The body is made of panels of pressed steel and there are strong steel rods, called impact bars, inside the doors to protect the passengers in a collision.

SEE FOR YOURSELF

This experiment shows how sodium chloride (a compound of sodium and chlorine) conducts electricity when dissolved in water. You need table salt, which is sodium chloride, half a jar of warm water, electric wire, a 4.5 volt battery and a 3.5 volt bulb and holder.*

NEVER USE ELECTRICITY FROM SOCKETS FOR EXPERIMENTS

Put four teaspoons of salt in the water and stir until dissolved.

Make sure the wires in the water do not touch each other.

Set up the experiment as shown here. The bulb should glow showing that the sodium chloride in the water conducts electricity between the wires.

**Periodic Table, 55; Setting up Experiments, 96   *Periodic Table, 55; Bases and Alkalis, 74   *Periodic Table, 55; Alloys, 58; Main Metals and Alloys, 59; Iron and Steel, 58

THE REACTIVITY SERIES

The reactivity series is a list of metals showing how reactive they are. The position of each metal is decided by how strongly it reacts with oxygen. The more reactive metals pull oxygen away from less reactive metals. Reactive metals are difficult to separate from the minerals in which they are found, while the least reactive metals can be found as pure metals.

Sodium and potassium are stored in oil as they react violently with air and water.

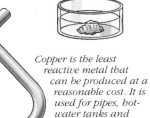

Copper is the least reactive metal that can be produced at a reasonable cost. It is used for pipes, hot-water tanks and electrical wiring.

Most reactive

Potassium
Sodium
Calcium
Magnesium
Aluminum
Zinc
Iron
Tin
Lead
Copper
Silver
Gold
Platinum

Least reactive

FLAME TESTS

When some metals burn, they produce distinctive colored flames. This can be used to test for the presence of a particular metal in a substance. The substance is held in a flame on a piece of unreactive platinum wire.

Compounds containing the metal sodium burn with a yellow flame, compounds of copper have blue-green flames, calcium compounds have red flames and potassium have lilac flames.

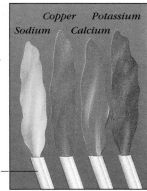

Sodium   Copper   Potassium
Calcium

Tubes containing metals

Fireworks contain metal compounds that burn with brilliant colors. Barium compounds create greens, strontium compounds make red, sodium are yellow and copper make blue-green colors.

THE DISCOVERY OF METALS

People probably discovered how to extract metals from their compounds by accident when rocks containing a metal were heated with charcoal in fireplaces. A chemical reaction called reduction* occurred which freed the metal from its compound. The same reaction is still used in blast furnaces today (see Iron and Steel*).

In about 4,000BC, Sumerian people in the Middle East made items such as this helmet and dagger from gold, silver and copper.

The first metals worked by people were copper, gold and silver, probably because these are noble metals (see left) and were found as pure metals. Later, in about 3,500BC, the Sumerians learned how to make bronze by combining copper and tin. Bronze is stronger than the pure metals. Iron was discovered later, probably because it needs higher temperatures to separate it from its compounds.

Gold dagger and sheath

Bronze axe-head made in 500 BC

Sumerian bronze bowl

Until 1735, the only known metals were copper, silver, gold, iron, mercury, tin, zinc, bismuth, antimony and lead. Aluminum was discovered in 1825. Now, scientists have re-created a number of metal elements, such as unnilennium, by combining uranium with neutrons and other nuclear particles in a nuclear reactor. The new elements are unstable and break down in a short time.

CORROSION

Corrosion is the chemical reaction that takes place when a metal is in contact with air and water. The metal reacts with oxygen in the air to form a compound called an oxide on the surface of the metal. The metal loses its shine and becomes tarnished. Metals high in the reactivity series (see above) corrode more quickly than less reactive metals.

Steel armor was rubbed with oil or beeswax to stop it from rusting. (Steel is made from iron.)

The steel body of a car is covered with several layers of paint to stop it from rusting.

On some metals, such as aluminum, the layer of oxide clings to the metal and protects it. When iron corrodes, it forms a flaky layer of iron oxide that combines with water to form rust. The rust flakes away and the metal underneath continues to corrode.

Steel food cans are plated with tin, a less reactive metal, to stop the steel from corroding.

Large objects, such as bridges, are painted to stop them from corroding.

Moving parts, such as gears and bicycle chains, are greased to stop them from rusting.

Galvanizing is a method of protecting steel by coating it with zinc. Zinc is more reactive than steel so it "pulls" the oxygen away from the steel (see Reactivity Series, above). If the layer of zinc is scratched, the oxygen in the air reacts with the zinc rather than the steel. Ships and oil rigs are protected by attaching a block of zinc or magnesium, which corrodes first and is called the sacrificial metal.

Galvanized nail

On most cars, the steel panels that make up the body are galvanized before they are painted to give them more protection against corrosion. The underneath may be sealed with plastics.

KEY TERMS

Atom The smallest particle of an element that still has the chemical properties of that element.
Bond A force that holds two or more atoms together.
Compound A substance made up of two or more elements that are chemically bonded together.
Element A substance made up of one kind of atom and which cannot be broken down by a chemical reaction to form simpler substances.
Minerals The naturally occurring compounds of which the rocks in the Earth's crust are made.

*Reduction, 72; Iron and Steel, 58

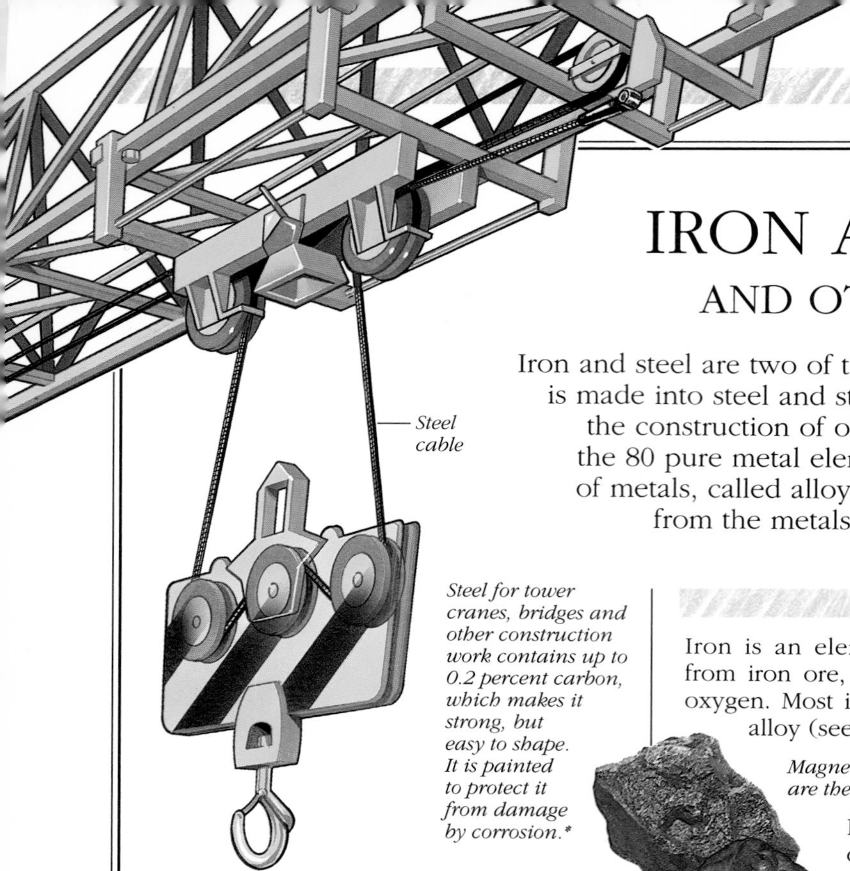

IRON AND STEEL
AND OTHER METALS

Iron and steel are two of the most important metals. Most iron is made into steel and steel has many different uses, from the construction of oil rigs to paperclips. As well as the 80 pure metal elements, there are many mixtures of metals, called alloys, that have different properties from the metals of which they are made.

Railway tracks are made of steel strengthened with manganese.

French TGV (Train à Grande Vitesse)

Steel cable

Steel for tower cranes, bridges and other construction work contains up to 0.2 percent carbon, which makes it strong, but easy to shape. It is painted to protect it from damage by corrosion.*

ALLOYS

An alloy is a mixture of two or more metals, or a metal and another substance. For example, brass is an alloy of copper and zinc. The addition of other metals makes brass harder than copper, but it is easily worked and does not corrode.*

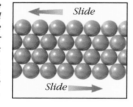

In pure metals, the atoms are arranged in tight rows. The rows can slide over each other and this makes the metal soft. Sudden changes in the rows make the metal brittle.

Slide

Slide

The atoms of the alloying metal help to strengthen the metal by stopping the rows from sliding over each other, and holding weak parts of the metal together.

Alloy atom

Atoms cannot slide

Many pure metals are too soft to be useful on their own, but alloys can be created that withstand great stress and extreme temperatures. Steel is an alloy made of iron and a nonmetal, carbon. There are also alloys of steel made by adding small amounts of other metals.

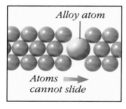

Stainless steel, such as that used for cutlery, is an alloy of steel, chromium and nickel.

Alloys of steel and manganese are very hard wearing and are used for industrial cutting equipment. Alloys of aluminum and magnesium are light, strong and corrosion resistant. They are used for aircraft and bicycle frames.

*Corrosion, 57

Iron is an element* and it is extracted from iron ore, a compound of iron and oxygen. Most iron is made into steel, an alloy (see left) of iron and carbon.

Magnetite (top) and hematite (below) are the two most common iron ores.

Iron is extracted from iron ore in a blast furnace by a process called smelting. In the furnace, iron ore, limestone and coke (coal heated to burn off oils and leave carbon) are blasted with very hot air. The carbon combines with oxygen in the air to form carbon monoxide. The carbon monoxide then becomes carbon dioxide by "pulling" the oxygen away from the iron ore, leaving the metal free. This is an example of a reduction* reaction.

Diagram of a blast furnace

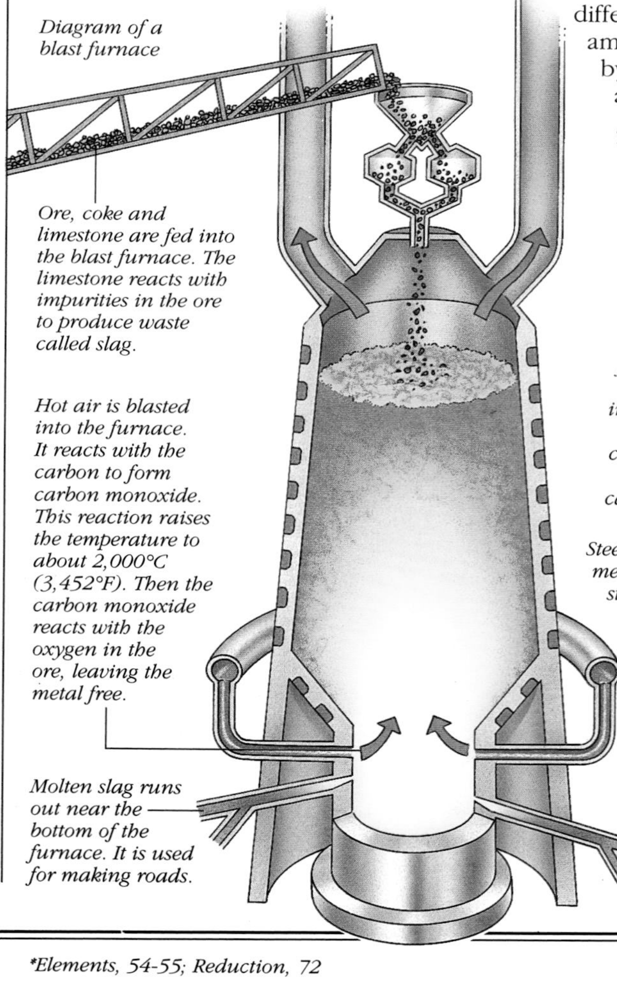

Ore, coke and limestone are fed into the blast furnace. The limestone reacts with impurities in the ore to produce waste called slag.

Hot air is blasted into the furnace. It reacts with the carbon to form carbon monoxide. This reaction raises the temperature to about 2,000°C (3,452°F). Then the carbon monoxide reacts with the oxygen in the ore, leaving the metal free.

Molten slag runs out near the bottom of the furnace. It is used for making roads.

The iron extracted from iron ore contains carbon (about four percent) and other impurities such as sulphur. These make the iron brittle, so most iron is made into steel by burning off the impurities as shown below.

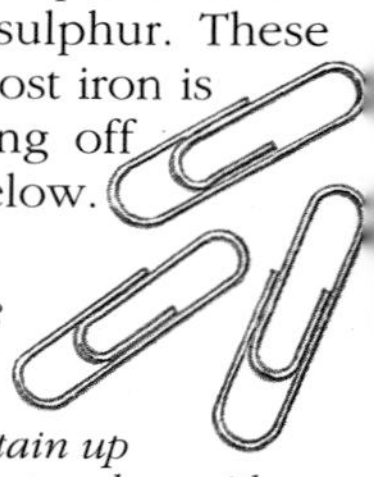

Steel paperclips contain about 0.08 percent carbon.

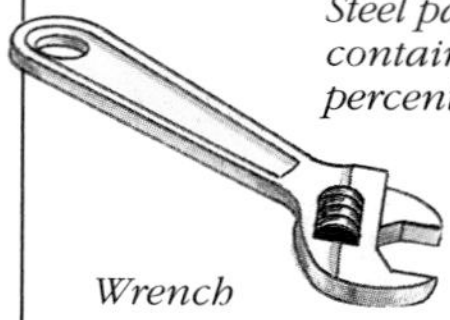

Wrench

Tools contain up to 1 percent carbon with chrome and vanadium to strengthen them.

Iron is converted to steel by blasting molten iron and some scrap steel with oxygen. The oxygen combines with the carbon in the iron to form the gas carbon monoxide, which is collected as a fuel. After refining, the steel may contain as little as 0.04 percent carbon, although different grades of steel have different amounts of carbon. Steel is also made by recycling scrap steel in an electric arc furnace, as shown below.

To convert iron to steel, molten iron and scrap steel are poured into a furnace called a converter.

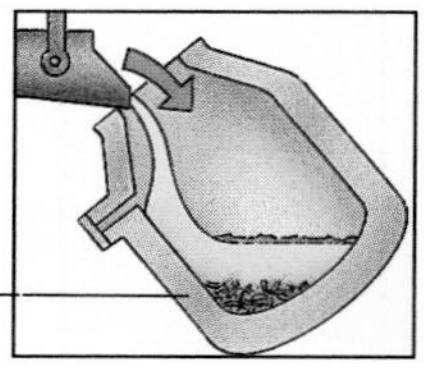

Converter

A high pressure jet of almost pure oxygen is blasted into the converter. The oxygen combines with the carbon, forming carbon monoxide.

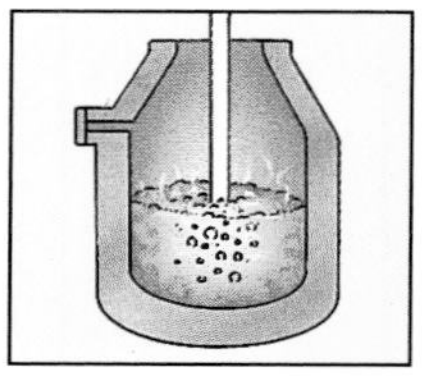

Steel is also made by melting down scrap steel in an electric arc furnace. The scrap is melted by a powerful current of electricity.

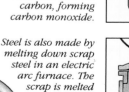

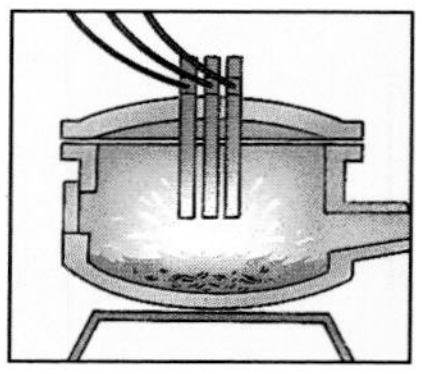

Molten iron is tapped off here. The blast furnace is kept alight for up to ten years until the lining of the walls starts to disintegrate. The walls are over 3m (10ft) thick and the furnace is 30m (100ft) tall.

*Elements, 54-55; Reduction, 72

MAIN METALS AND ALLOYS

Aluminum A very light, silvery-white metal that is resistant to corrosion. It is extracted from bauxite by electrolysis.* Aluminum is used for overhead electric cables, aircraft, ships, cars, drink cans and kitchen foil.

Aluminum drink cans are strong and light.

Brass An alloy of copper and zinc which is easy to shape and is used for decorative purposes, ornaments, musical instruments and screws and tacks.

Bronze An alloy of copper and tin known since ancient times. It resists corrosion and is easy to shape.

Calcium A malleable, silvery-white metal found in limestone and chalk. It also occurs in animals' bones and teeth. It is used to make high-grade steel, and in cement.

Calcium compounds are found in bones and teeth.

Chromium A hard, grey metal used to make stainless steel and for plating other metals to protect them or give them a shiny, reflective finish.

Copper A malleable, reddish metal used to make electrical wires, hot water tanks and the alloys brass, bronze and cupronickel.

Copper bar

Cupronickel An alloy made of copper and nickel from which most silver-colored coins are made.

Cupronickel coins

Gold A soft, unreactive, bright yellow element that is used for jewelry and in electronics.

Iron A malleable, silvery-white magnetic metal extracted mainly from the ore hematite by smelting in a blast furnace. It is used in building and engineering, and to make the alloy steel.

Iron is found in red blood cells.

Lead A heavy, malleable, poisonous blue-white metal extracted from the mineral galena and used in batteries, roofing and as a shield against radiation from X-rays.

Magnesium A light, silvery-white metal that burns with a bright white flame. It is used in rescue flares and fireworks and in lightweight alloys.

Fireworks contain magnesium and other metals.

Mercury A heavy, silvery-white, poisonous liquid metal used in thermometers, dental amalgam for filling teeth, and in explosives.

Thermometer

Platinum A malleable, silvery-white unreactive metal that is used as a catalyst* and in electronics and for making jewelry.

Platinum is unreactive and is used for making jewelry.

Plutonium A radioactive metal produced by bombarding uranium (see below) in nuclear reactors and used in nuclear weapons.

Potassium A light, silvery, highly reactive metal, compounds of which are used in fertilizers.

Silver A malleable, grey-white metal that is a very good conductor of heat and electricity. It is used for making jewelry, silverware and in photographic emulsions.

Photographic film

Solder An alloy of tin and lead that has a low melting point and is used for joining wires in electronics.

Sodium A very reactive, soft, silvery-white metal that occurs in common salt and is used in sodium vapor street lamps and in the chemical industry.

Steel An alloy of iron and carbon that is one of the most important metals in industry. Stainless steel, an alloy of steel and chromium, resists corrosion and is used in aerospace industries.

Tin A soft, malleable, silvery-white metal used for tin-plating steel to stop it corroding, and in the alloys bronze, pewter and solder.

Titanium A strong, white, malleable metal that is very resistant to corrosion and is used in alloys for spacecraft, aircraft and bicycle frames.

Tungsten A hard, grey-white metal used for lamp filaments and in electronics, and in steel alloys for making sharp-edged cutting tools.

Lamp filament

Uranium A silvery-white, radioactive metal used as a source of nuclear energy* and also in nuclear weapons.

Vanadium A hard, white, poisonous metal used to increase the strength and hardness of steel alloys and also as a catalyst* for making sulphuric acid.

Zinc A blue-white metal extracted from the mineral zinc blende. It is used for galvanizing* iron, and in batteries and alloys such as brass.

Zinc battery

RECYCLING METALS

Recycling is a way of conserving the Earth's resources by reusing the same raw materials, instead of mining new ones. Metals are easy to recycle because they can be melted down to make metal of the same quality as new metal extracted from ore. Steel and aluminum are both practical and economical to recycle, but other metals, such as copper, tin and lead, are also recycled.

Iron and steel are magnetic and can be separated from other waste with a very strong magnet.

Most steel for recycling comes from scrapped cars and machines, but it is also collected from household garbage, and factories save offcuts and return them to steelworks. Scrap steel is also mixed with molten iron to make new steel (see opposite page).

Aluminum is not magnetic, but it can be separated from other rubbish using an electromagnet* to repel the aluminum. Over 50 percent of drink cans are made of aluminum that has been recycled.

You can use a magnet to check whether a can is made of steel or aluminum. If it is attracted to the magnet it is steel, if not it is an aluminum can.

Recycling existing metal uses far less power than extracting new metal from ore - and it reduces the amount of waste that needs to be disposed of. In principle, there is no limit to the number of times that metal can be recycled.

Recycling aluminum cans uses only 5 percent of the energy needed to produce new aluminum.

KEY TERMS

Alloy A mixture of two or more metals, or a metal and a nonmetal.

Corrosion The way metals react with oxygen to form a layer of metal oxide on their surfaces.

Minerals The naturally occurring compounds of which the rocks in the Earth's crust are made.

Ore A mineral from which useful products, such as metals, can be extracted.

*Electrolysis, 73

*Catalysts, 71; Electroplating, 73; Nuclear Power, 11; Galvanizing, see Corrosion, 57; Electromagnets, 49

HYDROGEN
AND THE HALOGENS

Hydrogen is the most abundant element in the universe. The Sun and the stars are made of hydrogen gas, but on Earth, hydrogen is found only in compounds and does not occur naturally as a free element. The halogens are a group of five very reactive and poisonous elements, such as chlorine and fluorine, that form group 7 of the periodic table.*

Stars are globes of extremely hot hydrogen and other gases.

Halogen lamps contain compounds of bromine that make the lamps shine more brightly.

HYDROGEN

Hydrogen is a colorless, inflammable gas. It is very reactive and is found combined with many other elements. For example, water, the most plentiful compound on Earth, is a compound of hydrogen and oxygen. Fossil fuels, such as coal and oil, are compounds of hydrogen and carbon, and sugars and starch also contain hydrogen.

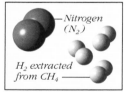

Sucrose ($C_{12}H_{22}O_{11}$), the sugar in sweets, is a compound of carbon, hydrogen and oxygen.

Hydrogen (H_2) can be made by reacting methane gas (CH_4) with steam (H_2O) as shown by the following chemical equation: $CH_4 + 2H_2O = 4H_2 + CO_2$. Most of the hydrogen is used to make ammonia (NH_3) for fertilizers. To make ammonia, hydrogen is combined with nitrogen* using the Haber process discovered by Fritz Haber in 1909.

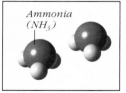

— Nitrogen (N_2)

H_2 extracted from CH_4 —

For the Haber process, nitrogen gas from the air and hydrogen extracted from methane (CH_4) are passed over a catalyst of iron.

Ammonia (NH_3)

Under very high pressure and at a high temperature, the gases react to produce ammonia gas (NH_3) that is cooled to form liquid ammonia.

KEY TERMS

Compound A substance made up of two or more elements that are chemically bonded together.
Element A substance made up of one kind of atom and which cannot be broken down by a chemical reaction to form simpler substances.

If hydrogen is mixed with air and then lit, it explodes. This can be used as a test for small amounts of gas in the laboratory. If the gas is hydrogen, it makes a small pop.

Hydrogen gas makes a small pop when tested with a burning splint.

If pure hydrogen is burned in air or oxygen, it burns quietly with a blue flame and forms steam, as shown in this equation: $2H_2 + O_2 = 2H_2O$. In theory, hydrogen is an ideal fuel as it produces a lot of energy when it burns and the only product is water, which is not a pollutant. But at present it is not suitable as an everyday fuel because it is difficult to store and transport.

On May 6, 1937, the Hindenburg, *an airship filled with hydrogen, caught fire. The hydrogen exploded and 36 people were killed.*

Compressed hydrogen, which is a liquid, is used as a rocket fuel.

— Oxygen tank
— Liquid hydrogen fuel tank

Liquid hydrogen is, however, used as a fuel for rockets.* In order for the fuel to burn in space, where there is no oxygen, rockets also carry separate tanks of oxygen. The liquid hydrogen and oxygen are fed into a combustion chamber where they burn safely.

The Sun is a massive ball of glowing hydrogen and helium gas. Fountains of gas flare up from the surface.*

THE HALOGENS

The group of elements called the halogens is made up of fluorine, chlorine, bromine, iodine and astatine. Astatine is an unstable, radioactive element that does not exist naturally.

Chlorine is a poisonous gas. It is very reactive and only occurs naturally in compounds such as sodium chloride (common salt). Chlorine is used as a disinfectant and to make hydrochloric acid and PVC (polyvinyl chloride) plastic.*

PVC juggling equipment

Bromine is a brown liquid. Traces of bromine are found in seawater and mineral springs. Fluorine is a poisonous gas. It is extracted from the mineral fluorite. Fluorides (compounds that contain fluorine) are added to toothpaste and drinking water to reduce tooth decay.

Fluorite shines in ultraviolet light and this effect is called fluorescence.

Iodine is a purple-black solid. It is used in medicine, photography and dyes and a solution of iodine is used as a test for starch.

Iodine is found in seaweed, and in vegetables and fruit. It is an essential part of our diet.

Leaves contain starch and when tested with a solution of iodine, the iodine turns blue-black.

*Nitrogen, 62; Rockets, 34; Sun, 32

*Periodic Table, 55; Plastics, 82-83

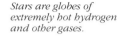

CARBON, SULPHUR
AND PHOSPHORUS

Carbon, sulphur and phosphorus are solid, nonmetal elements. Carbon is found in all living things, and also occurs as a free element in the form of diamond and graphite. Sulphur is found in underground deposits in volcanic areas, but phosphorus only occurs naturally in compounds such as the mineral apatite, and in bones and teeth.

Animal and plant proteins are compounds of carbon, oxygen, hydrogen and nitrogen.

Pure sulphur

Iron pyrites, a compound of iron and sulphur

CARBON

As an element, carbon is found in several different forms, or allotropes,* including diamond, graphite and fullerene (see below). In each form, the carbon atoms are bonded together in different ways and this gives the allotropes their very different physical properties.

Carbon is also found in a large number of different compounds. The study of carbon in compounds produced by living things is called organic chemistry.*

Most carbon atoms have existed since the world began. They circulate through animals, plants and the air in a process called the carbon cycle.

CARBON DIOXIDE IN THE AIR

Photosynthesis | Burning | Respiration

The Carbon Cycle

Decay | Decay

PLANTS → ANIMALS

Plants use carbon dioxide to make carbon compounds by photosynthesis. Animals eat plants (or other animals) and use the carbon compounds in their bodies. Carbon dioxide returns to the air when fuels burn and living things decompose, and as a result of respiration* - the way plants and animals break down sugars to release energy.*

In graphite, each atom of carbon is bonded to three other atoms, and the atoms are arranged in a network of plates that easily slide over each other.

Carbon atoms

In diamond, each carbon atom is bonded to four other atoms. This makes diamonds very hard and they are used in cutting and drilling equipment, as well as in jewelry.

Powdered graphite is mixed with clay to make pencil "lead". Hard pencils have more clay than soft ones.

Cut diamond

Silky threads of pure carbon, called carbon fibers, are used to reinforce plastics. They are eight times stronger than steel. Carbon fiber racing bike frames are very strong and light.

Each molecule of fullerene, an allotrope of carbon, contains 60 carbon atoms linked in the shape of a ball.

Charcoal is an impure form of carbon. It is used in filters and gas masks to trap poisonous gases.

World War I mask

SULPHUR

Sulphur is a bright yellow, crumbly solid. It is found as a free element and in the minerals iron pyrites and copper pyrites. It is also found in fossil fuels. Sulphur has two allotropes, called monoclinic sulphur and rhombic sulphur.

Left: rhombic sulphur, and far left: monoclinic sulphur

Most sulphur is obtained by desulphurizing fossil fuels. It is used for making sulphuric acid,* in vulcanization to harden rubber, and in medicines.

Below: sulphur dioxide is used to kill insects, and as a fungicide and a preservative for fruit.

PHOSPHORUS

The element phosphorus has three allotropes: a poisonous, flammable white solid form; a less reactive red form used in matches, pesticides, alloys and distress flares, and an unstable black form.

Matchheads contain phosphorus.

Plants need phosphorus for healthy growth and it is added to the soil in fertilizers.

The minerals apatite (top) and turquoise (below) contain phosphorus.

KEY TERMS

Allotrope One of two or more different forms of an element.

Compound A substance made up of two or more elements that are chemically bonded together.

Element A substance made up of one kind of atom and which cannot be broken down to form simpler substances.

*Allotropes, 65; Organic Chemistry, 78-79; Photosynthesis, see Reduction, 72; Respiration, see Oxidation, 72

*Sulphuric Acid, 75

THE AIR

The air is a mixture of gases that form a protective layer called the atmosphere around the Earth. Air is essential for life on Earth - for animals to breathe and for plants to make their food - and it also helps protect the Earth from the Sun's dangerous ultraviolet rays. The main gases in air are nitrogen and oxygen, but there are also traces of the noble gases (see right), and of carbon dioxide and solid particles such as soot and pollen.

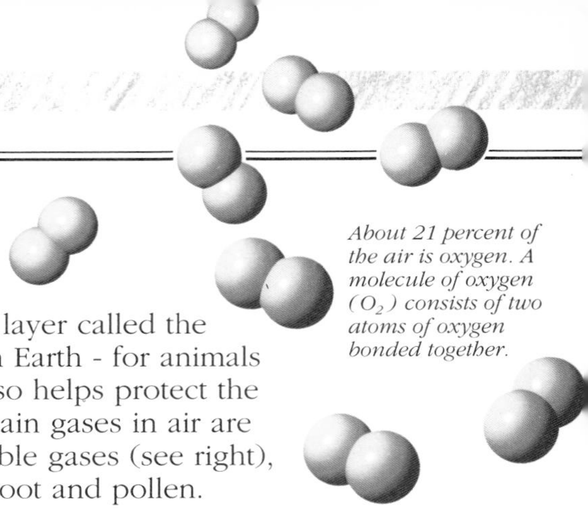

About 21 percent of the air is oxygen. A molecule of oxygen (O_2) consists of two atoms of oxygen bonded together.

All animals need air to breathe.

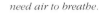

THE GASES IN THE AIR

The amounts of the different gases in the air vary slightly from place to place, season to season and day and night. The pie chart below shows the average volumes of the gases as percentages.

Nitrogen 78%
Oxygen 21%
Other gases - 1%

Nitrogen and oxygen are the main gases. The remaining one percent is noble gases, carbon dioxide, water vapor and pollutants such as nitrogen dioxide.

The different gases in the air can be separated by a process called fractional distillation.* The air is cooled until the gases become liquids. The mixture of liquids is heated. Each liquid boils at a different temperature and is collected separately as it evaporates.

Oxygen, nitrogen and carbon dioxide are continually removed and returned to the air by living things as part of natural cycles.

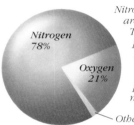

Animals take oxygen from the air when they breathe in and return carbon dioxide to the air when they breathe out (see Carbon Cycle).*

KEY TERMS

Atom The smallest particle of an element that still has the chemical properties of that element.
Compound A substance made up of two or more elements that are chemically bonded together.
Element A substance made up of one kind of atom and which cannot be broken down by a chemical reaction to form simpler substances.
Mixture Two or more substances (elements or compounds) that are not chemically bonded together.
Molecule Two or more atoms chemically bonded together to form the smallest particle of a substance.

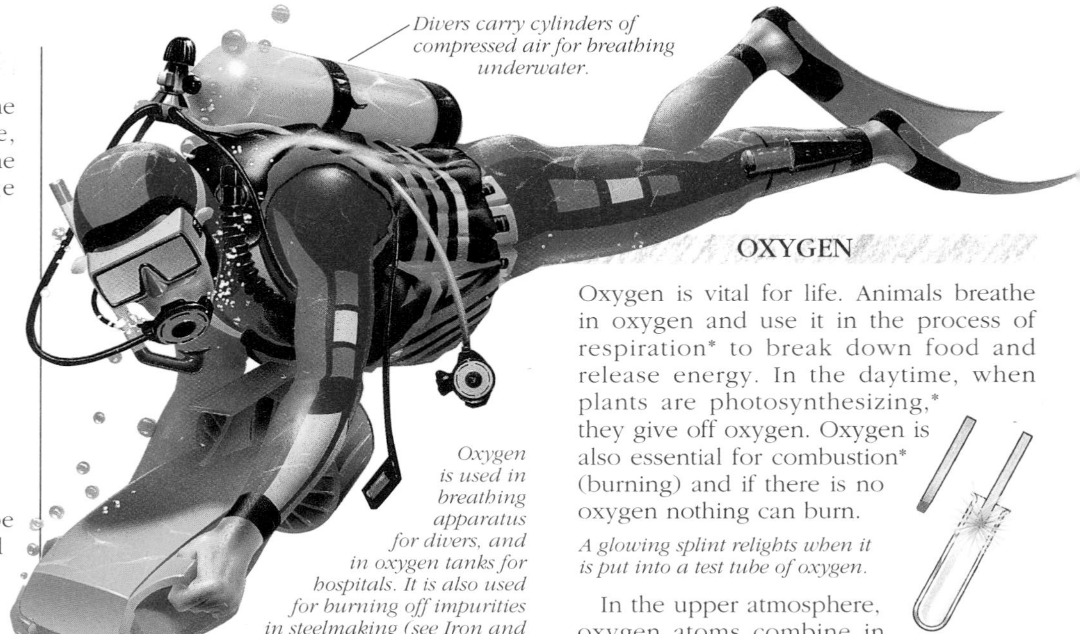

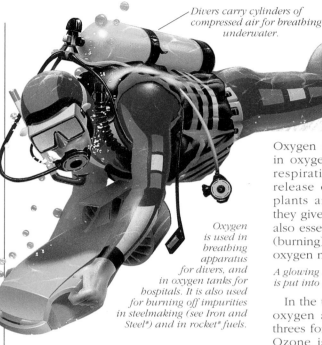

Divers carry cylinders of compressed air for breathing underwater.

Oxygen is used in breathing apparatus for divers, and in oxygen tanks for hospitals. It is also used for burning off impurities in steelmaking (see Iron and Steel) and in rocket* fuels.*

Nearly 50 percent of the compounds in the Earth's crust and oceans contain oxygen. A grain of white sand is a compound of silicon and oxygen.

OXYGEN

Oxygen is vital for life. Animals breathe in oxygen and use it in the process of respiration* to break down food and release energy. In the daytime, when plants are photosynthesizing,* they give off oxygen. Oxygen is also essential for combustion* (burning) and if there is no oxygen nothing can burn.

A glowing splint relights when it is put into a test tube of oxygen.

In the upper atmosphere, oxygen atoms combine in threes forming molecules of ozone (O_3). Ozone is an allotrope* (an alternative form) of oxygen. It is a poisonous gas, but in the upper atmosphere it forms a layer that absorbs most of the Sun's harmful ultraviolet radiation* and protects the Earth.

NITROGEN

Most of the air (over 78 percent) is nitrogen, and the proteins of which all living things are made contain nitrogen. The diagram below shows how nitrogen is continually being recycled between the air and living things.

The most important use of nitrogen is in the production of ammonia for making fertilizers. To do this, it is combined with hydrogen.* It is also used in packaging food such as bacon and chips, because ordinary air would cause the food to oxidize* and go bad. Human organs for transplants are preserved in liquid nitrogen because it is very cold and unreactive.

A molecule of nitrogen (N_2) is made up of two atoms of nitrogen bonded together.

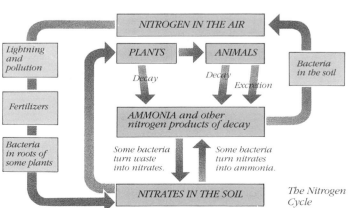

NITROGEN IN THE AIR

Lightning and pollution

PLANTS → ANIMALS

Bacteria in the soil

Fertilizers

Decay | Decay | Excretion

Bacteria in roots of some plants

AMMONIA and other nitrogen products of decay

Some bacteria turn waste into nitrates. | Some bacteria turn nitrates into ammonia.

NITRATES IN THE SOIL

The Nitrogen Cycle

Plants take in nitrogen in the form of nitrates from the soil and use them to make proteins. Animals eat plants and use the proteins in their own bodies. The nitrogen compounds return to the soil when animals die and decay, and in their waste.

In the soil, the nitrogen compounds are broken down by bacteria to form ammonia and then nitrogen. Other bacteria take nitrogen from the air and convert it into nitrates that plants can use.

*Distillation, see Separating Mixtures, 67; Carbon Cycle, 61   *Iron and Steel, 58; Rockets, 34; Hydrogen, 60; Respiration, see Oxidation, 72; Photosynthesis, see Oxidation, 72; Combustion, 72; Allotropes, 65; Oxidation, 72; Ultraviolet Radiation, 37

CARBON DIOXIDE

Carbon dioxide gas is a compound made of the elements carbon* and oxygen. The air contains about 0.003 percent carbon dioxide.

A molecule of carbon dioxide (CO_2) has two oxygen atoms and one carbon atom.

Carbon dioxide is part of the carbon cycle.* Plants use it for photosynthesis* and animals breathe out the carbon dioxide which they produce during respiration.*

Plants use carbon dioxide for photosynthesis.

Carbon dioxide is also produced when fuels containing carbon, such as wood and gasoline, burn. Because we now burn so much fuel in factories and vehicles, the amount of carbon dioxide in the air is increasing (see Greenhouse Effect).

Most substances will not burn in carbon dioxide and it is used in fire extinguishers.

Carbon dioxide is denser than air and suffocates a fire by preventing oxygen from reaching it.

Carbon dioxide fire extinguisher

Carbon dioxide is slightly soluble in water and it dissolves to form a weak solution of carbonic acid. Frozen carbon dioxide is called dry ice. When it melts, it becomes a gas and it is used to make clouds in theater productions.

SEE FOR YOURSELF

In this experiment, you can see how carbon dioxide gas prevents fire from burning.

Small jar or bottle

First, light a small tea candle. Then put five tablespoons of vinegar into a small jar or bottle and add half a tablespoon of baking soda.

As the mixture fizzes, hold the mouth of the bottle near the candle, making sure no liquid escapes.

The candle goes out as carbon dioxide gas from the reaction between vinegar (ethanoic acid) and baking soda prevents oxygen from reaching the flame.

AIR POLLUTION

Air pollution is caused by soot and poisonous gases such as carbon monoxide, nitrogen dioxide and sulphur dioxide. Carbon monoxide is formed when fuels burn. Most fuels burn so quickly it is difficult for them to get enough oxygen (see Combustion*), and carbon monoxide (CO) is produced instead of carbon dioxide (CO_2). Carbon monoxide is a very toxic gas that stops the red cells in animals' blood from carrying oxygen.

Carbon monoxide has only one atom of oxygen.

Exhaust fumes from car engines contain carbon monoxide, and nitrogen dioxide which causes acid rain.

Sulphur dioxide is produced by burning fossil fuels, especially coal. Sulphur dioxide is poisonous and causes breathing problems. It also dissolves in rain to make acid rain (see below).

Sulphur dioxide (SO_2)

Particles of soot and dust from industry, and lead compounds from car exhaust fumes, are other forms of pollution that can be breathed in and which settle on plants. Lead used to be added to gasoline to help it burn efficiently, but all cars now must use unleaded gasoline. Lead compounds are nerve poisons that build up in the body and can cause brain damage in young children.

ACID RAIN

Rain is always slightly acidic from dissolved carbon dioxide, but pollutants such as sulphur dioxide and nitrogen dioxide (see above) also make it more acidic. Acid rain corrodes metals and damages stone buildings, and makes the water in rivers and lakes more acidic.

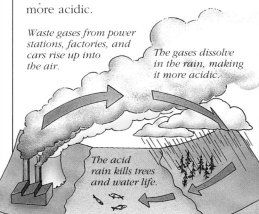

Waste gases from power stations, factories, and cars rise up into the air.

The gases dissolve in the rain, making it more acidic.

The acid rain kills trees and water life.

THE NOBLE GASES

The noble gases are six elements that form group 8 in the periodic table.* They are all very unreactive and are the only elements that exist as single atoms and do not form molecules. Because they are unreactive, several of the noble gases are used for filling the empty space inside light bulbs.

Neon

Argon

All the noble gases can exist as single atoms.

Helium

Xenon has no significant uses but argon is used in electric light bulbs and fluorescent tubes are filled with krypton. Neon emits an orange-red glow when an electric discharge passes through it. It is used with sodium in sodium vapor street lamps, and also in neon lights.*

Neon-filled lights are used for advertisements.

Radon is radioactive and occurs as a result of the radioactive decay of radium, a metal element. Helium is not known to form any compounds and it is thought to be completely unreactive. It is seven times less dense than air, so it is used in airships.

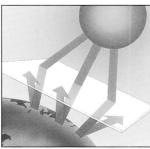

Balloons containing helium carry scientific instruments into the upper atmosphere.

GREENHOUSE EFFECT

This term is used to describe the way that increasing levels of carbon dioxide in the air are causing global warming - a rise in the average temperatures around the world.

Carbon dioxide in the air prevents heat energy from escaping from the Earth in the same way that the glass prevents heat escaping from a greenhouse.

As the carbon dioxide in the air is increasing, more heat is being trapped in the Earth's atmosphere. Even a slight rise in temperature causes the sea level to rise as the water expands, affects winds and weather patterns and melts some of the ice at the ice caps. Scientists believe that if the carbon dioxide increases at its present rate, average temperatures will rise by between 1.5°C and 4°C (3°F and 7°F) in the next fifty years.

*Carbon, 61; Photosynthesis, see Oxidation, 72; Respiration, see Oxidation, 72

*Combustion, 72

*Periodic Table, 55; Neon lights, see Fluorescence, 39

BONDING

The beautiful, symmetrical shapes of ice crystals and the hard, glittery surfaces of a diamond are due to the way the atoms in these substances are bonded together. The properties of a substance, and the way it reacts with other substances, depend on the type of bonds it forms. Bonding is a complicated subject and to understand it, you need a clear idea of the structure of an atom.*

Crystals of ice - the solid form of water

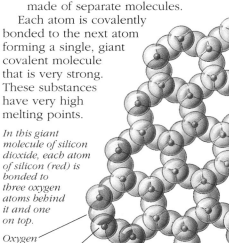

Oxygen atom
Hydrogen atom

The atoms in a molecule of water are held together by covalent bonds.

BONDS AND ATOMIC STRUCTURE

Atoms attempt to bond with other atoms in order to become stable. A stable atom is one that has a full outer energy level, or "shell", of electrons around its nucleus (see Atomic Structure*).

Argon has a full outer shell of electrons. It is stable and is not known to bond with any other atoms. Electrons

Most atoms have several shells of electrons. The first shell can have two electrons and the second and third shells can have eight, although some atoms in compounds can have up to 18 electrons in their third shells. When a shell is full, the electrons begin filling a new energy level. The arrangement of electrons around the nucleus is called the electron configuration.

Electron configuration can be written as numbers after an atom's name.

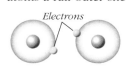

Hydrogen (1)
Fluorine (2,7)
Sodium (2,8,1)

To achieve a full outer shell, an atom may share its electrons with other atoms (covalent and metallic bonding - see right and opposite page) or give or take electrons from another atom (ionic bonding - see opposite page).

This model shows the electrons in the first three shells of an atom. The third shell can have up to 18 electrons. The gaps show where extra electrons would go.

COVALENT BONDING

Covalent bonds are created by atoms sharing electrons. For example, hydrogen atoms have one electron and a molecule of hydrogen is formed when two atoms share their electrons. This gives both atoms a full outer shell.

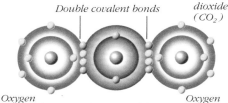

Electrons
Covalent bond
Hydrogen atoms (H)
Hydrogen molecule (H₂)

The atoms in the gas carbon dioxide are also held together by covalent bonds. In this case, each of the atoms shares two electrons with its partner. This is called a double bond.

Double covalent bonds
Carbon dioxide (CO₂)

Oxygen atom (O)
Carbon atom (C)
Oxygen atom (O)

Nonmetal elements, and compounds made only of nonmetals, tend to form covalent bonds. In most covalent compounds the atoms are bonded together in groups called molecules. Although the covalent bonds between the atoms in a molecule are strong, the attraction between the molecules is not so strong. Because of this, covalent substances usually have very low melting and boiling points, and many are liquids or gases at room temperature.

Right: these models represent molecules of water (H₂O). The attraction between the molecules is not as strong as the bonds between the atoms, so water is a liquid at room temperature.

Shell models, like the one on the left, are useful for understanding the chemical behavior of an atom, but atoms do not actually look like this and the positions of the electrons cannot be pinpointed with such accuracy.

As well as having low melting and boiling points, many covalent substances, for example, oil, do not dissolve in water and, apart from graphite, they do not conduct electricity.

Ice is the solid form of water. Heat weakens the attraction between the water molecules and makes the ice melt.

Some covalent elements, such as carbon, and many covalent compounds are not made of separate molecules.

Each atom is covalently bonded to the next atom forming a single, giant covalent molecule that is very strong. These substances have very high melting points.

In this giant molecule of silicon dioxide, each atom of silicon (red) is bonded to three oxygen atoms behind it and one on top.

Oxygen
Silicon

KEY TERMS

Atomic number The number of protons in the nucleus of an atom.
Electron A negatively charged particle that exists around the nucleus of an atom.
Electron configuration The number of electrons that exist in each of the shells around an atom.
Ion An atom (or a molecule) that has lost or gained an electron and is no longer electrically neutral.
Molecule Two or more atoms chemically bonded together to form the smallest particle of a substance.
Proton A positively charged particle in the nucleus of an atom.
Shell A region in which a certain number of electrons can exist around the nucleus of an atom.

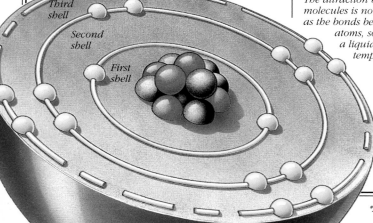

Third shell
Second shell
First shell

Atomic Structure, 4; Atoms and Molecules, 4-5

IONIC BONDING

Ionic bonds are created by atoms giving up or receiving electrons. Compounds made of a metal and a non-metal form ionic bonds. The metal atoms give electrons from their outer shells to the outer shells of the non-metal atoms.

An atom that has gained or lost electrons is called an ion. Ions have an electrical charge as they no longer have an equal number of positively charged protons and negatively charged electrons (see Atomic Structure*).

Sodium cation

An atom that has lost electrons is called a cation and it has a positive charge. Here, sodium is giving chlorine an electron. The sodium cation has a positive charge as it has 11 protons and only 10 electrons.

Electron transfer

Atoms that have gained electrons are called anions. An anion has a negative charge as it has more electrons than protons. The chlorine anion has 17 protons and 18 electrons. It is called a chloride ion.

Chloride anion

The strength of the charge is written after the ion's name. For example, Na^+ shows that sodium has lost an electron, Cl^- shows chlorine has gained an electron and O^{2-} shows oxygen has gained two electrons (electrons have a negative charge).

Ions with opposite charges are pulled toward each other and this creates the ionic bond that holds them together. Ionic compounds are not made up of separate molecules. Instead, all the ions cling together in a regular arrangement called a lattice.

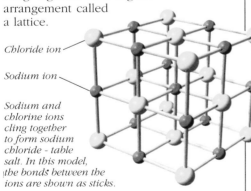

Chloride ion

Sodium ion

Sodium and chlorine ions cling together to form sodium chloride - table salt. In this model, the bonds between the ions are shown as sticks.

The bonds holding the ions together are strong, so ionic compounds have high melting and boiling points, and are solids at room temperature. Most ionic compounds dissolve in water, but not in organic solvents such as oil. When they are dissolved, the ions are free to move, so solutions of ionic compounds are electrolytes - they can conduct electric current (see Electrolysis*).

METALLIC BONDING

Metallic bonding is the type of bonding found in metal elements. The atoms cling together to form a metallic lattice which is a regular arrangement of metal cations (atoms that have lost electrons and so have a positive charge), with free electrons traveling between them. The forces between the electrons and the cations are strong, so most metals have high melting and boiling points, and because the electrons can move, metals can conduct heat and electricity.

Free-moving electrons

Metal cation

VALENCY

The number of electrons an atom needs to gain or lose to form a complete outer shell of electrons is called its combining power, or valency.

Sulphur

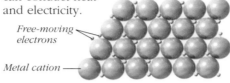

Sulphur needs to gain two electrons. Its valency is 2. Sodium (below) needs to lose one electron. Its valency is 1.

Valencies tend to be related to the position of an element in the periodic table.* For example, all group 1 elements need to lose one electron and have a valency of 1. Group 2 elements need to lose two electrons and have a valency of 2. Elements in groups 5, 6 and 7 (the nonmetals) need to gain electrons and they have valencies of 3, 2 and 1, respectively.

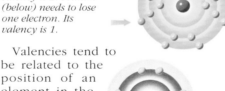

Sodium

Fluorine, in group 7, has seven electrons in its outer shell. It needs to gain one electron to have a full shell so its valency is 1. *Extra electron*

Phosphorus, in group 5, has five electrons in its outer shell and needs to gain 3 to form a full shell, so its valency is 3.

The valency of an ion (see Ionic Bonding) is the same as the strength of its charge. For example, the oxide ion has a negative charge of 2 (O^{2-}) and its valency is 2. Some elements, for example, iron, have two different ions (Fe^{2+} and Fe^{3+}), so they have more than one valency. Roman numerals after an ion's name, e.g. iron (II) and iron (III) indicate the valency.

ALLOTROPES

Some elements can exist in different physical forms because their atoms can bond together in different ways. The different forms are called allotropes. Diamond and graphite are both allotropes of the element carbon.*

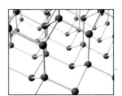

In diamond, each carbon atom is linked to four other carbon atoms and the atoms are packed tightly together. Because of this, diamond is very strong.

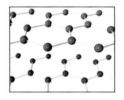

In graphite, each atom of carbon is bonded to three other carbon atoms. The atoms form layers and the bonds between the layers are quite weak, making graphite flaky.

Carbon has a third allotrope, called fullerene, in which 60 carbon atoms are bonded together to make a hollow sphere. Many other elements, for example, phosphorus,* tin and sulphur* also have allotropes.

"Molecular man" was created by scientists at IBM by bonding together 28 molecules of carbon monoxide. Over twenty thousand such "men" holding hands would be only as wide as a human hair.

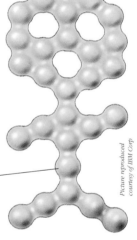

Carbon monoxide molecule with carbon atom in front concealing oxygen atom

Picture reproduced courtesy of IBM Corp

SEE FOR YOURSELF

Can you calculate the electron configurations (see Bonds and Atomic Structure) of these atoms? They all have up to two electrons in the first shell, and up to eight in the second and third shells. Remember, an atom has an equal number of protons and electrons, so the atomic number also shows the number of electrons. See if you can also work out the valencies of these atoms. (Answers on page 96).

Magnesium (atomic number 12)
Argon (atomic number 18)
Nitrogen (atomic number 7)
Potassium (atomic number 19)
Silicon (atomic number 14)

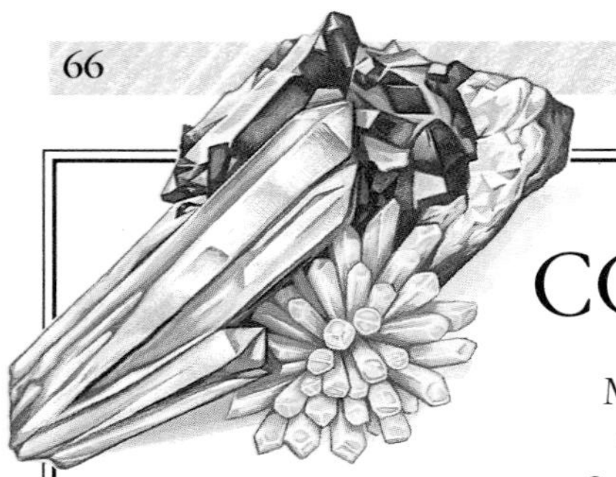

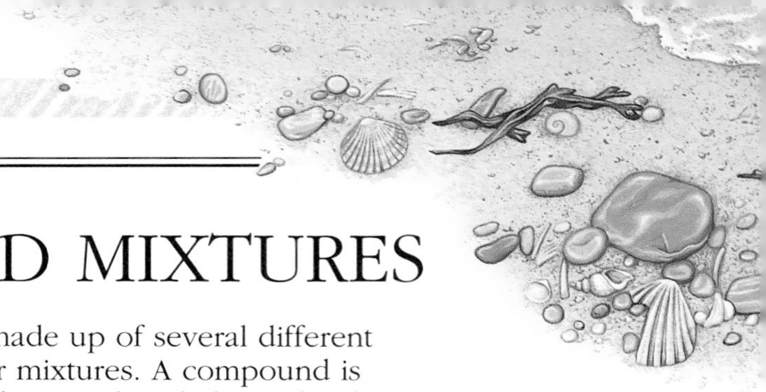

COMPOUNDS AND MIXTURES

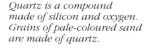

Quartz is a compound made of silicon and oxygen. Grains of pale-coloured sand are made of quartz.

Most of the substances around us are made up of several different elements and are either compounds or mixtures. A compound is a substance that contains two or more elements bonded together by a chemical reaction. In a mixture, such as sea water or the air, the substances exist side by side, but they are not chemically bonded.

The sand on the seashore is a mixture of tiny particles of quartz, seashell and organic matter.

COMPOUNDS

A compound contains atoms from two or more elements bonded* together by a chemical reaction to form a new and different substance.

Carbon dioxide gas is a compound. It is made of atoms of carbon and oxygen bonded together.

Carbon — Oxygen

The elements in a compound cannot be separated by physical means, such as filtering or evaporation, and the compound has different properties from the elements of which it is made.

When a mixture of iron and sulphur is heated, the two elements react together and form a compound called iron sulphide.

Iron and sulphur

After the reaction, the iron and sulphur can no longer be separated. Unlike iron, iron sulphide is not magnetic and unlike powdered sulphur, it sinks in water.

Every sample of a compound contains the same proportions of the elements of which it is made. The chemical formula shows the proportions of the elements in the compound. The formula for iron sulphide is FeS because each atom of iron joins with one atom of sulphur.

KEY TERMS

Atom The smallest particle of an element that still has the chemical properties of that element.
Bond A force that holds two or more atoms together.
Element A substance made up of one kind of atom and which cannot be broken down by a chemical reaction to form simpler substances.
Solution A mixture that consists of a solid dissolved in a liquid.
Solvent The liquid in which a solid substance is dissolved.
Suspension A mixture of solid particles floating in a liquid or gas.

Although there are only just over a hundred different elements, they combine together in many different ways to make at least two million different compound substances.

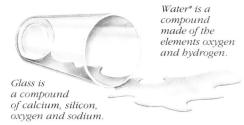

Water* is a compound made of the elements oxygen and hydrogen.

Glass is a compound of calcium, silicon, oxygen and sodium.

Compounds can be organized into groups according to their chemical properties, for example, acids and bases* are separate groups. Compounds can also be classified according to the atoms they contain. For example, hydrides are compounds that contain hydrogen, chlorides contain chlorine and oxides contain oxygen.

This picture shows sodium reacting with chlorine to form a compound called sodium chloride - common salt. Chlorine is a poisonous gas and sodium is a very reactive metal. When they join together to form sodium chloride, they lose these dangerous properties.

Chlorine gas

Cloud of minute pieces of sodium chloride

Sodium

Organic compounds* are compounds that contain the element carbon. Fossil fuels, such as crude oil,* and all living things are made of organic compounds. They are also used in the manufacture of other compounds such as plastics, paints, detergents and medicines.

Before it is cooked, a cake is a mixture of several different compounds, including eggs, flour and fat. When the cake is baked, the ingredients react together to form a different compound - cake.

Salt is a compound called sodium chloride.*

MIXTURES

Most of the natural substances around us are mixtures. They contain different substances (which may be elements or compounds) mixed together without a chemical reaction.

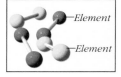

A mixture may contain two or more elements (substances made up of only one type of atom) as shown in this diagram.

— Element
— Element

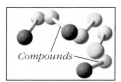

A mixture may contain two or more different compounds, that is, substances made up of different atoms bonded together.

Compounds

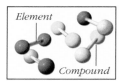

Other mixtures may contain elements and compounds. Air is a mixture of elements, such as oxygen, and compounds such as pollen and soot.

Element

Compound

The ingredients in a mixture are not chemically bonded together and they can usually be separated quite easily. For example, iron can be removed from a mixture of iron filings and sulphur with a magnet. Other methods of separating mixtures are shown opposite.

Iron is magnetic and can be separated from a mixture of iron and sulphur with a magnet.

A mixture may contain any proportion of the substances of which it is made. The substances keep their own properties, and the mixture has all the properties of the substances.

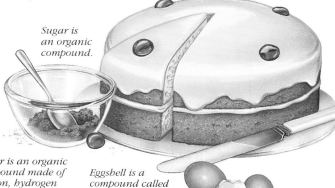

Sugar is an organic compound.

Butter is an organic compound made of carbon, hydrogen and oxygen.

Eggshell is a compound called calcium carbonate.

*Water, 68; Acids, Bases and Alkalis, 74-75; Organic Compounds, 78; Crude Oil, 81; Sodium Chloride, 76

Sea water is a solution of salt (sodium chloride) and water.

TYPES OF MIXTURES

A mixture can be any combination of solids, liquids and gases. For example, air is a mixture of gases and sea water is a mixture of a solid (salt) and a liquid.

Brass is a mixture of two solids: copper and zinc. Mixtures of metals are called alloys.*

A mixture of a solid dissolved in a liquid, such as salt in water, is called a solution. The liquid is called the solvent and the solid is called the solute. A solid that dissolves easily is said to be soluble, while a solid that will not dissolve is insoluble.

Salt is soluble - it dissolves to leave a clear solution.

A mixture of solid particles floating in a liquid or a gas is called a suspension. Blood, milk and smoke are suspensions.

Milk is a suspension of fat particles in water.

Fizzy drinks are a mixture of two liquids, water and flavouring, and a gas, carbon dioxide. The gas makes the fizzy bubbles.

Liquids that mix easily, such as ink and water, are called miscible liquids. Liquids that do not mix easily, such as oil and water, are said to be immiscible. They can be made to mix by adding an emulsifier. The emulsifier makes the oil break up into minute droplets in the water. The resulting liquid is called an emulsion. Mayonnaise is an emulsion of oil and vinegar. *Mayonnaise*
The emulsifier is egg yolk. Emulsion paint is an emulsion of water and droplets of oil and coloured pigment.

Flour, sugar and butter are organic compounds made of carbon, hydrogen and oxygen. Eggs contain carbon, nitrogen, phosphorus, hydrogen, oxygen and sulphur.

Lemon juice is a mixture of citric acid and water.

SEPARATING MIXTURES

Chemists use a number of different methods to separate the substances in a mixture. The method chosen depends on the type of mixture to be separated.

Decantation is a simple method of separating solid particles from a liquid by leaving the particles to settle.

Muddy water contains particles of sand, soil and organic matter that settle in layers at the bottom of the jar.

Filtration is another method of separating solid particles from a liquid. The mixture is poured through a filter that traps the particles and only allows the molecules of liquid to pass through. This method is used in waterworks* as part of the process of creating clean drinking water.

The liquid that passes through the filter is called the filtrate and the solid that remains behind is the residue.

Filter paper traps the residue

Filtrate

Chromatography is used to analyze the substances in a mixture. The mixture is dissolved in a solvent and and a sample of the solution is placed on a piece of filter paper. The different substances in the solution are absorbed at different rates and form bands of colour, called a chromatogram.

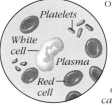

Chromatogram of different chemicals in brown food colouring

Scientists can identify the substances in the sample by comparing their chromatograms with those of known substances. This method can be used to identify the colourings used in foods.

Evaporation is a method of separating a solid from the solution in which it is dissolved. The solution is heated until it boils and the liquid evaporates, leaving the solid behind.

Lemon juice is a solution of citric acid and water. Boiling the juice causes the water to evaporate, leaving solid crystals of citric acid.

Distillation is used to obtain pure solvent, such as water, from a solution. The process is similar to evaporation (see above), except that the evaporated liquid (the solvent) is collected after cooling. The picture belows shows how distilled water is made in a laboratory.

Water evaporates and becomes water vapour.

Solution

Vapour cools and becomes droplets of pure water in test tube.

Spirit burner

Centrifuging separates solid particles from a liquid. The liquid is spun around very quickly in a machine called a centrifuge. This forces the solid particles to the sides of the container and the liquid can be poured or filtered off. A spin-drier is an example of a centrifuge.

Platelets

White cell

Plasma

Red cell

Hospitals use a centrifuge to separate the red blood cells from blood, which is a suspension of platelets and red and white cells in a liquid called plasma.

SEE FOR YOURSELF

You can use chromatography to separate the different coloured chemicals in inks. You need a piece of filter paper or kitchen towel, some water and some felt-tip pens.

1. Put some spots of ink about 3cm (1in) from the bottom of the paper.

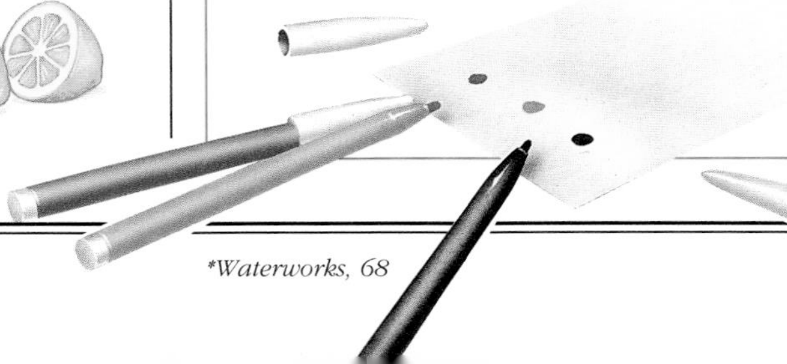

2. Hang the paper over a bowl of water so the water touches the paper but not the ink spots.

3. As the water is absorbed by the paper, it carries the inks with it. Some of the chemicals travel farther up the paper than others, making a chromatogram.

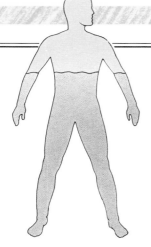

About 65 percent of our bodies is water.

WATER

Water is one of the most common compounds on Earth. As well as the water in rivers and seas, all living things contain water and cannot survive without it. Water is a very good solvent - other substances dissolve easily in it - and blood and plant sap are mainly water. All the water on Earth has existed since the world began and it is continually being recycled between the Earth, the atmosphere and living things.

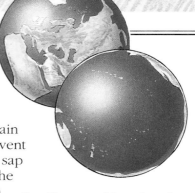

Over 70 percent of the surface of the Earth is covered with water.

WHAT IS WATER?

Water is a compound substance: each molecule of water contains two atoms of hydrogen bonded to an atom of oxygen. The chemical formula for water is H_2O. The chemical name for water is hydrogen oxide and water is formed when hydrogen* burns in air.

A model of a molecule of water

Pure water, that is, water that does not contain any dissolved substances, has a boiling point of 100°C (212°F) and it freezes at 0°C (32°F). If water contains any dissolved substances, the boiling and freezing points change. This is one way of testing whether or not a liquid is pure water.

Pure water that contains no dissolved substances boils at 100°C (212°F) and freezes at 0°C (32°F).

When water boils it forms a gas called water vapor (steam), and when it freezes, it forms a solid called ice. Unlike most other substances, water expands when it freezes, so ice is less dense than water and it floats on the water.

Ice is the solid form of water.

Ice floats because it is less dense than water. Because of this, fish and other creatures can live in the water under the ice in the Arctic.

Ice floe

In polar regions, animals such as these crabeater seals can survive by diving under the ice floes that float on the ocean. They catch fish and other sea creatures to eat.

THE WATER CYCLE

The water in rivers, lakes and seas is continually evaporating and becoming tiny droplets of water vapor in the air. The droplets form clouds and fall again as rain. This is the water cycle.

When vapor in clouds cools, it falls as rain, hail or snow.

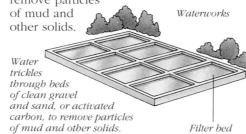

Evaporation

Clouds

Reservoir

Sewage works

Storage reservoir

Waterworks

Houses and factories

Rain water drains into rivers and flows back to the sea.

Water from houses and factories is cleaned in a sewage works before it is pumped back into the sea.

Water from rivers and reservoirs is cleaned in a waterworks and piped to houses and factories.

WATERWORKS

Water that has flowed over the land and through rocks contains impurities that have to be removed in a waterworks. The water is stored in reservoirs to allow solid matter to settle and then, in the waterworks, the water is filtered to remove particles of mud and other solids.

Waterworks

Water trickles through beds of clean gravel and sand, or activated carbon, to remove particles of mud and other solids.

Filter bed

After filtering, the water is treated with chlorine to kill harmful bacteria and then pumped to storage tanks and piped to houses and factories.

Sewage (waste water) should be cleaned before it is pumped back into the sea. In a sewage works, the water is filtered to remove garbage, and then left in sedimentation tanks for the solid particles to settle. Bacteria decompose any remaining organic matter and break it down into harmless substances.

PURIFYING WATER

Water is a good solvent (see right), so it usually contains several different dissolved substances. Pure water can be obtained by distillation (see Separating Mixtures*), but a more efficient method is by deionization. Ions are atoms or molecules that have lost or gained an electron and so have a positive or negative electrical charge.

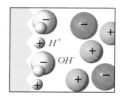

For deionization, a substance called an ion exchange resin has positively charged hydrogen ions (H^+) and negatively charged hydroxide (OH^-) ions clinging to it.

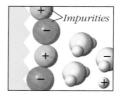

Impurities

When impure water passes through the ion exchange resin, the ions of the impurities are replaced by the hydrogen and hydroxide ions from the resin.

The hydrogen and hydroxide ions combine together to form new droplets of water and the water that trickles out of the resin contains no impurities.

WATER AS A SOLVENT

Water is a very good solvent, that is, many substances dissolve easily in water to form a solution. This is why water is rarely found in a pure state.

Many substances dissolve easily in water.

Water molecules have a slight electrical charge because their hydrogen atoms are grouped together on one side of the molecule. Because of this, ionic compounds (compounds that are made up of ions) dissolve easily in water. Their ions have an electrical charge and they are attracted to the charges on the water molecules.

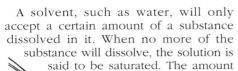

The electrons at this end of the water molecule create a slight negative charge.

The two hydrogen atoms give a slight positive charge at this end.

A solvent, such as water, will only accept a certain amount of a substance dissolved in it. When no more of the substance will dissolve, the solution is said to be saturated. The amount of solid that will dissolve in a liquid usually increases when the liquid is heated.

It is easier to dissolve sugar in a hot drink than in a cold one.

Soft drinks are made by dissolving carbon dioxide gas in water. The amount of gas that can be dissolved in a solution increases when the pressure of the solution is increased. This is why the carbon dioxide bubbles out of soft drinks when you open them and release the pressure. If the solution is heated, though, it can hold less gas.

River and sea water normally contain about 0.04g (0.0014oz) dissolved oxygen gas per 1kg (2.2lb) water. This is enough for plants, fish and other water creatures to live.

HARD WATER

The term "hard" is used to describe water that contains dissolved minerals from the rocks it has flowed over. Soap does not lather well in hard water because the minerals react with the soap to form scum. There are two types of hard water, depending on which minerals it contains.

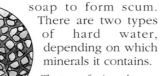

The type of minerals in water depends on the rocks it has flowed over.

Temporary hard water is caused by a chemical reaction between limestone and rainwater. Limestone is made of calcium carbonate, which is insoluble, and rainwater is a weak solution of carbonic acid. The acid reacts with the calcium carbonate to form calcium hydrogen-carbonate which then dissolves in the water, making it hard.

When temporary hard water boils or evaporates, some of the minerals are left behind and can be seen as a chalky deposit inside kettles, and as stalactites and stalagmites in caves.

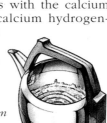

Permanent hard water contains calcium and magnesium compounds from rocks such as gypsum. These minerals cannot be removed by boiling.

SOFTENING WATER

The minerals that make water hard (see above) can be removed by adding washing soda, or by ion exchange, which is similar to deionizing water to purify it (see opposite page).

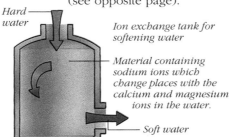

Hard water

Ion exchange tank for softening water

Material containing sodium ions which change places with the calcium and magnesium ions in the water.

Soft water

In an ion exchange tank, hard water containing calcium and magnesium compounds is passed through a material such as zeolite, which is sodium aluminum silicate. In the zeolite, the calcium and magnesium ions are swapped for sodium ions that do not make the water hard.

Washing soda is sodium carbonate. When added to hard water, it reacts with the calcium and magnesium compounds and changes them into insoluble compounds that do not make scum.

WATER POLLUTION

Water pollution is caused by untreated water from houses and factories flowing into rivers and the sea. When water contains a lot of waste, the bacteria that normally exist and break down organic waste matter become very numerous and use up most of the oxygen. The water becomes lifeless, except for harmful bacteria that can survive in water without oxygen.

When the level of dissolved oxygen in the water falls, fish and plants die and the water becomes lifeless.

Pollution is also caused by litter, pesticides and nitrates from fertilizers, and by poisonous substances such as lead and mercury.

Poisonous substances, such as metals, build up in the bodies of fish and may be passed on to other animals and to people. Pesticides kill microorganisms and larger animals and disturb the balance between the living things.

Oxygen in the water can also be used up by excessive plant growth caused when fertilizers from farmland, and detergents that contain phosphates, drain into rivers. The oxygen in the water is used up by the plants and by bacteria that feed on the plants when they die.

KEY TERMS

Atom The smallest particle of an element that still has the chemical properties of that element.

Bond A force that holds two or more atoms together.

Compound A substance made up of two or more elements that are chemically bonded together.

Element A substance made up of one kind of atom and which cannot be broken down by a chemical reaction to form simpler substances.

Insoluble A substance that will not dissolve.

Ion An atom (or a molecule) that has lost or gained an electron and is no longer electrically neutral.

Molecule Two or more atoms chemically bonded together.

Solvent The liquid in which a solid substance is dissolved.

When there is lightning, nitrogen in the air reacts with oxygen to form nitrogen dioxide.

CHEMICAL REACTIONS

Chemical reactions are happening around us all the time - when we digest our food, bake a cake or drive a car. During a chemical reaction, the atoms in the substances (the reactants) are rearranged to form different substances (the products). The way substances react together depends on the elements of which they are made.

Stalactites

Stalagmites

WHAT HAPPENS IN A REACTION

During a chemical reaction, the bonds* between the atoms of the substances are broken. The atoms rearrange themselves and form bonds with new partners. The pictures below show what happens when water and carbon dioxide react together to form carbonic acid.

Each molecule of water (H_2O) is made of two atoms of hydrogen and one atom of oxygen. Carbon dioxide (CO_2) is made of two atoms of oxygen bonded to one atom of carbon.

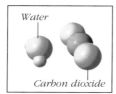

Water

Carbon dioxide

The atoms in the substances separate and combine with each other to form a molecule of carbonic acid, as shown in this equation: $H_2O + CO_2 = H_2CO_3$.

Carbonic acid

Energy* is needed to break bonds and creating new bonds releases energy, so there is always an exchange of energy with the environment during a chemical reaction. This is usually heat energy, although some reactions give off or take in light. A reaction that produces heat is called an exothermic reaction. If heat is taken in, it is an endothermic reaction.

Deep-sea viper fish have luminous cells that give off light as a result of chemical reactions that take place in their cells.

When you exercise, heat energy from chemical reactions in your cells makes you feel hot. They are exothermic reactions.

Most chemical reactions also need a certain amount of energy, usually in the form of heat, to start them off. This makes the molecules in the substances move around so they collide and can react together. The minimum amount of energy needed to start off a reaction is called the activation energy.

Striking a match activates the chemical reaction that takes place when the match burns.

The chemicals on a safety match will only react and burn if they are struck against the red phosphorus on the match box.

TYPES OF REACTIONS

These pictures show examples of some chemical reactions that take place in a laboratory, and others that happen naturally around us.

Copper sulphate solution

When an iron nail is placed in copper sulphate solution, the iron "pushes" the copper out of the solution and replaces it with iron. The copper collects around the nail. This is an example of a reactive element (iron) displacing a less reactive element (copper).

In this reaction, hydrogen peroxide breaks down very easily to form oxygen and water. The reaction can be speeded up by the addition of a catalyst (see opposite) such as manganese dioxide.

Many different chemical reactions take place when food is digested in our intestines. The reactions break down the food to make simpler substances that can be absorbed by the body.

Limestone caves, and stalactites and stalagmites, are formed as a result of a chemical reaction that takes place between the calcium carbonate of which the rock is made, and rainwater that contains dissolved carbon dioxide.

Batteries contain substances (usually zinc, ammonium chloride and manganese dioxide) that react together and produce electrical energy.

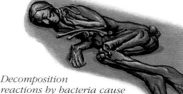

Decomposition reactions by bacteria cause organic matter to rot and decompose - but this 2,000 year old "bog man" was preserved because the bacteria could not survive in the airless mud where he was found.

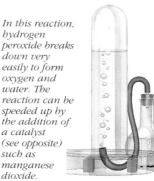

Many deep-sea fish produce light from chemical reactions in their cells as there is no light in the deep water where they live.

When limestone (calcium carbonate) is heated, it breaks down to form calcium oxide (quicklime) and carbon dioxide. This is a thermal decomposition reaction.

Luminous cells

Burning is a chemical reaction called combustion. When wood burns, it combines with oxygen in the air to produce carbon dioxide, water and charcoal or ash.*

Photosynthesis, the process by which plants make their food, is an endothermic reaction - it takes in energy in the form of sunlight.

Rusting is a form of corrosion. Corrosion is a chemical reaction that takes place when metals react with oxygen in the air.*

*Bonding, 64; Energy, 6   *Combustion, 72   *Corrosion, 57

LAW OF CONSERVATION OF MASS

Matter cannot be created or destroyed during a chemical reaction. This is the law of conservation of mass, also called the law of constant composition.

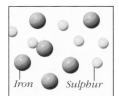 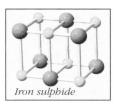

Iron   Sulphur   Iron sulphide

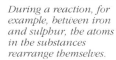

During a reaction, for example, between iron and sulphur, the atoms in the substances rearrange themselves.

After the reaction there are exactly the same number of atoms and therefore the same amount of matter.

CHEMICAL EQUATIONS

Chemical reactions can be written as equations using the chemical formulae* of the substances. In an equation, the substances that react together (the reactants) are written on the left and the products (the substances produced by the reaction) are written on the right.

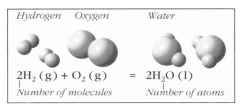

Hydrogen   Oxygen   Water

$$2H_2\,(g) + O_2\,(g) = 2H_2O\,(l)$$

Number of molecules   Number of atoms

This equation and pictures show how hydrogen and oxygen react to form water. Both sides of the equation must have the same number of atoms.

The products and reactants are separated by an arrow or equals sign. If a catalyst is used (see right), it is shown above the arrow. An equation may also show the physical states of the substances (g for gas, l for liquid, s for solid and aq for aqueous, that is, dissolved in water). Because of the law of conservation of mass (see above), both sides of an equation must balance: the reactants and the products must contain the same number of atoms.

KEY TERMS

Catalyst A substance that changes the rate of a chemical reaction, but is itself left unchanged.
Endothermic Used to describe a reaction that takes in energy.
Enzyme A catalyst that speeds up a chemical reaction in living things.
Exothermic Used to describe a reaction that gives off energy.
Products The substances produced as a result of a chemical reaction.
Reactants The substances that react together in a chemical reaction.

RATES OF REACTION

Some chemical reactions, such as rusting, take place slowly over a long period of time. Others, such as the chemical reaction that takes place when gunpowder explodes, are almost instantaneous.

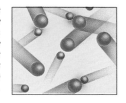

Limestone is slowly eaten away by a reaction between the rock and carbonic acid in rainwater.

The speed of a reaction is affected by the reactivity of the substances - very reactive elements react more quickly than less reactive elements (see Reactivity Series*). During a chemical reaction, the atoms of the substances must come into contact with each other in order to form new bonds, so gases and liquids, in which the molecules are free to move around, are more reactive than solid substances.

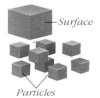

Heating the substances gives them more energy than the minimum needed to start off the reaction. This makes more of the particles move fast enough to collide and react.

Only the molecules on the surface of a solid are able to react with another substance. Grinding the solid into smaller particles increases the surface area and so increases the reaction speed.

— Surface

Particles

Increasing the concentration of a substance also speeds up the chemical reaction. Over the last 20 years, the amount of acid in rain* has increased and is causing more damage to trees and stonework, as shown on the left.

MOLES

Chemists measure chemicals in moles. One mole is 600,000 billion, billion particles. This can be written as 6×10^{23} and it is called the Avogadro number. It is the number of atoms found in a mass of 12g (0.42oz) of carbon-12. A mole of a different element will have a different mass, but the same number of particles. A mole of magnesium has a mass of 24g (0.85oz) because magnesium atoms are larger than carbon atoms.

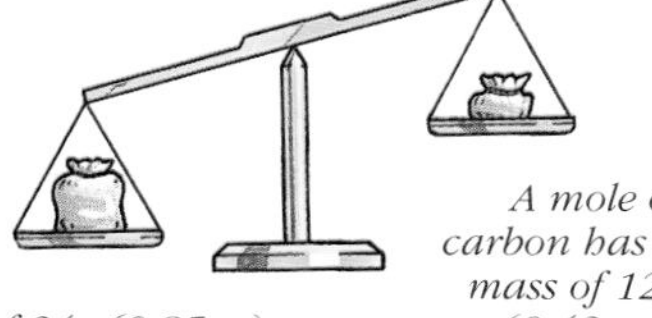

A mole of magnesium has a mass of 24g (0.85oz).

A mole of carbon has a mass of 12g (0.42 oz).

CATALYSTS

Catalysts are substances that can change the rate of a chemical reaction, but are themselves left unchanged. Some catalysts speed up reactions while others, called inhibitors, slow them down. Chemical reactions that take place in living things are speeded up by catalysts called enzymes.

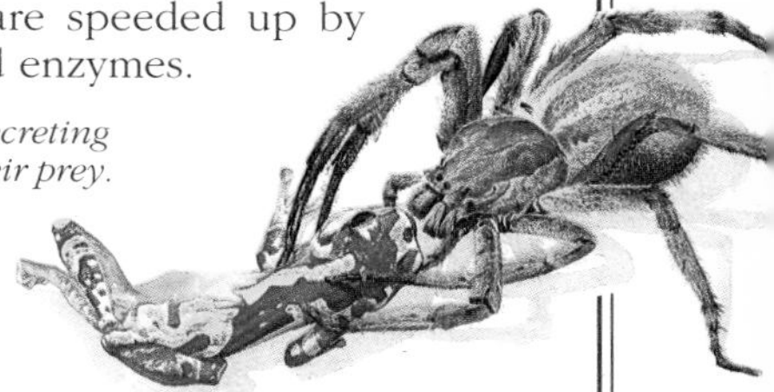

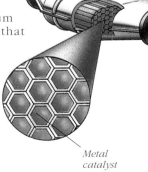

Spiders feed by secreting enzymes onto their prey. The enzymes speed up chemical reactions that break down the food.

Catalysts work by lowering the activation energy of a reaction, that is, the minimum amount of energy needed to set off the reaction (see What Happens in a Reaction). They make it easier for the reaction to take place. A catalyst is not a special substance, but one that assumes a particular role in a reaction. Metals are often used as catalysts. Catalytic converters, which remove toxic gases from car exhausts, contain two metals, platinum and rhodium, that act as catalysts.

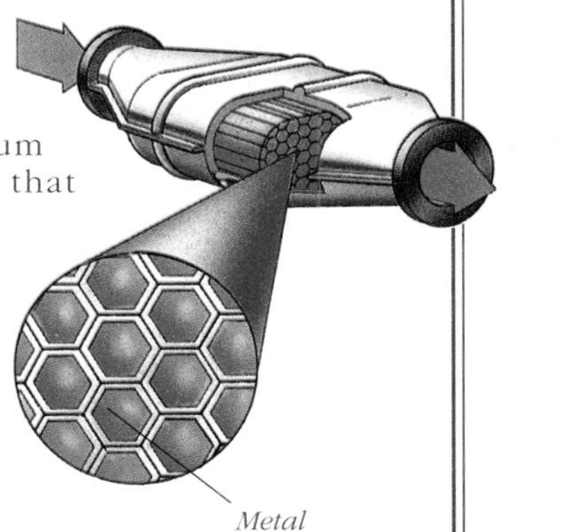

In a catalytic converter, toxic carbon monoxide and hydro-carbons cling to the metals and react together to form carbon dioxide and water.

Metal catalyst

Enzymes, and many other catalysts, are action specific. Each speeds up only one type of reaction. Many different enzymes in the digestive system of animals, such as the spider shown above, help speed up the chemical reactions that break complex foods into simpler substances.

Scientists believe that the increase in the size of the hole in the layer of ozone in the upper atmosphere around the Earth is being speeded up by chlorine* acting as a catalyst for the breakdown of oxygen*(O_2) to ozone (O). The chlorine comes from the decomposition of chemicals known as chlorofluorocarbons (CFCs).

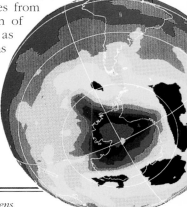

The hole in the ozone layer (shown red in this satellite picture) allows the Sun's harmful ultraviolet rays to reach the Earth.

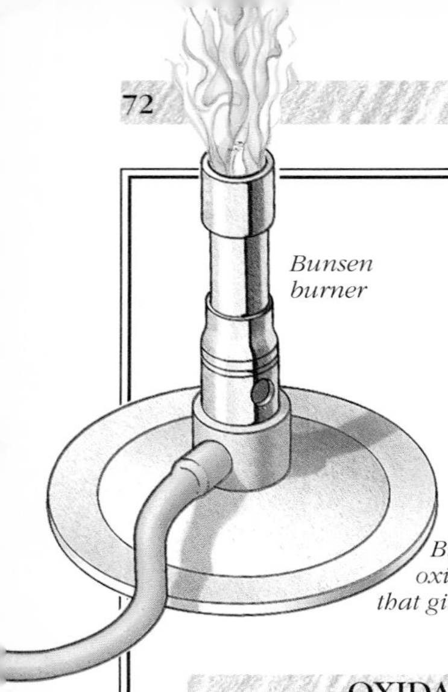

Bunsen burner

OXIDATION AND REDUCTION

Oxidation and reduction are processes that take place during certain types of chemical reactions.* During oxidation, a substance combines with oxygen, or loses hydrogen or electrons. When wood or gas burns, fireworks explode, or a car's engine is running, oxidation is taking place. Reduction is the opposite of oxidation. During reduction, a substance loses oxygen or gains hydrogen or electrons.

Burning is an oxidation reaction that gives off heat and light.

Oxidation reactions in the body produce energy.

OXIDATION

The term oxidation was originally used to describe chemical reactions in which a substance combines with oxygen to form a compound called an oxide. For example, when iron is exposed to air and water, it forms a compound called iron oxide, the chemical term for rust.

Rusting, and other forms of corrosion, are oxidation reactions.*

Iron   Water   Oxygen   Rust

Oxidation also describes reactions in which substances lose hydrogen or electrons. For example, when magnesium and chlorine combine to form magnesium chloride ($MgCl_2$), magnesium loses two electrons (see Ionic Bonding*) and is said to be oxidized.

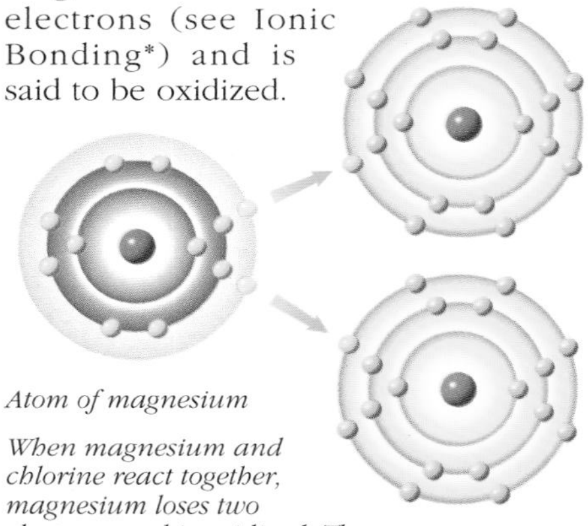

Atom of magnesium

When magnesium and chlorine react together, magnesium loses two electrons and is oxidized. The transfer of electrons creates an ionic bond between the atoms.*

Two atoms of chlorine

Respiration, the process by which animals and plants break down food to release energy, is an oxidation reaction. In fact, it is a slow form of combustion (see right). This is the equation for respiration: $C_6H_{12}O_6 + 6O_2 = 6CO_2 + 6H_2O$.

Animals absorb oxygen from the air they breathe. The oxygen oxidizes glucose ($C_6H_{12}O_6$) in their cells to give energy, water and carbon dioxide.

COMBUSTION

Combustion is the scientific term for burning. It is an oxidation reaction that gives off energy in the form of heat. When a substance burns, it combines with oxygen and forms a compound called an oxide. Most fuels, for example, gasoline and wood, contain hydrogen and carbon and produce water and carbon dioxide when they burn.

When fuels containing hydrogen and carbon burn, the hydrogen and carbon combine with oxygen in the air to form carbon dioxide and hydrogen oxide (water).

Because we now burn so much fuel for energy, the level of carbon dioxide in the air is increasing and may be causing changes in the weather (see Greenhouse Effect*).

Gas burning inside a motorcycle's engine is another example of combustion, called internal combustion.

Exhaust fumes contain carbon dioxide.

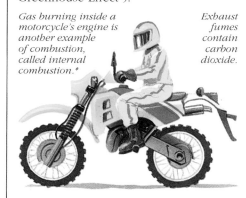

KEY TERMS

Combustion The scientific term for all forms of burning.
Electron A negatively charged particle that exists around the nucleus of an atom.
Oxide A compound made up of an element bonded with oxygen.

REDUCTION

Reduction is a chemical reaction in which a substance loses oxygen - or gains hydrogen or electrons. Reduction is the opposite of oxidation and it occurs at the same time as oxidation.

When copper oxide (a compound of copper and oxygen) reacts with carbon, the carbon pulls the oxygen away from the copper oxide, as shown below.

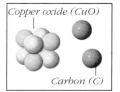

Copper oxide (CuO)
Carbon (C)

The carbon reduces the copper oxide to pure copper, and the copper oxide oxidizes the carbon to form carbon dioxide: $2CuO + C = CO_2 + 2Cu$.

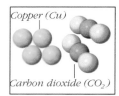

Copper (Cu)
Carbon dioxide (CO_2)

If one substance (the oxidizing agent) loses oxygen, another substance (the reducing agent) must gain it. This process is called the redox reaction. Smelting, the method by which iron* is extracted from its ore in a blast furnace, is a reduction reaction.

Iron ore is a compound of iron and oxygen. During smelting, carbon is used as a reducing agent to pull the oxygen from the iron.

Photosynthesis, the process by which plants make their food, is also a reduction reaction. In photosynthesis, plants build glucose ($C_6H_{12}O_6$) from carbon dioxide and water, using energy from sunlight. Photosynthesis is the opposite of respiration (see far left). This is the equation for photosynthesis: $6CO_2 + 6H_2O = C_6H_{12}O_6 + 6O_2$.

When they are photosynthesizing, trees and other plants produce oxygen. They use some for respiration (see far left) and the rest goes back into the air.

*Corrosion, 57; Ionic Bonding, 65   *Chemical Reactions, 70; Internal Combustion, 28; Greenhouse Effect, 63   *Iron and Steel, 58

ELECTROLYSIS

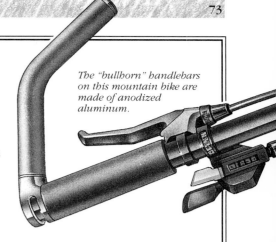

The "bullhorn" handlebars on this mountain bike are made of anodized aluminum.

Electrolysis is a method of separating the elements in a compound by passing an electric current through the compound when it is molten or in a solution. Electrolysis has many industrial uses. It is used to separate very reactive metals from their ores, to purify metals, and also to plate objects with a thin coating of metal.

The metal front of this guitar has been plated with chrome by electrolysis.

HOW ELECTROLYSIS WORKS

Only ionic compounds (compounds held together by ionic bonds*) can conduct electricity during electrolysis. This is because the atoms in these substances have lost or gained electrons and become ions - particles that have an electrical charge.

When an ionic compound, such as copper chloride, is in solution, the ions are free to move. Copper chloride has positively charged copper ions and negatively charged chloride ions.

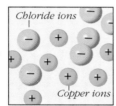

Chloride ions
Copper ions

Electrodes carry the current to the solution, which is called the electrolyte. The cathode is the electrode with a negative electrical charge and the anode has a positive charge.

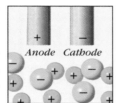

Anode   Cathode

Because opposite charges attract each other, the negatively charged ions in the electrolyte move toward the anode and the positively charged ions move toward the cathode.

During electrolysis, the ions of each of the elements collect around different electrodes and so the elements in the solution are separated.

ELECTROPLATING

Electroplating uses electrolysis to cover objects with a thin layer of metal. The object that is to be plated is used as an electrode (see How Electrolysis Works) and during electrolysis, it becomes coated with metal from the electrolyte.

Electroplating is used to protect cheap, but reactive metals with a layer of less reactive metal. For example, steel is plated with tin or chromium to protect it.

Steel food cans are plated with a very fine layer of tin.

ELECTROREFINING

This is a method of purifying metals by electrolysis. To purify copper, impure copper is used as an anode and the cathode is pure copper. The electrolyte is a solution of copper sulphate. Positively charged electrons from the impure copper anode collect around the cathode and form copper ions.

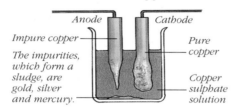

Anode   Cathode
Impure copper
Pure copper
The impurities, which form a sludge, are gold, silver and mercury.
Copper sulphate solution

METAL EXTRACTION

Very reactive metals, such as sodium and aluminum, are extracted by electrolysis. Aluminum is mined as bauxite, which is mainly aluminum oxide. For electrolysis, the aluminum oxide is dissolved in cryolite to help it melt. The tank is lined with carbon, which forms the cathode. Aluminum ions are attracted to the cathode and become atoms of molten aluminum.

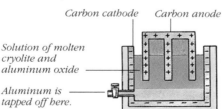

Carbon cathode   Carbon anode
Solution of molten cryolite and aluminum oxide
Aluminum is tapped off here.

KEY TERMS

Anode   In electrolysis, the electrode with a positive charge.
Cathode   In electrolysis, the electrode with a negative charge.
Electrode   A piece of metal, or other substance, that carries the current to an electrolyte.
Electrolyte   A solution or molten substance that conducts electricity.
Ion   An atom (or a molecule) that has lost or gained an electron and is no longer electrically neutral.

ANODIZING

Electrolysis can be used to coat a metal, such as aluminum, with a thin layer of its oxide (the compound it forms when it reacts with oxygen). This is called anodizing. The oxide forms a protective layer that prevents the metal from further corrosion.*

The aluminum object is used as the anode and placed in a solution of sulphuric acid, which is the electrolyte. Oxide ions from the acid collect at the anode and they react with the aluminum to form a layer of aluminum oxide. The oxide can later be dyed.

Anodized aluminum camping flasks

SEE FOR YOURSELF

You can use electrolysis to split water,* which is a compound of hydrogen and oxygen, into bubbles of hydrogen and oxygen gas. Set up the equipment* as shown here.

Pencils sharpened at both ends
Wire must touch pencil leads.
Paper to support pencils.
Tap water
4.5 volt battery

Impurities in the water conduct electricity between the pencil leads. Bubbles of hydrogen form on the pencil connected to the negative battery terminal because hydrogen forms positive ions. The bubbles on the other pencil are oxygen. There are more hydrogen bubbles because each molecule of water (H_2O) contains two atoms of hydrogen and one oxygen atom.

*Ionic Bonding, 65

*Corrosion, 57; Water, 68; Setting up Experiments, 96

ACIDS, BASES AND ALKALIS

The word acid comes from the Latin word *acer*, which means "sour". Some of the sour substances that we eat, for example, vinegar and lemon juice, are acids. A base is the chemical opposite of an acid, and when a base is mixed with an acid, it produces a neutral substance called a salt.* Bases that are soluble in water are called alkalis.

The poison in a bee's sting is an acid. It can be neutralized with soap - a base.

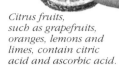

Citrus fruits, such as grapefruits, oranges, lemons and limes, contain citric acid and ascorbic acid.

ACIDS

Acids are compounds that contain hydrogen and which dissolve in water to produce hydrogen ions (H+). Ions are particles that have an electrical charge (see Ionic Bonding*). The ions give acids their special properties, but they only exist in solution, so an acid only displays its properties when it is dissolved.

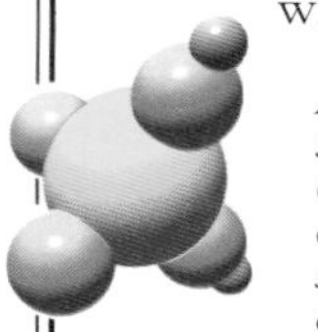

A molecule of sulphuric acid (H_2SO_4) is made of hydrogen, sulphur and oxygen.

Hydrochloric acid (HCl) is made from hydrogen and chlorine.

A strong acid is one in which most of the molecules separate to form a large number of hydrogen ions when it is in solution. Hydrochloric, sulphuric and nitric acid are all strong acids. The strength of an acid is measured in pH numbers, which stands for "power of hydrogen" (see right). Strong acids are very corrosive, that is, they burn away the surface of an object, or the skin.

The containers of strong acids are marked with the international warning symbols shown here, which mean harmful (left) and corrosive (right).

Acids, such as citric acid and ethanoic acid, that are produced by living things are called organic acids.* Acids are important in the chemical industry and in the manufacture of food, synthetic fibers and medicines.

Tomatoes contain an organic acid called salicylic acid.

Vinegar, which is made from grapes, contains a weak acid called ethanoic or acetic acid (see Organic Acids).*

The colorful markings on the skin of sea slugs contain distasteful acids that discourage predators from eating them.

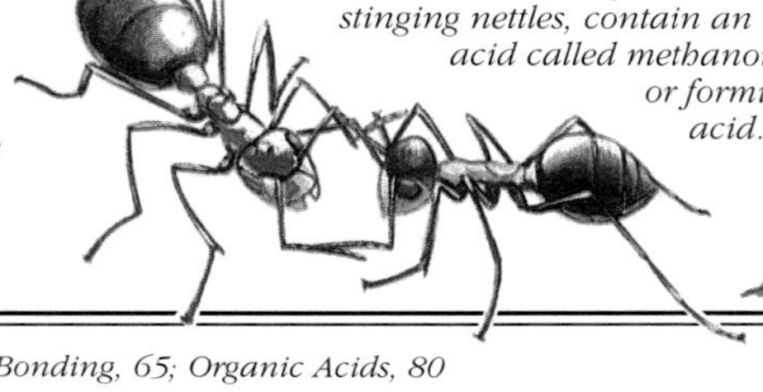

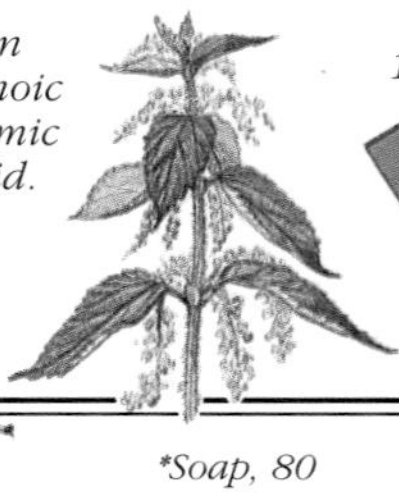

In chemistry, acids are known for the way they react with other substances. For example, acids react with bases to form a neutral substance called a salt* and water, and they react with most metals to form salts and hydrogen gas. They also react with carbonates to give a salt, carbon dioxide gas and water. Baking powder, which is used in cake-making, contains a type of carbonate called sodium hydrogen carbonate, and tartaric acid.

When liquid is added to a cake mixture containing baking powder, the acid and carbonate in the baking powder react to produce bubbles of carbon dioxide that help the cake to rise.

BASES AND ALKALIS

A base is the chemical opposite of an acid and a base that can dissolve in water is called an alkali. When a base is mixed with an acid, it neutralizes (cancels out) the properties of the acid and the reaction produces a salt.*

Toothpaste is a base that neutralizes the acids produced by food in your mouth.

Household liquid cleaners contain alkalis that dissolve dirt.

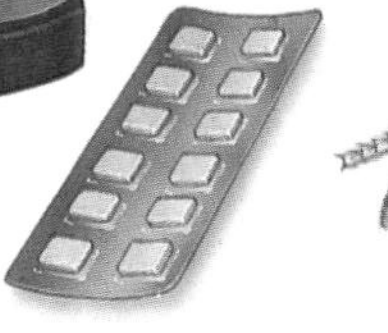

Indigestion tablets (below) contain alkalis that neutralize the acid produced by indigestion.

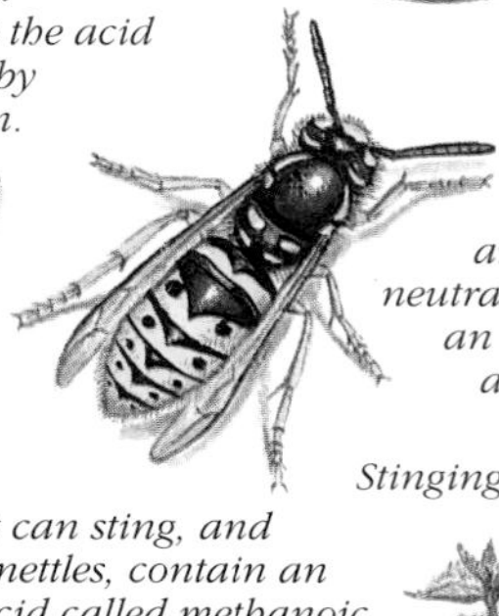

A wasp's sting contains an alkali and can be neutralized with an acid such as vinegar.

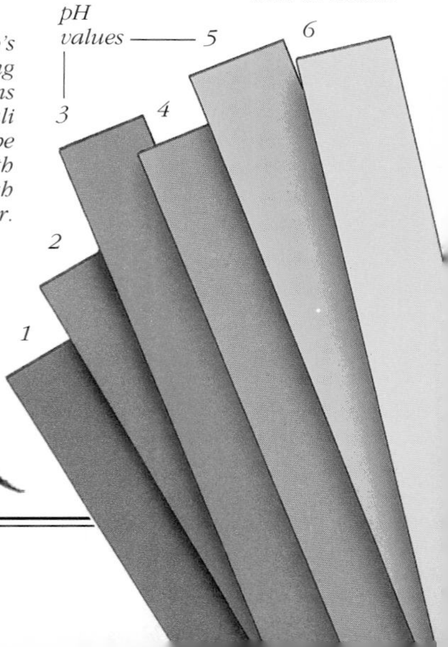

Stinging nettle

Ants that can sting, and stinging nettles, contain an acid called methanoic or formic acid.

In chemical terms, bases are substances that can accept the hydrogen ions (H+) of an acid (see left). The oxide ion (O^{2-}) and the hydroxide ion (OH-) are able to combine with the H+ ions in acids, so metal oxides, such as magnesium oxide, and metal hydroxides, such as sodium hydroxide (caustic soda), are bases.

Sodium hydroxide (NaOH) is made from sodium, oxygen and hydrogen.

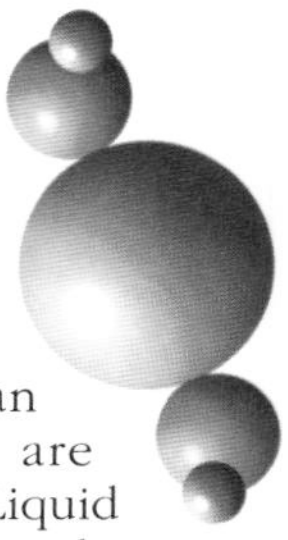

Magnesium hydroxide ($Mg(OH)_2$) is made from magnesium, oxygen and hydrogen.

Many bases and alkalis can be very dangerous as they are caustic (dissolve the flesh). Liquid floor cleaners contain alkalis, such as ammonium hydroxide, that dissolve dirt. Sodium hydroxide is used in paper-making to dissolve the resin in wood and leave the natural fibers of cellulose that are used to make paper.

This photograph shows sheets of paper being lifted out of a tank of sodium hydroxide.

The alkali sodium hydroxide (caustic soda) is used to make oven cleaners, and sodium hydroxide and potassium hydroxide are used to make soap.*

Soap is a base made by reacting an alkali with the acids in vegetable fats.

Below: strips of paper dyed with indicator for testing the strength of an acid or alkali.

pH values —— 5

6

3

4

2

1

*Salts, 76; Ionic Bonding, 65; Organic Acids, 80

*Soap, 80

pH VALUES AND INDICATORS

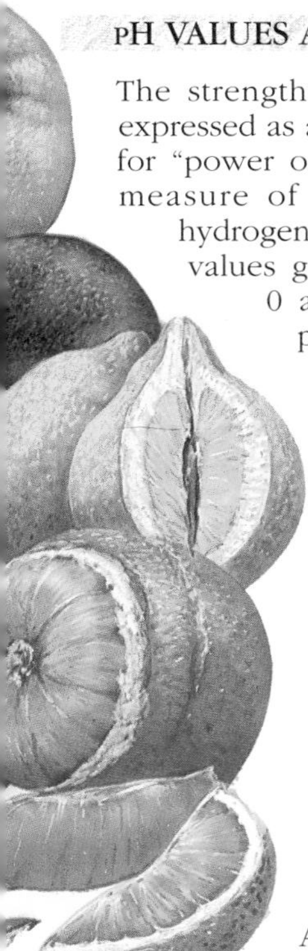

The strength of an acid or base is expressed as a pH number. pH stands for "power of hydrogen" and it is a measure of the concentration of hydrogen ions in a solution. pH values generally range between 0 and 14. The lower the pH number, the greater the concentration of hydrogen ions. A solution with a pH value of less than 7 is an acid.

Orange juice has a pH value of 4, so it is an acid.

Substances with a pH value of 7 are neutral and those with pH values higher than 7 are bases or alkalis.

The pH number of an acid or an alkali can be found with an indicator. An indicator is a substance whose colour changes when it is placed in an acid or an alkali. One indicator, called litmus, turns red in an acid and blue in an alkali.

Blue litmus paper
Acid
Red litmus paper
Alkali

Acids turn blue litmus paper red and alkalis turn red litmus paper blue or purple.

Litmus is an extract of plant-like organisms called lichens. Other plants, for example, hydrangeas (see right) and red cabbage, are also natural indicators.

Another indicator, called universal indicator, is a mixture of several different dyes that change colour according to the pH scale as shown in the picture below.

Universal indicator changes colour according to the pH value of a solution. It turns red, orange or yellow in an acid, green or yellow in a neutral substance and blue or purple in an alkali. The numbers beside each colour show the pH value.

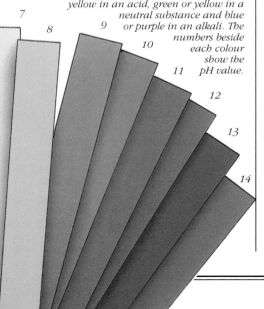

7
8
9
10
11
12
13
14

SULPHURIC ACID

Sulphuric acid is an important chemical used in many different industries, the most important of which is the production of superphosphates and ammonium sulphate for fertilizers. It is also used in the manufacture of synthetic fibres such as rayon, dyes, plastics, drugs, explosives and detergents, and in car batteries.

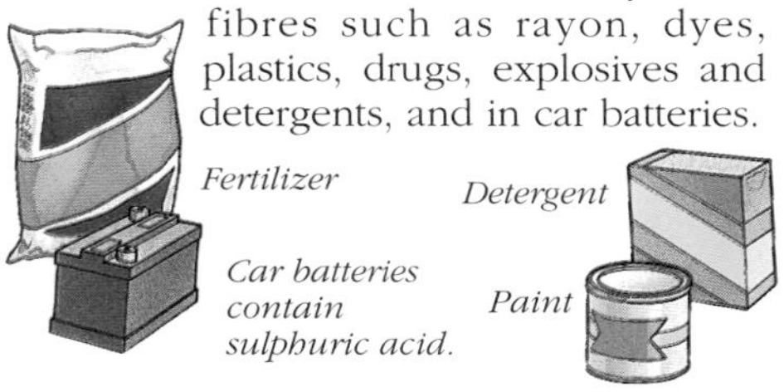

Fertilizer
Detergent
Car batteries contain sulphuric acid.
Paint

Sulphuric acid was originally called a mineral acid, because it is made from sulphur,* an element found as a mineral in the Earth's crust.

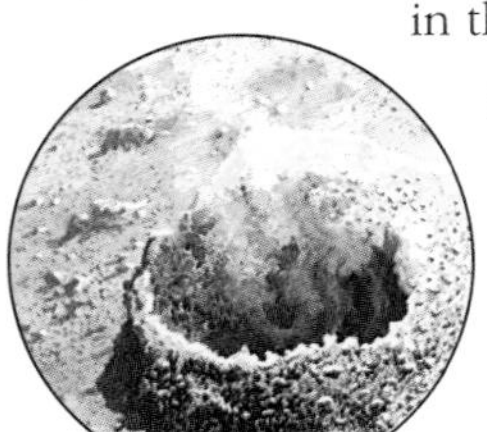

Yellow crystals of sulphur around the vent of a volcano. Sulphur is mainly found in volcanic areas.

Sulphuric acid is very reactive and highly corrosive. It produces a large amount of heat when dissolved in water and must always be added to the water, not the other way around. This way, the acid is rapidly diluted and the heat is absorbed by the water. It is a powerful oxidizing agent, that is, it gives oxygen to other substances during oxidation reactions.* It is also a dehydrating agent, which means that it removes water that is chemically combined in another substance (see Water of Crystallization*).

Sugar
Sulphuric acid H_2SO_4
Carbon Water

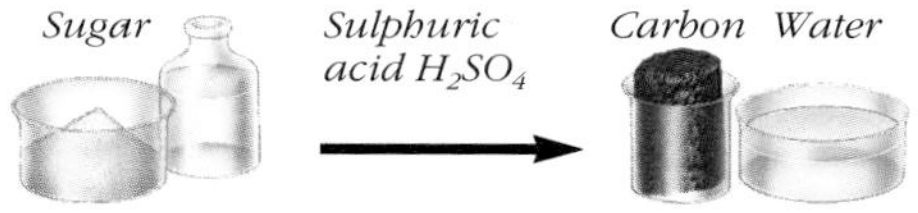

When sugar ($C_{12}H_{22}O_{11}$) is warmed with concentrated sulphuric acid, the acid removes water from the sugar, leaving a foamy mass of black carbon ($12C$) and water ($11H_2O$).

KEY TERMS

Compound A substance made up of two or more elements that are chemically bonded together.

Indicator A substance that changes colour in the presence of an acid or an alkali.

Ion An atom (or a molecule) that has lost or gained an electron and is no longer electrically neutral.

Neutralization The chemical reaction between an acid and a base that produces a salt.

Salt A neutral substance that is neither an acid nor a base.

ACIDS IN THE SOIL

The acidity of the soil depends on the type of rocks from which it is formed and the plants that grow in it. In chalk or limestone areas, the soil is usually alkaline, but in moorlands, sandstone and forested areas, it is more acidic. Acid rain* also adds to the acidity of the soil. Neutral or slightly acid soils with pH values of 6.5 to 7.0 (see left) are the best for farming.

When leaves die and decompose, they form an organic acid called humic acid that adds to the acidity of the soil.

In areas where the soil is too acidic, it is improved by adding powdered limestone or slaked lime (calcium hydroxide), which are bases that neutralize (cancel out) the acidity.

Tractor adding lime to the soil to make it less acidic

Some plants, such as rhododendrons and azaleas, grow well in acid soil and some, such as hydrangeas, have blue flowers in acid soils and pink ones in alkaline soils.

Hydrangeas are natural indicators (see left). They have blue flowers in acid soils and pink ones in alkaline soils.

SEE FOR YOURSELF

This experiment shows how acidic your rain is.* First you need to make an indicator (see left) from red cabbage. Chop three large cabbage leaves and boil them in 0.5l (1pint) of water for ten minutes. Cool, strain and pour a little of this indicator into three jars. Add half a teaspoon of bicarbonate of soda to one jar, some vinegar to another jar and some rainwater to the third jar.

Bicarbonate, an alkali, turns the indicator blue/green.

Compare the colour of the rainwater jar to the other two jars.

Vinegar, an acid, turns the indicator pink.

The cabbage-water will turn pink for an acid and green for an alkali.

*Sulphur, 61; Oxidation, 72; Water of Crystallization, 77; Acid Rain, 63

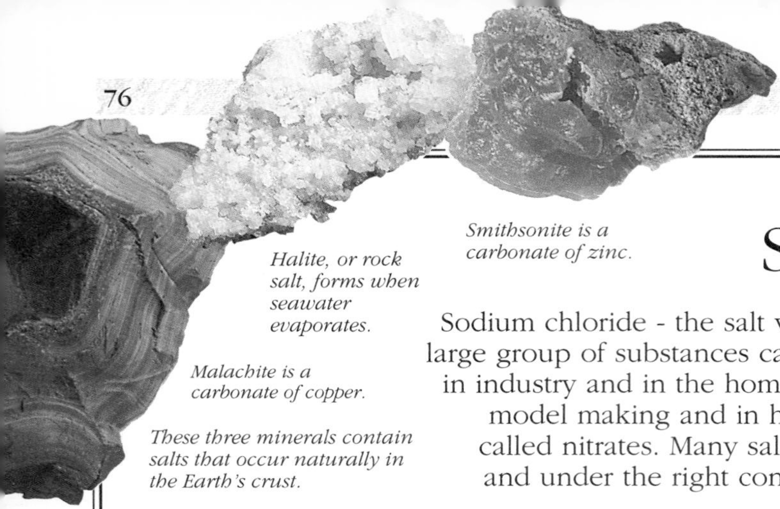

Halite, or rock salt, forms when seawater evaporates.

Malachite is a carbonate of copper.

These three minerals contain salts that occur naturally in the Earth's crust.

Smithsonite is a carbonate of zinc.

SALTS

Sodium chloride - the salt we eat with our food - is just one of a large group of substances called salts that have many different uses in industry and in the home. Plaster of Paris is used in decorating, model making and in hospitals, and fertilizers contain salts called nitrates. Many salts occur naturally in the Earth's crust and under the right conditions, they form beautiful crystals.

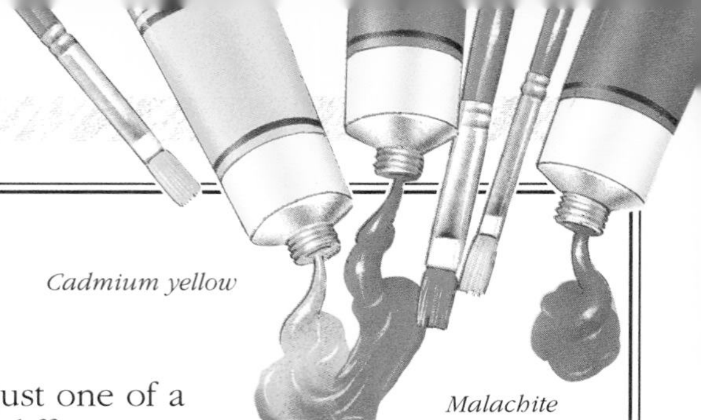

Cadmium yellow

Malachite green

Vermilion red

The salts vermilion, cadmium sulphide, and malachite are used to make artists' colors.

WHAT IS A SALT?

In chemical terms, compounds made of a metal and a nonmetal bonded together are salts. They are ionic compounds, that is, they are made up of ions (particles with an electric charge) held together by ionic bonds.*

Sodium chloride, or common salt, is an ionic compound made of sodium, a metal, and chlorine, a non-metal.

Salts are made when the hydrogen ions in an acid are replaced by a metal. They are neutral substances, that is, they are neither acidic nor alkaline (see Acids, Bases and Alkalis*) and one way to make a salt is by mixing an acid with an alkali.

Hydrochloric acid and sodium hydroxide (an alkali) react together to form sodium chloride, a salt. The solutions have been colored with litmus to show whether they are acidic, alkaline, or neutral.

Sodium chloride

There are several "families" of salts made with different acids. Sulphates are made with sulphuric acid, chlorides are made with hydrochloric acid, nitrates are made with nitric acid and carbonates with carbonic acid.

Bath salts and washing soda are sodium carbonate. They react with magnesium and calcium salts in hard water to form insoluble particles of calcium carbonate.*

Soluble salts are those, such as washing soda, that dissolve in water to form a solution.
Insoluble salts are ones that do not dissolve in water. Limestone and chalk are made of calcium carbonate, which is an insoluble salt.

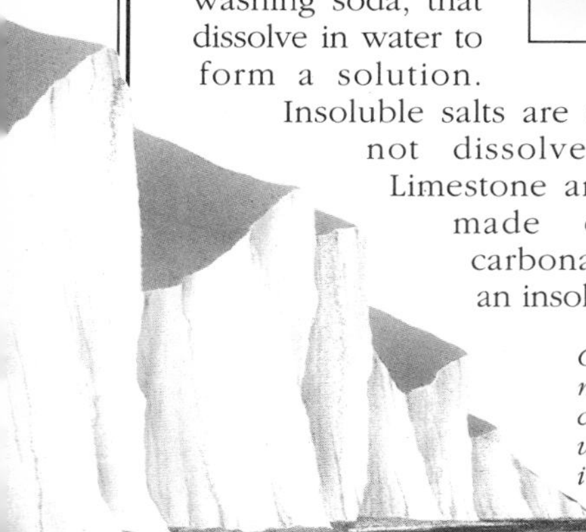

Chalk cliffs are made of calcium carbonate, which is an insoluble salt.

MAKING SALTS

There are several ways of making salts in the laboratory. Soluble salts can be made by the reaction between an acid and a metal, or metal oxide (a base).

Copper sulphate is made by adding copper oxide to dilute sulphuric acid. Excess copper oxide is added to make sure the acid is used up.

Copper oxide

The mixture is then filtered to remove excess copper oxide. The filtrate is a solution of copper sulphate.

Filtrate

The solution is heated to remove excess water, then left to form crystals of copper sulphate.

Insoluble salts are made from two soluble salts that react together to form a precipitate (solid particles of salt) in a solution. The solution is then filtered to remove the precipitate.
Salts can also be made by combining two elements. For example, iron sulphide is made by heating iron with sulphur (see Compounds*).

The picture on the right shows plaster of Paris, a salt that sets hard when it is mixed with water, being used to make a cast of an animal track. Plaster of Paris is also used for setting broken limbs.

KEY TERMS

Acid A compound that forms hydrogen ions when it dissolves in water.
Akali A base (see below) that is soluble in water.
Base A substance that can accept the hydrogen ions of an acid.
Precipitate An insoluble solid that separates from a solution during a chemical reaction.

FERTILIZERS

Many fertilizers contain salts, such as nitrates, phosphates and potash, that are soluble in water and can be absorbed by plants' roots. The salts contain elements, such as nitrogen and phosphorus, that are essential for healthy plant growth.

Left: a plant with small, pale leaves due to nitrogen deficiency. Right: a healthy plant.

Nitrates contain nitrogen, phosphates contain phosphorus and potash contains potassium salts, all of which are needed for healthy plant growth.

SODIUM CHLORIDE

Sodium chloride is the chemical name for common salt. It is a soluble salt and a strong solution of sodium chloride in water is called brine.

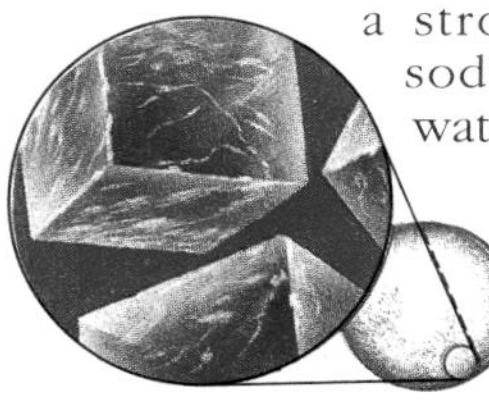

If you look closely at salt, you can see the crystals of which it is made.

Salt can be extracted by evaporation from seawater, and it is also found in solid form as rock salt or halite (see above). It is used to flavor and preserve food and is essential to animal life, although too much salt can be harmful.

Reptiles, such as lizards, that live in deserts and do not drink much water, have special glands to excrete salt.

Salt is an important raw material and it is used in the manufacture of hydrochloric acid, chlorine, sodium hydroxide (caustic soda) and sodium carbonate (washing soda). It is sprinkled on roads in winter to lower the freezing point of water and stop ice from forming.

When one liter (1.75 pints) of seawater evaporates, about 35g (1.25oz) of salts are left behind, most of which is sodium chloride.

*Ionic Bonding, 65; Acids, Bases and Alkalis, 74-75; Hard Water, 69; Compounds, 66

CRYSTALS

Amethyst crystals form from the mineral quartz.

Gemstones are crystals that have been cut along their cleavage planes.

When allowed to form slowly, salts, and many other substances, form crystals. A crystal is a solid that has a definite geometrical shape with straight edges and flat surfaces. Most solids, even metals, are made up of crystals but they are so small you cannot see them. Many of the minerals in the Earth's crust form crystals, for example, diamonds and emeralds.

Uncut natural emerald in limestone

The world's largest cut diamond, the "Star of Africa", in the British Royal Sceptre.

HOW CRYSTALS FORM

Some substances form crystals as they cool and solidify. Others crystallize when the water in which they were dissolved evaporates. The shape of the crystals depends on the regular arrangement and bonding* of the particles in the substance. Different substances form different shaped crystals and the main crystal shapes are shown in the picture

Calcite forms rhombohedral crystals.

Cubic

Tetragonal

Crystals of apatite, the substance of which teeth are made.

Monoclinic

Quartz crystal

Rhombohedral

Hexagonal

Crystals split along their cleavage planes, leaving the flat surfaces of the crystal. The cleavage planes are the boundaries between the particles in the crystal. If a crystal is not split along its cleavage plane, it will shatter.

Light shining through a calcite crystal is refracted (bent). This creates a double image of an object seen through the crystal.

LIQUID CRYSTAL DISPLAYS

Liquid crystals are crystals that, when they are heated, change color and become cloudy liquids before they become true liquids. They are used in displays in watches and calculators. When an electric voltage is placed across the crystals, their molecules line up and block the light, creating the pattern of the display.

This digital cassette player has a liquid crystal display that shows which track is playing.

WATER OF CRYSTALLIZATION

When water combines and chemically bonds with another substance it is called water of crystallization. Many salts (see opposite page) combine with water to form crystals.

If you heat washing soda crystals, the water of crystallization separates to form a solution of washing soda.

In a crystal, the water is chemically bonded with the atoms of the substance, unlike in a solution when the atoms of the substance are mixed but not bonded with the molecules of water.

Copper sulphate solution ($CuSO_4$) becomes $CuSO_4.5H_2O$ when it bonds with water and forms crystals.

When water combines with another substance the substance is said to be hydrated. The water can be made to separate from the solid by heating. This is called dehydration and the solid is said to be anhydrous.

White, anhydrous copper sulphate goes blue when water is present and copper sulphate can be used to test for the presence of water.

KEY TERMS

Bond A force that holds two or more atoms together.

Minerals The naturally occurring compounds of which the rocks in the Earth's crust are made.

Salt An ionic compound made of a metal and a nonmetal.

Saturated solution A solution in which no more of a solid can be dissolved.

QUARTZ CRYSTALS

Quartz crystals are crystals of the mineral quartz that form in the Earth's crust. When a current of electricity is passed through a quartz crystal, it vibrates at a precise frequency (rate). This is called a piezoelectric effect. The vibrations can be used to measure time in a clock.

Battery

Exploded view of a quartz crystal watch

Quartz crystal

Electronic circuits control the rate of vibrations to one pulse per second.

In a quartz watch, a current from a battery makes the quartz crystal vibrate 32,768 times a second.

SEE FOR YOURSELF

You can grow some crystals using alum (a sulphate of potassium and aluminum) from a chemist. They take about three weeks to grow.

Alum

1. Gently warm 100g (4oz) of alum over a low heat until it dissolves, then add more alum until no more will dissolve (about 75g or 3oz).

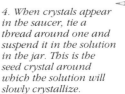

2. Pour a little of this saturated solution into a saucer and leave for three days.

3. Keep the rest of the solution in a clean, covered jar.

4. When crystals appear in the saucer, tie a thread around one and suspend it in the solution in the jar. This is the seed crystal around which the solution will slowly crystallize.

Seed crystal

ORGANIC CHEMISTRY

Organic compounds are used to make paints.

Organic chemistry is the study of organic compounds - carbon compounds produced by living organisms. Carbon can form over two million different organic compounds that are sorted into groups such as alkanes, alkenes and alcohols.* Many of these compounds are found in crude oil,* which is the fossilized remains of organisms that lived long ago, and are important for producing plastics,* paints, cosmetics and medicines.

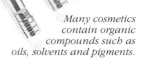

Many cosmetics contain organic compounds such as oils, solvents and pigments.

ORGANIC COMPOUNDS

Organic compounds are made up of carbon atoms bonded to atoms of other elements such as hydrogen and oxygen. The atoms are held together by strong covalent bonds (see right and Bonding*). Compounds that contain only carbon and hydrogen atoms are called hydrocarbons.

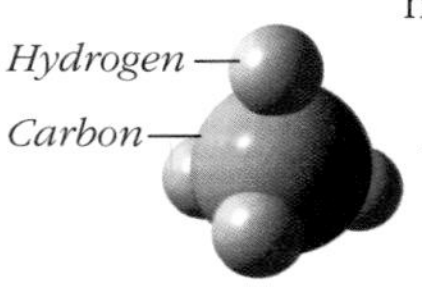

Hydrogen —
Carbon —
Model of a molecule of methane

Methane (CH₄), the main compound in natural gas, is a simple hydrocarbon.

Flare of burning methane at an oil rig

Organic compounds are grouped in families called homologous series. Alkanes and alkenes (see opposite page) are two different homologous series. Each series contains thousands of compounds that can be arranged according to the number of carbon atoms in their molecules.

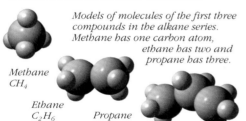

Models of molecules of the first three compounds in the alkane series. Methane has one carbon atom, ethane has two and propane has three.

Methane CH₄
Ethane C₂H₆
Propane C₃H₈

The names of compounds whose molecules contain one carbon atom start with "meth". Those with molecules containing two carbon atoms start with "eth" and those with three carbon atoms begin with "prop". The compounds in each homologous series have the same chemical properties, but their physical properties change from gas to liquid to solid as the molecules increase in size.

Brightly coloured synthetic dyes, such as those used on these ballet shoes, are made from an organic compound called aniline, which is found in coal tar.

COVALENT BONDS

A huge number of organic compounds is possible because atoms of carbon can link together to form long chains or rings. The atoms are held together by strong covalent bonds which are created by two atoms sharing the electrons in their outer shells (see Bonding*).

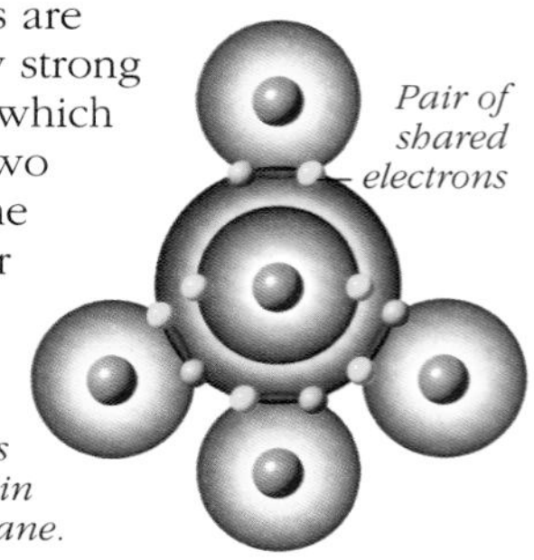

Pair of shared electrons

This diagram shows the covalent bonds in a molecule of methane.

Carbon can form single, double, or even triple covalent bonds. In single bonds, each pair of atoms shares one pair of electrons, in double bonds they share two and in triple bonds they share three pairs of electrons. In diagrams of the molecules, the bonds can be shown as sticks between the atoms.

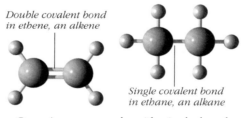

Double covalent bond in ethene, an alkene

Single covalent bond in ethane, an alkane

Organic compounds with single bonds are said to be saturated, or "full up", as they have no free bonds to join with other atoms. Compounds with double bonds are unsaturated as the double bonds can open up and make space for additional atoms.

Ballet shoes coloured with synthetic dyes

When saturated organic compounds react with other compounds, the bonds in their molecules break open and some of their atoms are replaced by different atoms. This is called a substitution reaction. For example, freon (CF₂Cl₂) is made by replacing the hydrogen atoms in methane with fluorine (F) and chlorine (Cl).

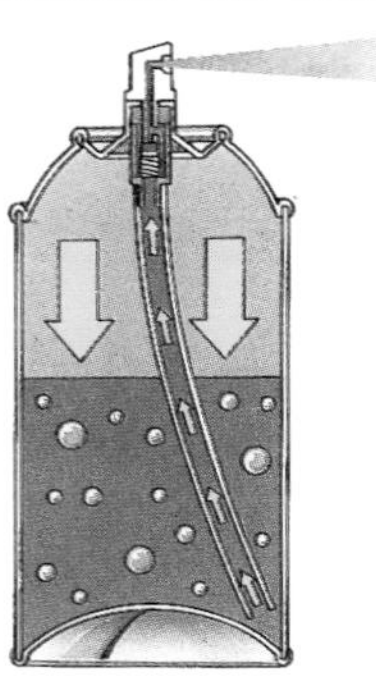

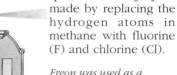

Freon was used as a propellant in aerosols, but it is a chlorofluorocarbon (a compound of chlorine, fluorine and carbon) and is believed to damage the atmosphere (see Catalysts). Other propellants are now used in aerosols.*

Unsaturated compounds are more reactive than saturated compounds. They can form bonds with other atoms without their molecules breaking up. This is called an addition reaction.

When ethene reacts with bromine, its double bonds open up, making space for the bromine atoms.

Ethene

Ethene and bromine react to form 1,2-dibromoethane, an important additive in petrol.

Bromine (Br₂)

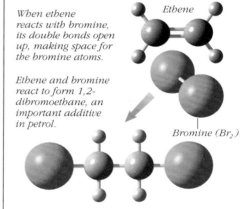

By studying the way different organic compounds react, chemists have been able to copy substances that occur naturally by synthesizing (making) them in laboratories.

Chemists make vitamin tablets by copying the structure of vitamins, which are naturally occurring organic compounds.

Chemists have also created new synthetic compounds that are used to make plastics,* pesticides, dyes, solvents, paints, varnishes and medicines.

Plastic bike helmet and synthetic gloves

*Bonding, 64

*Alcohols, 80;
Crude Oil, 81; Plastics, 82-83; Bonding, 64

*Catalysts, 71; Plastics, 82-83

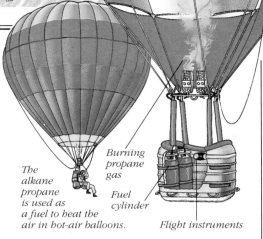

ALKANES

The alkanes are a homologous series of hydrocarbons whose carbon atoms are held together by single covalent bonds (see left). Alkanes are found in the Earth's crust in crude oil* and natural gas, and many are used as fuels.

Methane, the main compound in natural gas, is used as a fuel for cooking and heating.

Molecules of the first three alkanes, methane, ethane and propane, are shown on the opposite page. Alkanes with small molecules, such as methane, are gases, but as the molecules get larger, they become liquids, such as kerosene and petrol. Alkanes with more than 16 atoms of carbon are solids.

Kerosene is used as an aircraft fuel. It is a mixture of alkanes with 9-15 carbon atoms in their molecules.

Wax crayons are a mixture of solid alkanes.

Fuel tanks in wings

Alkanes burn easily and many are used as fuels. Petrol is a mixture of alkanes, and propane and butane are used in caravans and camping stoves, stored under pressure as liquids in portable cylinders.

Alkanes are used to make many other organic chemicals. For example, the hydrogen atoms in methane can be replaced with chlorine and fluorine to make compounds called chlorofluorocarbons.

Monochloromethane (right) is used to make paint-stripper.

Chlorine atom

Fluorine atom

Chlorine atom

Dichlorodifluoromethane (left) can be used as a coolant in refrigerators, as a propellant in aerosols and to make bubbles in expanded polystyrene (see Plastics).*

However, many chlorofluoro-compounds are no longer used as they are believed to damage the atmosphere (see Catalysts*).

The alkane propane is used as a fuel to heat the air in hot-air balloons.

Burning propane gas

Fuel cylinder

Flight instruments

ALKENES

Alkenes are a homologous series of hydrocarbons whose carbon atoms are held together by double covalent bonds (see left). The names of the compounds in this series end in "ene". Ethene (C_2H_4) is the first alkene. "Methene" does not exist as all alkenes must have at least two carbon atoms to form a double bond.

Double bond

Ethene C_2H_4

These are diagrams of the molecules of the first two compounds in the alkene series.

Propene C_3H_6

Alkenes are more reactive than alkanes because their double covalent bonds make them unsaturated compounds. Each carbon atom can give up one of its double bonds to other atoms without the molecules breaking open. They are used in industry to make plastics,* such as polythene, by joining many molecules together with addition reactions. Alkenes are not found naturally in great quantities and are obtained by breaking up large alkane molecules that are found in crude oil (see Cracking*).

Plastics are made by addition reactions using molecules of compounds such as ethene.

Charvel U.S.A. 84MH — *Plastic guitar plectrums*

Rubber tyres reinforced with fabric and steel

Racing cars are made of a very strong, rigid material called Kevlar, which is plastic reinforced with synthetic fibres. It is much lighter than metal.*

Steel suspension springs

HYDROGENATION

Hydrogenation is a chemical reaction in which atoms of hydrogen are added to unsaturated molecules, such as those of alkenes, to fill up the double covalent bonds. The new compounds are saturated as they contain only single covalent bonds. Hydrogenation is an addition reaction (see Covalent Bonds).

Ethene and hydrogen react together to form ethane. The hydrogen fills up the spare bonds in the double covalent bond.

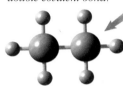

Ethene

Hydrogen

Ethane is an alkane and it is a saturated compound.

Vegetable oils, such as sunflower, peanut and coconut oil, are liquids containing alkenes, so they are unsaturated compounds. To make solid fats, such as margarine, the alkenes in the oil are converted to saturated alkanes by hydrogenation. Using a nickel catalyst to speed up the reaction, hydrogen is bubbled through the oil. The new saturated compound can be spread as it is solid at room temperature.

The oil in peanuts is made up of alkenes.

Saturated vegetable oils can be spread on bread.

KEY TERMS

Addition reaction A chemical reaction in which new atoms are added to an unsaturated compound.
Homologous series A group of organic compounds with the same chemical structure and properties.
Hydrocarbons Organic compounds made of hydrogen and carbon.
Saturated compound An organic compound whose carbon atoms are joined by single covalent bonds.
Substitution reaction A chemical reaction in which the molecules break open and some of the atoms are replaced by different atoms.
Unsaturated compound An organic compound whose carbon atoms have double covalent bonds.

ALCOHOLS AND ORGANIC ACIDS

Alcohols and organic acids are organic compounds* (carbon compounds produced by living things). Drinks such as wine and beer contain an alcohol called ethanol, but there are many other types of alcohols, and in industry, they are important solvents (substances that dissolve other substances). Organic acids behave like typical acids.* They turn litmus paper red and they form salts* when they react with alkalis. Soap is a salt made by mixing an organic acid with sodium hydroxide, an alkali.

Alcohol is used as a solvent in perfume.

Soap bubbles

ALCOHOLS

Alcohols are organic compounds* that contain carbon, oxygen and hydrogen. They are a homologous series, that is, a group of compounds with the same chemical properties. The oxygen and hydrogen form a hydroxyl group that gives the alcohols their special properties.

Ethanol (C_2H_5OH) has one hydroxyl group.

Hydroxyl group (OH)

In industry, ethanol is made by fermentation (see below), or by reacting ethene (see Alkenes*) with steam ($C_2H_4 + H_2O = C_2H_5OH$). Ethanol is used as a solvent for paints, varnishes and perfumes. In Brazil it is made by fermenting sugar cane and used as a fuel.

Glycerol, another alcohol, is used in explosives.

FERMENTATION

Fermentation is a chemical reaction that has been used for thousands of years to produce alcoholic drinks. It is now an important industrial process for producing the alcohol ethanol.

Bubbles of carbon dioxide gas

Fermentation mixture - yeast, sugar and water

During fermentation, glucose in fruit or grain is converted into ethanol (an alcohol) and carbon dioxide by enzymes (catalysts that speed up chemical reactions in living things) produced by yeast, a fungus.

The sugar in grapes is fermented to make wine, cider is made from apples and whisky is made from cereals.

ORGANIC ACIDS

Ethanoic acid, which gives vinegar its sour taste, and formic acid, the poison in the sting of some ants, are organic acids. They belong to a group called carboxylic acids. Other complex carboxylic acids, called fatty acids, are found in animal fats and plant oils.

Ant about to squirt poison

Coconut oil contains fatty acids.

Organic acids can be made by oxidizing* (adding oxygen to) alcohols. Vinegar has been made for thousands of years by allowing wine, which contains the alcohol ethanol, to oxidize and form ethanoic acid.

Ethanoic acid is used in the production of synthetic fibers such as polyester. As vinegar, it is used to preserve, or pickle, food.

Synthetic thread

When carboxylic acids react with alcohols, they produce compounds called esters, and water. Esters give fruit and flowers their flavors and smells. Fats and oils are esters made of glycerol or glycol (alcohols) combined with fatty acids.

Fatty acid

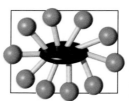

Glycerol

Above: a molecule of fat

The scents that attract insects to flowers are esters - compounds of fatty acids and alcohols.

SOAPS AND DETERGENTS

A detergent is a substance that enables water to remove dirt. Soaps are a type of detergent, but there are also soapless detergents.

Detergents reduce the attraction between the water molecules (see Surface Tension) so the water spreads easily over the washing.*

Soap is made from vegetable oils, which contain fatty acids (see left). When the oils are boiled with sodium hydroxide, an alkali, the acids react with the alkali to produce a salt,* which is soap.

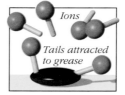

Ions

Tails attracted to grease

Soaps and detergents are made of particles called ions that have a charge at one end. This end is attracted to water and the other end (the "tail") is attracted to grease.

The tails attach themselves to grease and form a "bridge" between the water and the grease. Their attraction to water pulls the grease away from the washing.

Soapless detergents work in the same way and are not affected by the minerals in hard water,* which form a scum with soap. But soapless detergents contain phosphates and these encourage excess plant growth in ponds and rivers.

KEY TERMS

Acid A compound that contains hydrogen and that dissolves in water to produce hydrogen ions.
Alkali A solution that neutralizes the acidity of an acid.
Organic compound A compound that contains the element carbon and is produced by living things.
Salt A neutral substance produced when an acid reacts with an alkali.
Solvent A substance capable of dissolving other substances.

*Organic Compounds, 78; Acids, 74-75; Salts, 76; Alkenes, 79

*Oxidation, 72; Surface Tension, 13; Salts, 76; Hard Water, 69

CRUDE OIL

Crude oil is an important raw material from which fuels such as gasoline and natural gas are obtained, as well as many different chemicals for industry. It is a mixture of hydrocarbons, which are organic compounds* made up of carbon and hydrogen. The different compounds are separated in oil refineries by a process called fractional distillation.

Oil is the fossilized remains of microscopic sea organisms.

The energy* released when oil burns came originally from the Sun.

HOW OIL AND GAS FORMED

Oil and natural gas formed from the bodies of microscopic organisms that lived in the sea millions of years ago.

The microscopic organisms from which oil formed were similar to the plankton that live in the sea today.

When the organisms died, their bodies sank to the bottom of the sea and became buried in sand and mud. As the layers of sand and mud built up and became rock, the minute organisms rotted and formed oil and gas.

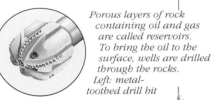

Porous layers of rock containing oil and gas are called reservoirs. To bring the oil to the surface, wells are drilled through the rocks. Left: metal-toothed drill bit

Nearly a third of all oil reservoirs are found under the seabed. To extract the oil, an oil platform is built.

An offshore oil platform may pipe oil from 20 wells.

Rig's legs are fastened to the sea floor.

— Drill pipes

FRACTIONAL DISTILLATION

In an oil refinery, the different compounds of which oil is made are separated by fractional distillation.* The oil is heated until the compounds become gases at about 340°C (644°F). The gases are piped into a tower called a fractionating column and as they rise up the tower, they cool and condense (become liquids again) and are collected.

The compounds with the largest, heaviest molecules condense first and are collected near the bottom of the tower. Compounds with smaller, lighter molecules have lower boiling points, so they rise higher up the tower before they condense. The mixture of compounds that condense at each level is called a fraction.

Furnace where crude oil is heated until it boils and the compounds become gases

Diagram of a fractionating column

0°C (32°F) — Refinery gases (1-4 carbon atoms per molecule). Used as fuels for heating and cooking.

110°C (230°F) — Gasoline compounds (5-10 carbon atoms per molecule). Used for gasoline and for making medicines, plastics, paints, and chemicals.

180°C (356°F) — Kerosene compounds (11-14 carbon atoms per molecule). Used for heating, lighting and jet fuels.

260°C (500°F) — Diesel oils (15-19 carbon atoms in each molecule). Used as fuels for trucks and trains.

340°C (644°F)

500°C (932°F) — Residue compounds (20-40 carbon atoms in each molecule). Used for heating oil, candle waxes, polishes, lubricants and bitumen for surfacing roads.

CRACKING

Cracking is a method by which compounds with large molecules, such as decane, an alkane,* are converted to compounds with smaller molecules that are more useful and can be used as fuels or in the chemicals industry.

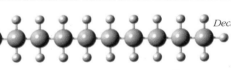

Decane

When heated and mixed with steam and a catalyst, the large molecules break up to make smaller, lighter molecules.

Ethene

Although new deposits of oil are being discovered all the time, geologists estimate that we have already used about 20 percent of the oil that can be extracted.

KEY TERMS

Hydrocarbon An organic compound that contains only the elements hydrogen and carbon.
Molecule Two or more atoms chemically bonded together to form the smallest particle of a substance.
Organic compound A compound that contains carbon and which is produced by living things.

*Organic Compounds, 78; Energy, 6; Distillation, see Separating Mixtures, 67; Alkanes, 79

Caption: Plastic can be made into any shape by pouring it into moulds.

PLASTICS
AND NATURAL POLYMERS

Polymers are substances made of many small molecules joined together to make long chains. Plastics and synthetic fibres, such as nylon, are polymers made from chemicals found in crude oil.* As well as synthetic polymers, there are natural polymers, such as rubber, starch, wool and silk - and the hair on your head.

Caption: Plastic fairing

Caption: Plastics reduce vehicle weight and help save fuel.

HOW PLASTICS ARE MADE

Plastics are synthetic polymers made from the organic compounds* found in crude oil.* Many different types of plastic, for example polythene, PVC and polystyrene, are made using ethene, which belongs to the group of organic compounds called alkenes.*

Caption: PVC drinks bottles are light and shatterproof.

Caption: Polythene can be made into thin sheets for wrapping food.

Caption: Polythene and polystyrene can be moulded to make shapes such as cups.

Ethene is an unsaturated compound, that is, it contains double covalent bonds that can open up and form bonds with other atoms. In a double covalent bond, two atoms share two pairs of electrons (see Covalent Bonds*).

Each molecule of ethene (C_2H_4) contains two atoms of carbon joined by a double covalent bond.

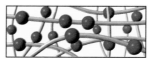

Caption: Double bond

Caption: Carbon atoms

Caption: The double bonds can open up and form bonds with other atoms.

Using heat, pressure and catalysts, ethene molecules can be made to react together. Their double bonds open up and the carbon atoms join together to form long chains that are giant molecules of polythene.

Joining molecules together to make polymers is called polymerization. The small molecules of which a polymer is made are called monomers.

Caption: A giant molecule of polythene contains up to 20,000 atoms of carbon.

Different types of plastics can be made by changing some of the atoms in the monomers. PVC (polyvinylchloride) is made by replacing one of the hydrogen atoms in ethene with an atom of chlorine to make chloroethene.

Caption: Chloroethene

PVC is a polymer made of long chains of chloroethene monomers.

Caption: Chlorine atom

Plastics can be divided into two groups. Thermoplastics can be melted and used again, while thermosetting plastics form in the mould and can only be moulded once.

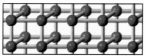

In thermoplastics, the polymer chains are not linked together.

In thermosetting plastics the polymers are linked firmly together.

Thermoplastics are flexible but they are not heat resistant. Polythene, polystyrene, nylon and Terylene are all thermoplastics. This type of plastic can be recycled, but this is not yet carried out on a large scale.

Fibres for clothing can be made from recycled PVC bottles.

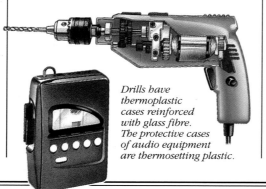

Thermosetting plastics can only be moulded once. They have a rigid structure and are hard and heat resistant. Melamine, from which mugs, plates and kitchen work surfaces are made, is a thermosetting plastic.

Caption: Drills have thermoplastic cases reinforced with glass fibre. The protective cases of audio equipment are thermosetting plastic.

SYNTHETIC FIBRES

Some plastics can be drawn out to make fibres. Nylon, polyester and acrylic are three different types of plastic used to make fibres. They can be spun and woven, often together with natural fibres such as wool and cotton, to make clothes, carpets, ropes and strong fabrics for sails and parachutes.

Caption: Synthetic fibres, such as Lycra, are very smooth and light. They help to reduce weight and friction with the air for dancers and athletes.

Synthetic fibres are stronger and lighter than natural fibres such as wool and cotton. Synthetic fibres can also be drawn out to make very long threads, unlike most natural fibres that have to be spun to make long lengths (see Natural Polymers, right).

Caption: Nylon threads

Caption: Nylon is made from an organic chemical called benzene.

KEY TERMS

Monomer Small molecules that are joined together to make polymers.
Organic compound A compound that contains the element carbon and is produced by living things.
Polymer A substance made of small molecules called monomers.
Synthetic Used to describe compounds made artificially by chemical reactions in a factory.

*Crude Oil, 81; Organic Compounds, 78; Alkenes, 79; Covalent Bonds, 78

PROPERTIES OF PLASTICS

Some of the many useful properties of plastics are described on this page. Some of their properties also create problems. Plastics do not rot or corrode, so they are difficult to dispose of, and some produce poisonous fumes when they burn. However, new types of plastic that are biodegradable have been developed.

The first plastics were made over 150 years ago. After early experiments, celluloid and later Bakelite were developed.

Bakelite clock

Early in the 20th century, Bakelite was used to make new equipment such as wirelesses and telephones.

Bakelite telephones

Modern phones are made of much lighter types of plastic than Bakelite.

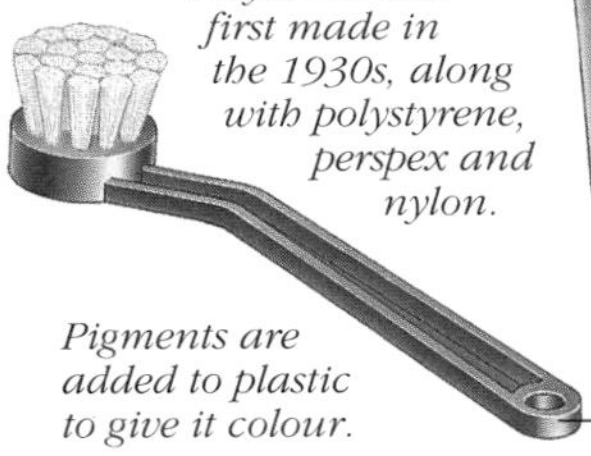

Polythene was first made in the 1930s, along with polystyrene, perspex and nylon.

Pigments are added to plastic to give it colour. — *Polythene*

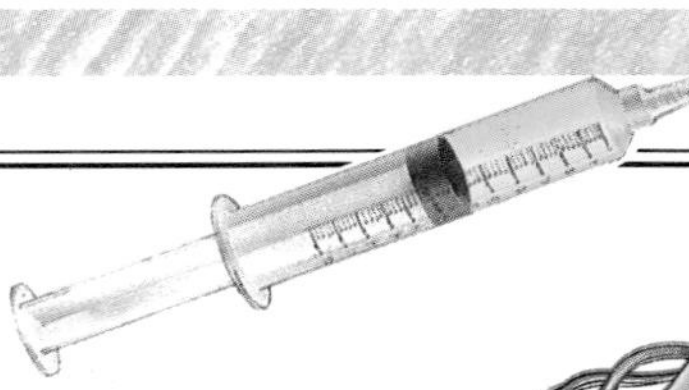

Polystyrene cup

Expanded polystyrene is very light and it is a good insulator. It is used for packaging food and fragile equipment.

Polystyrene packaging keeps food warm.

Plastic disposable syringes are hygienic and cheap to produce.

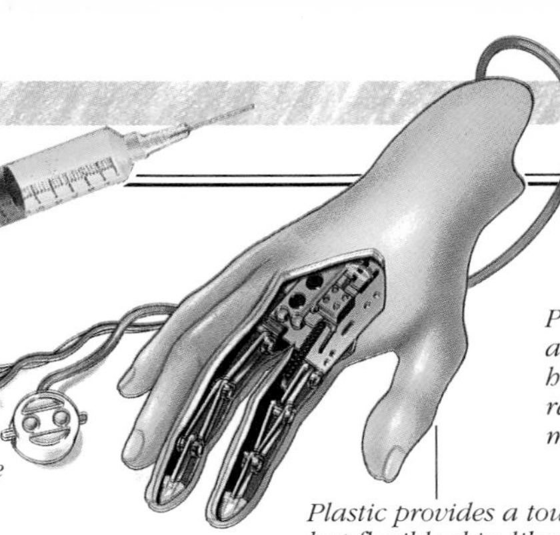

Helmets for racing drivers are made of thermosetting plastic reinforced with synthetic fibres. The gloves are made of fire-resistant synthetic fibres.

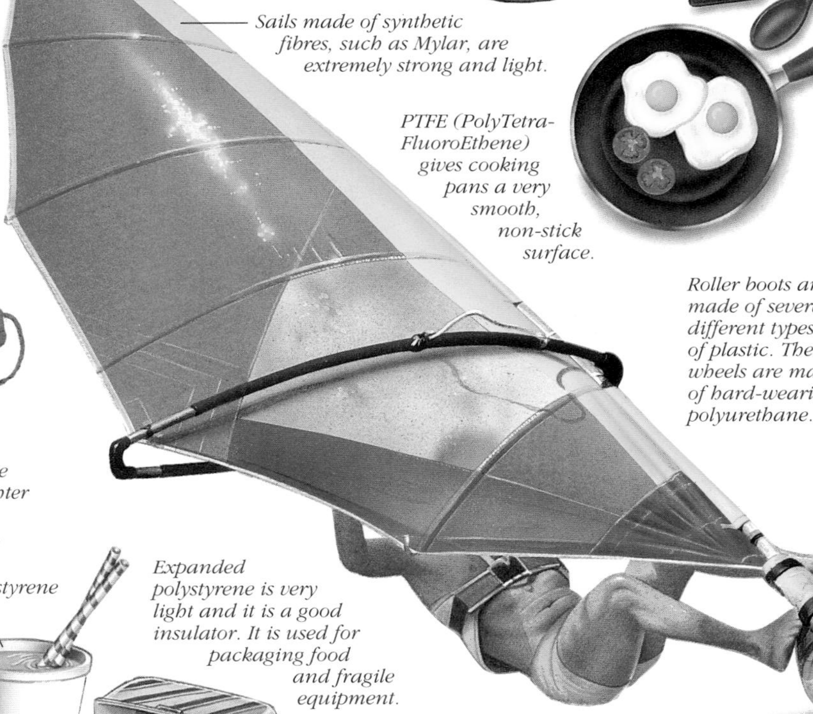

Sails made of synthetic fibres, such as Mylar, are extremely strong and light.

PTFE (PolyTetra-FluoroEthene) gives cooking pans a very smooth, non-stick surface.

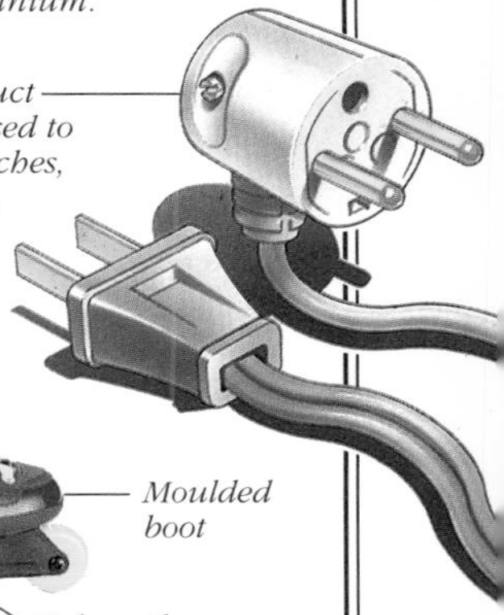

Composites, such as plastics reinforced with glass fibres, are being developed for the aerospace industry.

Flaps and control surfaces made of plastic help to reduce the overall weight of an aircraft.

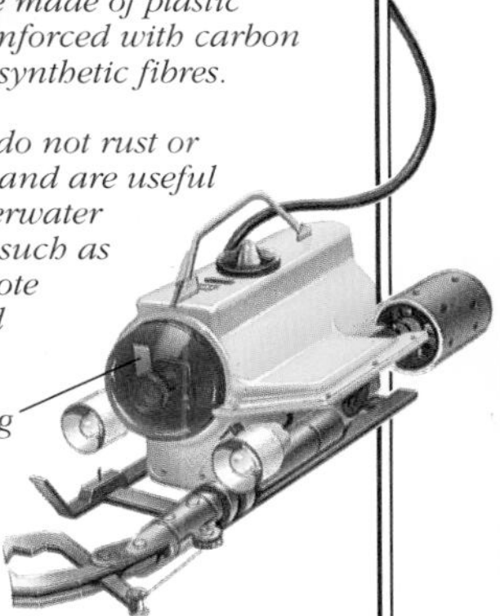

Plastic provides a tough but flexible skin-like finish for artificial limbs.

PVC gloves are used for handling radioactive material.

Substances can be added to plastics to make them fire-resistant.

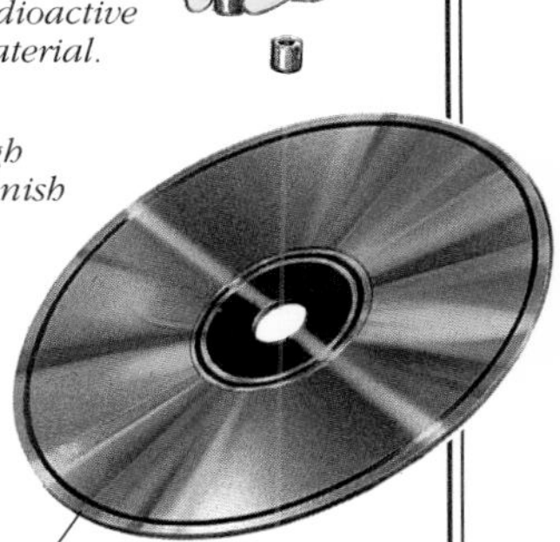

Compact discs are made of polycarbonate plastic covered with a thin layer of aluminium.

Plastics do not conduct electricity and are used to make plugs and switches, and to insulate wire.

Roller boots are made of several different types of plastic. The wheels are made of hard-wearing polyurethane.

Moulded boot

Polyurethane wheels

Windsurfing boards are made of plastic reinforced with carbon or synthetic fibres.

Plastics do not rust or corrode and are useful for underwater vehicles such as this remote operated vehicle.

PVC covering for video camera

NATURAL POLYMERS

Before the invention of plastics, natural polymers such as wool, and the fibres of plants such as cotton and jute were used for weaving. Like plastics, natural polymers are chains of simple molecules. Proteins are also natural polymers.

Rubber is made from a natural polymer called latex, a milky fluid that seeps out of the bark of rubber trees. Rubber is strengthened by heating it with sulphur.* This is called vulcanized rubber and is used mainly for making tyres.

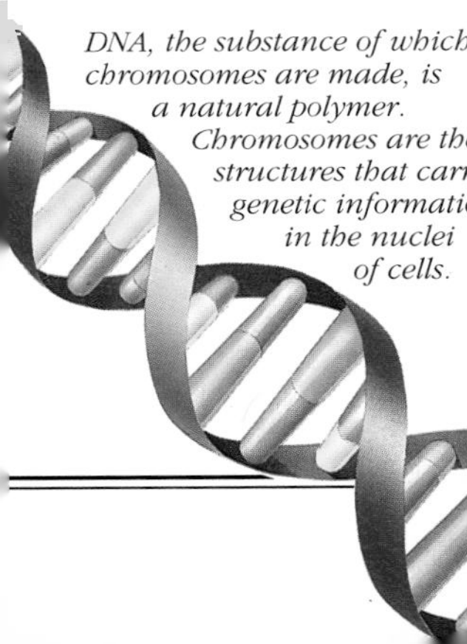

DNA, the substance of which chromosomes are made, is a natural polymer. Chromosomes are the structures that carry genetic information in the nuclei of cells.

Wool and hair are natural polymers.

Latex is a natural polymer produced by rubber trees.

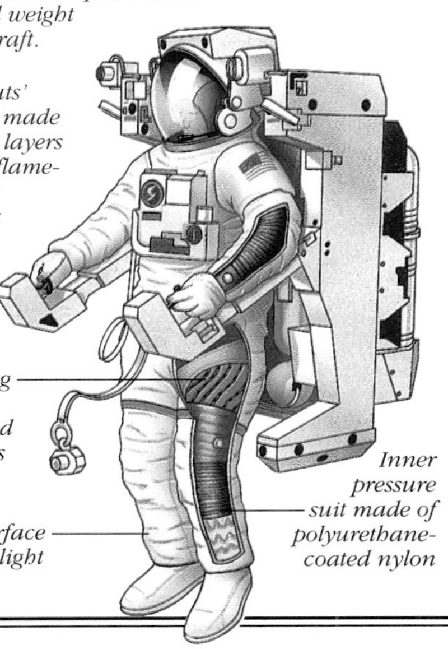

Astronauts' suits are made of 8 or 9 layers of light, flame-resistant synthetic fabrics.

Insulating layers of metallized synthetics

White surface to reflect light

Inner pressure suit made of polyurethane-coated nylon

*Sulphur, 61

SCIENTIFIC DATA

METRIC AND IMPERIAL MEASUREMENTS

Imperial equivalents of metric units

1cm	=	0.39 inches
1m	=	3.28 feet
1km	=	0.62 miles
1 square cm	=	0.16 square inches
1 square m	=	10.76 square feet
1 square km	=	0.39 square miles
1 cubic cm	=	0.061 cubic inches
1 liter	=	1.76 pints 0.22 gallons
1 gram	=	0.04 ounces
1kg	=	2.20 pounds
1 tonne	=	0.98 tons

Metric equivalents of imperial units

1 inch	=	2.54cm
1 foot	=	0.30m
1 mile	=	1.61km
1 square inch	=	6.45 square cm
1 square foot	=	0.09 square m
1 square mile	=	2.59 square km
1 cubic inch	=	16.39 cubic cm
1 pint	=	0.57 liters
1 gallon	=	4.55 liters
1 ounce	=	28.35 grams
1 pound	=	0.45 kilograms
1 ton	=	1.02 tonnes

TEMPERATURE SCALES

Celsius	Fahrenheit	Kelvin
100	212	373
90	194	363
80	176	353
70	158	343
60	140	333
50	122	323
40	104	313
30	86	303
20	68	293
10	50	283
0	32	273
-10	14	263
-20	-4	253

MATHEMATICAL FORMULAE

In these formulae, b = base, h = height, r = radius, π = pi (3.142), θ = an angle.

Area of circle	=	πr^2
Circumference of circle	=	$2\pi r$
Area of sector	=	$\dfrac{\theta \pi r^2}{360}$
Length of arc	=	$\dfrac{\theta \pi r}{180}$
Volume of cylinder	=	$\pi r^2 h$
Volume of cone	=	$\frac{1}{3}\pi r^2 h$
Volume of sphere	=	$\frac{4}{3}\pi r^3$
Area of sphere	=	$4\pi r^2$
Area of triangle	=	$\frac{1}{2}bh$
Area of parallelogram	=	bh
Volume of pyramid	=	$\frac{1}{3}h \times$ base area

SI UNITS

SI units are an internationally agreed system of units used for scientific purposes.

Quantity	Unit	Abbreviation
Distance	meter	m
Mass	kilogram	kg
Time	second	s
Force	newton	N
Energy	joule	J
Power	watt	W
Voltage	volt	V
Current	ampere	A
Resistance	ohm	Ω

PHYSICS EQUATIONS

Average speed (m/s)	=	$\dfrac{\text{distance moved (m)}}{\text{time taken (s)}}$
Force (N)	=	mass (kg) × acceleration (m/s²)
Acceleration (m/s²)	=	$\dfrac{\text{change in velocity (m/s)}}{\text{time taken for this change (s)}}$
Momentum (kgm/s)	=	mass (kg) × velocity (m/s)
Work done (Nm or J)	=	force (N) × distance moved in the direction of the force (m)
Pressure (N/m²)	=	$\dfrac{\text{force (N)}}{\text{area (m}^2\text{)}}$
Density (kg/m³)	=	$\dfrac{\text{mass (kg)}}{\text{volume (m}^3\text{)}}$

MOH'S SCALE OF HARDNESS

The ten minerals in Moh's scale represent different levels of hardness.

1. Talc (softest)
2. Gypsum
3. Calcite
4. Fluorite
5. Apatite
6. Orthoclase
7. Quartz
8. Topaz
9. Corundum
10. Diamond

ELECTRICAL AND ELECTRONIC SYMBOLS

The symbols below show many of the components found in electrical and electronic circuits. Alternative symbols are sometimes used in other countries.

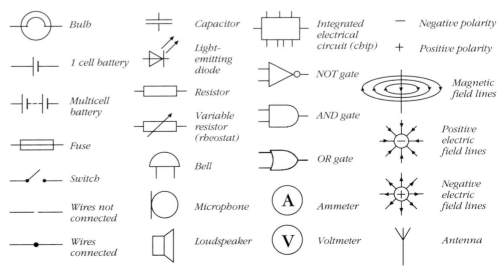

THE PLANETS

	Mercury	Venus	Earth	Mars	Jupiter	Saturn	Uranus	Neptune	Pluto
Distance from Sun									
millions of km	57.9	108.2	149.6	227.9	778.3	1,427	2,870	4,497	5,913
millions of miles	36.0	67.2	93	141.5	483.3	886.1	1,782	2,774	3,672
Diameter									
km	4,879	12,104	12,756	6,786	142,984	120,536	51,118	49,528	2,284
miles	3,033	7,523	7,928	4,222	88,784	74,914	31,770	30,757	1,419
Mass (Earth=1)	0.056	0.82	1	0.107	318	95	14.5	17	0.002
Surface gravity (Earth=1)	0.38	0.9	1	0.38	2.64	0.925	0.79	1.12	0.05
"Year" (Time to orbit Sun)	88 days	224.7 days	365.3 days	687 days	11.9 yrs	29.5 yrs	84 yrs	164.8 yrs	248.5 yrs
"Day" (Time to turn 360°)	58.7 days	243 days	23h 56m	24h 37m	9h 55m	10h 39m	17h 14m	16h 7m	6.4 days

GEOMETRICAL SHAPES AND FIGURES

Planes

Flat shapes are called planes and have two dimensions: length and breadth. Polygons, triangles and circles are planes.

1. Polygons

A polygon is a flat shape with three or more straight sides.

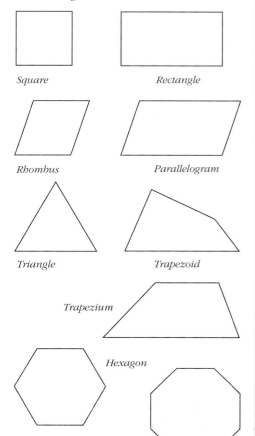

Square

Rectangle

Rhombus

Parallelogram

Triangle

Trapezoid

Trapezium

Hexagon

Octagon

2. Triangles

A triangle is a three-sided plane. Each side is a straight line.

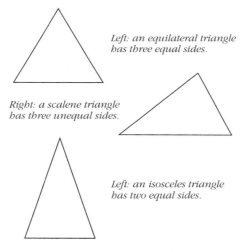

Left: an equilateral triangle has three equal sides.

Right: a scalene triangle has three unequal sides.

Left: an isosceles triangle has two equal sides.

3. Circles

A circle is a curved line on which all points are equally distant from the center. The parts of a circle are shown below.

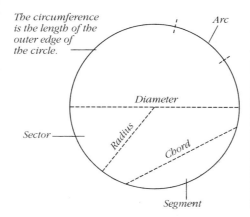

The circumference is the length of the outer edge of the circle.

Arc

Diameter

Sector

Radius

Chord

Segment

Solid Shapes

Solids have three dimensions: length, breadth and width. Some of the main solids are represented below.

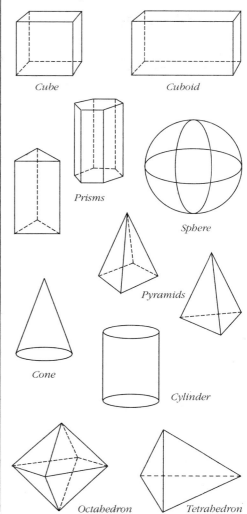

Cube

Cuboid

Prisms

Sphere

Pyramids

Cone

Cylinder

Octahedron

Tetrahedron

SCIENTISTS AND INVENTORS

Ampère, André Marie (1775-1836) A French mathematician and physicist who did pioneering work on electricity and magnetism. The unit of electric current called the ampere is named after him.

Archimedes (c.287-212BC) A Greek scientist who formulated the scientific principle that explains how a floating object displaces its own weight in water.

Babbage, Charles (1792-1871) An English mathematician and inventor who built a calculating machine called the Analytical Engine. The machine anticipated the modern computer.

Baird, John Logie (1888-1946) A Scottish engineer who invented the television (1926).

Bell, Alexander Graham (1847-1922) A Scottish-American inventor who invented the telephone (1872-76).

Benz, Karl (1844-1929) A German inventor who designed the first car to be driven by an internal combustion engine.

Bohr, Niels (1885-1962) A Danish physicist who applied the quantum theory of physics to Rutherford's structure of the atom (1913).

Boyle, Robert (1627-1691) This Irish scientist advanced the science of chemistry by proposing that matter is made up of tiny particles. He also formulated Boyle's law, which states that the pressure and volume of a gas are inversely proportional.

Brown, Robert (1773-1858) A Scottish biologist who noted the apparently random motion of particles suspended in liquids.

Celsius, Anders (1701-1744) A Swedish astronomer who invented the centigrade thermometer and the Celsius scale.

Chadwick, James (1891-1974) An English physicist who worked on radioactivity and discovered the neutron.

Charles, Jacques (1746-1823) A French physicist who formulated Charles Law, the relation between heat and volume in gases.

Copernicus (1473-1543) This Polish astronomer developed the theory that the planets move around the Sun, not around the Earth (1530).

Curie, Marie (1867-1934) A pioneering Polish scientist who conducted work in radiation and discovered the radioactive material radium (1910).

Dalton, John (1766-1844) This English chemist suggested that elements are made of atoms that combine to form compounds.

Edison, Thomas (1847-1931) This American inventor made over a thousand devices including the phonograph, an early version of a gramophone.

Einstein, Albert (1879-1955) A German-born physicist who published the *Special Theory of Relativity* (1905) and *General Theory of Relativity* (1916), revising previous ideas of time and space.

Fahrenheit, Gabriel (1686-1736) A German physicist who invented the mercury thermometer (1714) and devised the fahrenheit temperature scale.

Faraday, Michael (1791-1867) An English scientist who invented the dynamo, generating an electric current by spinning a coil of wire in a magnetic field.

Ford, Henry (1863-1947) An American automobile engineer who built the Ford Model T and pioneered mass-production techniques in industry.

Galilei, Galileo (1564-1642) An Italian astronomer and scientist who made many discoveries. His studies of motion supported the Copernican theory that the planets move around the Sun.

Halley, Edmund (1656-1742) An English astronomer and mathematician who charted and predicted the orbit of a comet. Halley's Comet is named after him.

Hawking, Stephen (1942-) This English physicist has advanced the understanding of the origin of the Universe.

Hertz, Heinrich (1857-1894) This German physicist began the research that demonstrated the existence of radio waves.

Hooke, Robert (1635-1703) An English physicist and chemist who discovered the relationship between elasticity and force, as formulated by Hooke's law.

Hubble, Edwin (1889-1953) An American astronomer who proved the existence of galaxies beyond our own. The Hubble telescope is named after him.

Joule, James (1818-1889) An English physicist who did important work on heat, and helped to establish the principle of the conservation of energy. The joule, a unit of measurement of work and energy, is named after him.

Kelvin, Lord see Thomson, William

Lovelace, Ada (1815-52) An English mathematician, Lovelace worked on the Analytical Engine designed by Charles Babbage, devising "programs" which anticipated computer programming.

Maimam, Theodore (1927-) An American scientist who built the first laser.

Marconi, Guglielmo (1874-1937) An Italian physicist, Marconi developed radiotelegraphy and succeeded in sending signals across the Atlantic (1901).

Maxwell, James Clerk (1831-1879) A Scottish physicist who established the presence of electromagnetic radiation.

Mendeleyev, Dmitri (1834-1907) This Russian chemist devised the Periodic Table of Elements.

Newcomen, Thomas (1663-1729) An English inventor who built the first atmospheric steam engine.

Newton, Isaac (1642-1727) This English physicist and mathematician formulated fundamental laws of gravity and motion.

Nipkow, Paul (1860-1940) A German engineer and pioneer of television who invented the Nipkow disc, a mechanical scanning device.

Ohm, Georg (1787-1854) A German physicist who researched electric resistance. The unit of electric resistance called the ohm is named after him.

Pascal, Blaise (1623-1662) A French mathematician and physicist who made contributions to hydraulics and the study of atmospheric pressure. The unit of pressure called the pascal is named after him.

Pythagoras (6th century BC) A Greek scientist who made many discoveries including Pythagoras' theorem, a formula for calculating the unknown length of one side of a right-angled triangle.

Rutherford, Ernest (1871-1937) A British physicist who demonstrated the structure of the atom.

Savery, Thomas (c.1650-1715) An English engineer who built the first practical steam engine.

Sikorsky, Igor (1889-1972) A Russian-born American aeronautical engineer who built the first successful helicopter (1939).

Stephenson, George (1781-1848) An English inventor who invented the first successful steam locomotive (1814).

Thomson, William (Lord Kelvin) (1824-1907) A British mathematician and physicist who did important work in thermodynamics, and established the Kelvin scale of temperature.

Torricelli, Evangelista (1608-1647) An Italian physicist who in 1644 discovered the principle of the barometer.

Volta, Alessandro (1745-1827) An Italian physicist who built the first electric battery. The volt, which measures electric potential, is named after him.

Watt, James (1736-1819) A Scottish inventor who improved the steam engine and introduced the sun-and-planet gear.

Wright, Orville (1871-1948) and Wilbur (1867-1912) American aviation pioneers who built the first powered aircraft (1903).

KEY DATES IN SCIENCE

This chart shows some of the most important dates in the history of scientific invention and discovery.

BC Dates

c.7500BC Boats were being made out of hollowed-out tree trunks.
c.4000BC Bronze, an alloy of copper and tin, was first made in Mesopotamia.
c.3500BC The first wheels were made out of sections of tree trunks.
c.3000BC The Babylonians divided the day into 24 hours, the first formal measurement of time.
c.1600BC The first records were made of the study of astronomy.
c.1500BC Iron smelting technology was first developed in Asia Minor (Turkey).
c.530BC The Greek mathematician Pythagoras made various discoveries, including Pythagoras' theorem.
c.500BC The Greek philosopher Thales of Miletus described the magnetic properties of lodestone.
c.400BC Invention of the pulley in Italy.
c.335BC Aristotle made many important scientific observations, including work on levers.
c.300BC Gears were first used in Egypt.
c.235BC Archimedes invented the Archimedes screw, which could move water upwards. It was used for bailing out water from flooded ships.

AD Dates

200 Earliest known use of cast iron, used to make a Chinese cooking stove.
635 Quill pens were used for writing.
700 The Catalan forge was used in Spain for smelting iron. It was an early version of the modern blast furnace.
950 Gunpowder was used by the Chinese to make fireworks and signals.
1000 The optical properties of lenses were first observed by the Arab physicist Ibn-al-Haytham.
1088 The first known clock, which was water-powered, was invented in China by Han Kung-Lien.
1090 Compasses were first used by the Chinese and the Arabs to navigate at sea.
1230 In China, gunpowder was first used as an explosive, to make bombs for attacking city walls.
1289 Earliest recorded description of spectacles to correct sight, in Italy.
1326 Early guns were in use in Italy.
1451 Johann Gutenberg invented the printing press in Germany.
1500 The Italian artist and scientist Leonardo da Vinci designed many devices, including one like a helicopter.
1540 The first artificial limbs were developed for wounded soldiers by the French doctor Abroise Paré.
1543 Copernicus published his theory that the planets revolve around the Sun, not the Earth, to a hostile reaction.
1590 The microscope was invented in the Netherlands.
1592 Galileo invented the first thermometer based on the expansion and contraction of air.
1608 The telescope was first demonstrated in the Netherlands.
1610 Galileo used a telescope to make astronomical observations.
1623 The first calculator, which worked mechanically, was invented by the German scientist Wilhelm Schickard.
1644 The principle of the barometer was discovered by Evangelista Torricelli.
1687 Isaac Newton published his book *Principia*, in which he set forward the laws of motion and gravity.
1704 Isaac Newton published *Opticks*, a book about prisms and light.
1712 The English inventor Thomas Newcomen built an early version of the steam engine.
1752 The American scientist Benjamin Franklin invented the lightning conductor to transfer the electrical energy of lightning safely into the ground.
1774 Joseph Priestley discovered and isolated oxygen gas.
1775 James Watt produced his improved steam engine, which was used in British mines.
1783 The first flight in a hot-air balloon took place in Paris, France.
1808 John Dalton published *A New System of Chemical Philosophy*, in which he set forward his theories of atomic structure.
1810 The first electric lamp was demonstrated in London, England.
1823 The electromagnet was invented.
1831 Michael Faraday invented the dynamo, which generated an electrical current by spinning a coil of wire in a magnetic field.
1833-4 Charles Babbage and Ada Lovelace worked on the Analytical Engine, a forerunner of the computer.
1837 Black and white photography was invented in England.
1837 The electric motor was invented.
1839 Invention of the electric telegraph, used to send messages along wires.
1852 Maiden flight of the first airship, powered by steam and filled with hydrogen, at Paris, France.
1856 Internal combustion engine invented in Italy.
1859 Invention of the battery.
1862 The first celluloid plastics were exhibited in London.
1869 The Russian scientist Dmitri Mendeleyev developed the first periodic table of the elements.
1876 Transmission of the first telephone message in Boston, Massachussetts, USA, by Alexander Graham Bell.
1877 The first sound recording made by Thomas Edison on his prototype phonograph machine.
1878 Invention of the microphone.
1879 Thomas Edison invented the light bulb.
1881 The first power station built in Surrey, England.
1883 The first synthetic fabric, an artificial silk made from cellulose, was produced in England.
1885 Invention of the petrol-driven motor car by the German Karl Benz.
1886 Heinrich Hertz demonstrated the existence of radio waves.
1895 Moving pictures first shown in public in France.
1895 X-rays were discovered in Germany and the first x-ray photograph was taken.
1895 Guglielmo Marconi developed and demonstrated radio transmission.
1903 The first controlled, powered aeroplane, the Flyer I, made its short maiden flight in North Carolina, USA.
1905 Albert Einstein published scientific works including the *Special Theory of Relativity*.
1911 Marie Curie won the Nobel prize for her work on radioactivity.
1926 John Logie Baird transmitted the first black and white television picture across the Atlantic.
1929 Edwin Hubble showed that galaxies are moving away from each other in space. This became the foundation of the Big Bang theory of the beginning of the universe.
1936 The first helicopter flight was made in Germany by the Focke Fa-61.
1937 Invention of the jet engine.
1939 Discovery of nuclear fission by the German scientist Otto Hahn.
1945 The USA tested the atomic (nuclear) bomb in New Mexico, USA, and used it on Hiroshima, Japan.
1953 Francis Crick and James Watson discovered the structure of the DNA molecule which forms living cells, later proved by Roselyn Franklin.
1957 The first satellite was launched.
1961 The first manned spacecraft, Vostok I, was launched. Yuri Gagarin became the first human in space.
1961 Invention of the integrated circuit.
1975 Launch of the first small home computer, the Altair.
1981 The first reusable spacecraft, the Space Shuttle, was launched.

GLOSSARY OF SCIENTIFIC TERMS

acceleration The change in an object's velocity over a certain amount of time.

acid A compound that contains hydrogen and that dissolves in water to produce hydrogen ions.

activation energy The minimum amount of energy needed to start off a chemical reaction.

addition reaction A chemical reaction in which the double bonds of an unsaturated compound open up and form bonds with different atoms.

aerodynamics The study of the way a gas, especially air, flows over a moving object.

airfoil The special wing shape that creates the force of lift.

alkali A soluble base that neutralizes the acidity of an acid.

allotrope One of two or more different forms of an element.

alloy A mixture of two or more metals, or a metal and a nonmetal.

alpha particle Radiation emitted from a nucleus as a cluster of two protons and two neutrons as a result of radioactivity.

alternating current An electric current that changes direction many times a second.

ampere The unit for measuring the strength of an electric current.

amplitude The height of a wave from rest position to peak.

analogue The term used to describe a continual signal that varies in proportion to another quantity which it represents.

anhydrous The term used to describe a solid that can be separated from water by heating.

anion An atom that has gained one or more electrons and so has a negative charge.

anode In electrolysis, the electrode with the positive charge.

anodizing A method of coating a metal with a thin layer of its oxide using electrolysis.

aqueous A substance that is dissolved in water.

atmospheric pressure The weight of the air pressing down on the Earth's surface.

atom The smallest particle of an element that still has the chemical properties of that element.

atomic number The number of protons in the nucleus of an atom.

Avogadro number The number of atoms found in 12g (0.42oz) of carbon-12, which is 600,000 billion billion, or 6×10^{23}.

base A substance that can accept the hydrogen ions of an acid and is the chemical opposite of an acid.

beta particles Radiation emitted as high energy electrons when a neutron changes into a proton in a radioactive nucleus.

binary A code consisting of only 0s and 1s which is used in electronic circuits to represent information.

biodegradable A term used to describe matter that can be decomposed by biological means.

bond A force that holds two or more atoms together.

catalyst A substance that changes the rate of a chemical reaction but is itself left unchanged.

cathode In electrolysis, the electrode with a negative charge.

cathode ray A beam of electrons coming from a cathode.

cation An atom that has lost one or more electrons and so has a positive charge.

caustic A term used to describe a substance, usually strongly alkaline, that can burn or corrode.

center of gravity The point where the whole weight of an object seems to act.

centripetal force A force that keeps an object moving in a circle.

CFCs Chlorofluorocarbons, that is, organic compounds containing carbon, fluorine and chlorine that are believed to damage the atmosphere.

chemical energy Energy that is stored in a substance and released during a chemical reaction.

chemical formula Symbols that show the atoms of which a substance is made and in what proportions.

chromatography A method of separating the substances in a mixture by the rate they are absorbed by filter paper.

color spectrum The separation of white light into the colors of the rainbow.

combustion The scientific term for all forms of burning.

commutator A device that causes the direction of an electric current to be reversed.

compound A substance made up of two or more elements that are chemically bonded together.

condensation The droplets of liquid that form as a gas cools to its boiling point.

conduction The way heat energy is transferred in a solid by the vibration of the solid's heated particles.

conductor A substance through which an electric current or heat can flow.

convection The way heat energy in liquids or gases is transferred by the movement of heated particles.

corrosion The way metals react with oxygen to form a layer of metal oxide on their surfaces.

corrosive A substance that burns away skin or the surface of an object.

covalent bond A bond created by atoms sharing electrons to give each atom a full outer shell of electrons.

cracking A method by which organic compounds with large molecules are converted to more useful compounds that have smaller molecules.

crystal A solid with a definite geometrical shape with straight edges and flat surfaces.

decantation A method of separating the solid particles from a liquid by leaving the particles to settle and pouring off the liquid.

dehydration The process by which water is removed from a solid by heating.

density A measure of how tightly packed the mass is in a substance. Relative density is the density of a substance in relation to water.

diffraction The way a wave bends around a barrier or spreads out after passing through a gap.

diffusion The spreading out of a gas to fill the available space.

digital The term used to describe a signal made up of separate pulses that can be used to represent the 0s and 1s of binary code.

direct current An electric current that flows in only one direction.

dispersion The splitting up of light into the color spectrum.

displacement reaction A chemical reaction in which one of the elements in a compound is replaced by a more reactive element.

distillation A method of obtaining a pure liquid from a solution by collecting the liquid as it evaporates.

drag The force that tries to slow down objects moving in air.

ductile The term used to describe metals that can be pulled out to make wire.

dynamo A machine for converting the energy of movement into electricity.

effort The force needed to operate a simple machine.

electric current The speed of flow of electrically charged particles from an area at high electrical potential to an area at low potential.

electrode A conductor through which an electric current enters or leaves an electrolyte, a gas, or a vacuum.

electrolysis A method of splitting the elements in a compound by passing an electric current through the compound when it is molten or in a solution.

electrolyte A solution or molten substance that can conduct an electric current.

electromagnet A magnet that can be switched on and off by an electric current.

electromagnetic spectrum The arrangement of electromagnetic waves in order of wavelength and frequency.

electromagnetic waves Waves made up of vibrations of ever-changing electric and magnetic fields, for example, light.

electromagnetism The forming of a magnetic field as an electric current flows through a wire.

electron A negatively charged particle that exists around the nucleus of an atom.

electron configuration The number of electrons that exist in each of the shells around an atom.

electroplating A method of covering an object with a thin layer of metal using electrolysis.

electrorefining A method of purifying metals using electrolysis.

element A substance made up of one kind of atom and which cannot be broken down by a chemical reaction to form simpler substances.

emulsifier A substance that helps liquids, such as oil and water, to mix by breaking up the oil into minute droplets.

emulsion A mixture of an oil-based and a water-based liquid that is made by using an emulsifier.

endothermic reaction A chemical reaction in which heat energy is taken in.

enzyme A catalyst that speeds up a chemical reaction in living things.

equilibrium The state of an object when the forces acting on it are balanced.

evaporation The process by which the surface molecules of a liquid escape into a vapor.

exothermic reaction A chemical reaction in which heat energy is given off.

fermentation A chemical reaction in which sugar is broken down by enzymes to produce alcohol and carbon dioxide.

ferromagnetic The term used to describe metals that can be magnetized.

filtrate The liquid that passes through a filter.

filtration A method of separating solid particles from a liquid by trapping them in a filter that allows only the molecules of liquid to pass through.

fluid Any liquid or gas.

fluorescence The ability of certain substances to absorb ultraviolet radiation, or other forms of energy, and give it out as bright light.

force One of several forms of push or pull on an object.

fossil fuel A fuel, such as coal, oil and natural gas, that is formed from fossilized remains of plants or animals

frequency The number of waves per second, measured in hertz (Hz).

friction The force that tries to slow down moving objects that are touching.

fulcrum (or **pivot**) The fixed point around which a turning effect takes place.

gamma rays Electromagnetic waves with a short wavelength and a high frequency that are given off from a nucleus as radiation during radioactivity.

gas A state of matter in which the substance expands to fill any container.

gravity The pulling force that attracts objects to each other.

halflife The average time taken for half the radioactive atoms in a sample to decay.

hertz (Hz) The unit of measurement for wave frequency.

homologous series A group of organic compounds with the same chemical structure and properties.

hydraulic Powered by liquid pressure.

hydrocarbon An organic compound that contains only hydrogen and carbon.

hydrogenation A chemical reaction in which atoms of hydrogen are added to unsaturated organic compounds.

immiscible The term used to describe two or more liquids that do not mix.

indicator A substance that changes color in the presence of an acid or alkali and which is used to test the strength of an acid or alkali.

inertia The tendency of objects to resist a change in their movement.

inflammable Liable to catch fire.

infrared Electromagnetic radiation just beyond the red end of the visible color spectrum.

insoluble The term used to describe a substance that will not dissolve.

insulator A substance that cannot conduct a current of electricity, or that does not conduct heat well.

internal energy The sum of the kinetic and potential energy of the particles in a substance.

ion An atom (or a molecule) that has lost or gained an electron and is no longer electrically neutral.

ionic bond A strong bond between atoms created by the atoms giving up or receiving electrons.

isotope An atom that has a different number of neutrons and so has a different mass number from the other atoms in an element.

joule (J) The unit of measurement for energy and work.

kinetic energy Energy that takes the form of movement.

laser An artificial beam of pure colored light where the waves are in phase and do not spread out like normal light.

lever A rod that turns at a fixed point.

lift The upward force created by an airfoil shape such as that of an aircraft's wings moving through air.

litmus An extract of plant-like organisms called lichens that is used as an indicator to test the strength of an acid or alkali.

load The force that a simple machine overcomes.

longitudinal waves Waves in which the particles vibrate in the same direction as the waves are traveling, for example sound waves.

luminous The term used to describe any object that gives off light.

magnetic field The area around a magnet in which the magnetic force operates.

malleable The term used to describe

metals that can be shaped by hammering.

mass The amount of matter an object contains.

mass number The total number of protons and neutrons in the nucleus of a particular atom.

medium The substance or space in which objects exist and phenomena, such as waves, take place.

microwaves Electromagnetic waves with wavelengths bween infrared and radio waves.

millibar The unit in which atmospheric pressure is measured.

minerals The naturally occurring compounds of which the rocks in the Earth's crust are made.

miscible The term used to describe two or more liquids that mix easily.

mixture Two or more substances (elements or compounds) that are not chemically bonded together.

mole An amount of substance that contains 600,000 billion, billion (the Avogadro number) atoms or molecules.

molecule Two or more atoms that are chemically bonded together to form the smallest particle of a substance.

molten A substance that has been melted and is in a liquid state.

moment The turning effect of a force, measured in newton meters (Nm).

momentum A measure of an object's tendency to continue moving, equal to its mass multiplied by its velocity.

monomer Small molecules that can be joined together to make polymers.

neutralization The reaction between an acid and a base that produces a salt.

neutron A subatomic particle with no electrical charge in the nucleus of an atom.

newton (N) The unit in which force is measured.

nuclear fission The splitting open of an atom's nucleus to form two or more new nuclei, releasing large amounts of energy.

nuclear fusion The joining of two small nuclei to form a larger one, usually releasing large amounts of energy.

nucleus The core section of an atom that contains protons and neutrons.

ohm The unit of measurement of electrical resistance.

opaque The term used to describe a solid object through which light cannot pass.

ore A mineral from which useful products, such as metals, can be extracted.

organic acid An acid produced by a living thing.

organic compound A compound that contains the element carbon and is produced by living things.

oscillate To move back and forth systematically many times a second.

oxidation A chemical reaction in which a substance combines with oxygen, or loses hydrogen or electrons.

oxide A compound made up of an element bonded with oxygen.

oxidizing agent A substance that provides oxygen or receives electrons or hydrogen in a redox reaction.

ozone layer A layer of the gas ozone in the atmosphere that absorbs harmful ultraviolet radiation from the Sun.

particle An atom, molecule or ion.

pascal (Pa) The unit in which pressure is measured.

penumbra Pale shadow illuminated by only part of a light source.

pH value The strength of an acid or alkali expresssed as a number on a scale from 0 to 14.

phosphor A chemical that glows when it absorbs energy.

phosphorescence A fluorescence that continues after the source of energy producing it has stopped.

photoelectric cell A device that turns light energy into electricity.

photosynthesis The process by which plants make their food.

piezoelectric effect The mechanical distortion produced by applying a voltage between the faces of a crystal like quartz.

pigment A substance that absorbs some colours of light and reflects others, which makes an object appear coloured.

pitch The highness or lowness of a musical note or other sound.

pixel Short for "picture element". A dot that forms part of a picture on a TV screen or monitor.

pneumatic Powered by the pressure of a gas, usually air.

polymer A substance made of many small molecules called monomers.

polymerization The process of joining monomers to make polymers.

potential difference The force needed to push a certain amount of electric charge along a conducting pathway between two points.

potential energy The energy an object has because of its position in a force field such as gravity.

power The rate that work is done or energy is used, measured in watts (W).

precipitate An insoluble solid that separates from a solution during a chemical reaction.

pressure The force exerted over a given area by a solid, a liquid or a gas.

primary colours Red, green and blue for light, or magenta, yellow and cyan for pigments.

proton A positively-charged subatomic particle in the nucleus of an atom.

radiation Electromagnetic energy that travels in waves, or the energy given off by radioactive substances.

radioactive decay The process by which a nucleus ejects particles through radiation and becomes the nucleus of a different element.

radioactivity The release of radiation

from the nuclei of unstable atoms.

radioisotope A radioactive isotope.

redox reaction A chemical reaction in which both reduction and oxidation take place.

reducing agent A substance that takes oxygen from another substance during a redox reaction, or loses electrons or hydrogen.

reduction A chemical reaction in which a substance loses oxygen, or gains hydrogen or electrons.

reflection The way a wave bounces off a different medium.

refraction The way a wave bends as it passes into a medium in which its speed is different.

relative atomic mass (RAM) The average mass number of the atoms in a sample of an element.

renewable energy resources Sources of energy, such as Sun, wind or water, that generate power without themselves being used up.

residue The solid particles that remain behind in a filter.

resistance The ability of a substance to resist the flow of electric current.

respiration The process by which animals and plants break down food to release energy.

resultant force The total effect of all the forces acting on an object.

salt A neutral substance that is neither an acid nor a base, which is produced when an acid reacts with a base.

saturated compound An organic compound whose carbon atoms are joined by single covalent bonds.

saturated solution A solution in which no more substance will dissolve.

scalar quantity A quantity that has magnitude but no direction.

secondary colour A colour made by mixing two or more primary colours.

semiconductor A substance that conducts electricity better than an insulator, but not as well as a good conductor.

shell A region in which a certain number of electrons can exist around the nucleus of an atom.

solenoid or **coil** A coil of wire that creates a magnetic field when a current passes through it.

solute A solid substance which is dissolved in a liquid.

solution A mixture that consists of a solid dissolved in a liquid.

solvent A substance capable of dissolving other substances and the liquid in which a solid is dissolved.

specific heat capacity The amount of heat needed to raise a specific amount of a substance by one degree in temperature.

speed The distance an object travels in a certain amount of time.

static electricity The electrical charge

that builds up when atoms lose electrons to other atoms.

subatomic The term used to describe the particles of which atoms are made.

sublimation The change from solid to gas without going through liquid form.

substitution reaction A chemical reaction in which some bonds in a saturated compound break open and the atoms are replaced by different atoms.

surface tension A force that pulls together molecules on the surface of a liquid.

suspension A mixture of solid particles floating in a liquid or gas.

synthetic The term used to describe compounds that are made artificially by chemical reactions in a factory.

terminal A point on a battery where it is connected to an electric circuit.

thrust The force that moves a plane or rocket forwards.

translucent The term used to describe substances that allow a little light to pass through them.

transparent A term used to describe substances through which light can pass.

transverse waves Waves in which the vibrations that make up the waves are at right angles to the direction of travel.

ultrasound Very high-pitched sounds above 20,000Hz.

ultraviolet radiation Electromagnetic waves just beyond the violet end of the colour spectrum.

umbra Dark shadow where no light reaches.

unsaturated compound An organic compound whose carbon atoms are joined by double covalent bonds.

upthrust The force pushing up on an object when it is placed in a fluid such as water or air.

vacuum A space with no air or other matter in it.

valency The number of electrons an atom must gain or lose to become stable.

vector quantity A quantity that has magnitude and direction.

velocity The speed an object travels in a particular direction.

virtual image An image made by reflection in a surface from which rays of light only appear to come.

volt The unit for measuring the potential difference between two points in an electrical circuit.

volume The amount of space a solid or liquid occupies.

water vapour The gas that forms when water boils and evaporates.

watt (W) The unit in which power is measured.

wavelength The length of a complete wave between two similar points.

weight A measure of the strength of the pull of gravity on an object.

work The distance an object moves times the force needed to move it.

INDEX

LIST OF ILLUSTRATORS

Simone Abel
Sophie Allington
Rex Archer
Paul Bambrick
Jeremy Banks
Andrew Beckett
Joyce Bee
Stephen Bennet
Roland Berry
Gary Bines
Isabel Bowring
Trevor Boyer
John Brettoner
Peter Bull
Hilary Burn
Andy Burton
Terry Callcut
Kuo Kang Chen

Stephen Conlin
Sydney Cornfield
Dan Courtney
Steve Cross
Gordon C. Davies
Peter Dennis
Richard Draper
Brin Edwards
John Francis
Mark Franklin
Nigel Frey
Peter Geissler
Nick Gibbard
William Giles
David Goldston
Peter Goodwin
Jeremy Gower
Teri Gower

Terry Hadler
Nick Hawken
Nicholas Hewetson
Christine Howes
Ian Jackson
Karen Johnson
Richard Johnson
Elaine Keenan
Aziz Khan
Steven Kirk
Richard Lewington
Brian Lewis
Jason Lewis
Steve Lings
Rachel Lockwood
Kevin Lyles
Chris Lyon
Kevin Maddison

Janos Marffy
Andy Martin
Josephine Martin
Rob McCaig
Joseph McEwan
David McGrail
Malcolm McGregor
Dee McLean
Annabel Milne
Robert Morton
Martin Newton
Louise Nevett
Louise Nixon
Justine Peek
Mick Posen
Barry Raynor
Mark Roberts
Michael Roffe

Michelle Ross
Mike Saunders
John Scorey
John Shackell
Chris Shields
David Slinn
Guy Smith
Peter Stebbing
Robert Walster
Craig Warwick
Ross Watton
Phil Weare
Hans Wiborg-Jenssen
Sean Wilkinson
Ann Winterbotham
Gerry Wood
David Wright

Computer images of atom and molecule models: Julian Mann/Arcana Graphics Ltd

PHOTOGRAPH CREDITS

p7: (Cinque Centro car) Fiat Auto (UK) Ltd
p17: (Magnified metals) ©Jeremy Burgess/ Science Photo Library
p17: (Air flow over car) ©Takeshi Takara/ Science Photo Library
p17: (Large tire, water channeled through tire treads) Goodyear
p18: (Porsche 959) Dr Ing hCF Porsche AG
p19: (Planets in solar system) ©David A. Hardy/Science Photo Library
p28: (Zetec engine) Ford Motor Company Limited, Photographic Department
P20: (Seashore) ©Images Colour Library
p30: (Ford Ka) Ford Motor Company Limited, Photographic Department
p30-31: (Cutaway Polo car) Volkswagen
p30: (Honda CBR900RR Fireblade motorbike) Honda UK
p32: (Solar flare) ©NASA/Science Photo Library
p32: (Sun spots) ©Hale Observatories/Science Photo Library
p33: (Satellite picture of Humber Estuary) National Remote Sensing Centre Ltd.
p34: (Saturn's rings) ©Tim Furniss/Genesis Photo Library
p36: (Waves produced from drop of water)

©Martin Dohrn/Science Photo Library
p37: (Infra-red image of Hurricane Andrew) ESA/RAL/NERC/BNSC
p38: (Sunbeams) Maurice Nimmo, National Meteorological Society
p38: (Refraction of light through water) ©Jerome Wexler/Science Photo Library
p39: (Neon light, Sunset) Robin Farrow
p40: (Needle and thread) ©Dr. Tony Brain and Tony Parker/Science Photo Library
p41: (Stills of woman with a parasol) Eadweard Muybridge Collection/Kingston Museum & Heritage Service; BFI Stills, Poster and Design
p42: (Walkie Talkie) Motorola Ltd
p42: (Mobile phone) Picture Courtesy of Nokia Mobile Phones
p45: (Electronic keyboard) Yamaha-Kemble Music (UK) Ltd
p51: (Pentium® Pro processor) Intel Corporation UK Ltd
p52: (Animatronic robotic dinosaur) The Natural History Museum, London
p53: (CAD wire frame, rendered jet, bicycle and engine parts) Images produced in Autosketch for Autodesk. Copyright Autodesk Ltd

p53: ("Manny" Android) ©US Department of Energy/Science Photo Library
p53: (Concept 90 Flight Simulator) Thomson Training & Simulation
p53: (Animated monster) SOFTIMAGE
p53: (Crash test dummy) Volvo Cars UK Ltd
p71: (Hole in ozone layer) ©NASA/image from British Antarctic Survey
p74: (Hand papermaking) Wookey Hole Paper Mill
p76: (Salt on fries) Robin Farrow
p76: (Digital Compact Cassette Player) PHILIPS
p82: (Jacket made from recycled plastic) Karrimor International Limited

OTHER PHOTOGRAPHERS

Howard Allman
John Bellenis
David Cannon
 (All-Sport UK)
Bill Cooper
Mike Freeman

Amanda Heywood
Rob Jewell
Mark Mason
Bob Martin
 (All-Sport UK)
Tony McConnell

ACKNOWLEDGEMENTS

The publishers would like to thank the following organizations for their help in the preparation of this book:

Applied Environmental Research Center
Balfour Beatty Civil Engineering Ltd.
BMW (GB) Ltd
British Rail

Center for Alternative Technology, Powys, Wales
Copper Development Federation
Diam Trading
Friends of the Earth
Kimbolton Fireworks
Johnson Matthey Plc
Rob Mackie, Ae Fisheries
Mitsui Machinery Sales

National Asthma Campaign, UK
PHILIPS
RAF Brize Norton
The Science Museum, London
Supertramp Trampolines
Tower of London
Volkswagen

ELECTRICAL EXPERIMENTS

Here are some tips to help you set up experiments that need electrical wire and batteries:

Use thin electrical wire such as bell wire.

Carefully strip off about 1cm (0.5in) of the plastic insulation from each end of the wire to expose the metal inside.

Twist the metal ends of the wires around the battery terminals, or the terminals of the bulb holder. You can also use sticky tape to hold the wires in place.

Only use batteries and bulbs with the voltages specified in the experiment.

REMEMBER
Never use mains electricity for experiments

PROPELLER SHAPE

This is the propeller shape to trace for the experiment on page 9.

Trace this shape onto a piece of thin writing paper.

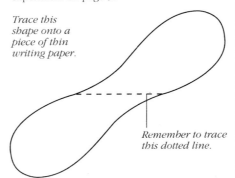

Remember to trace this dotted line.

Cut out your tracing of the propeller shape and fold it along the dotted line. Then unfold it and balance it on a pencil as shown on page 9.

PUZZLE ANSWER

Answers to quiz on page 67:

	Electron configurations:	Valencies:
Magnesium	2,8,2	Magnesium (II)
Argon	2,8,8	Argon (0)
Nitrogen	2,5	Nitrogen (V) or (III)
Potassium	2,8,8,1	Potassium (I)
Silicon	2,8,4	Silicon (IV)